PAPER TIGERS

PAPER TIGERS

The Ideal Fictions of
Jorge Luis Borges

JOHN STURROCK

CLARENDON PRESS · OXFORD
1977

Oxford University Press, Walton Street, Oxford OX2 6DP

OXFORD LONDON GLASGOW NEW YORK
TORONTO MELBOURNE WELLINGTON CAPE TOWN
IBADAN NAIROBI DAR ES SALAAM LUSAKA ADDIS ABABA
KUALA LUMPUR SINGAPORE JAKARTA HONG KONG TOKYO
DELHI BOMBAY CALCUTTA MADRAS KARACHI

© *Oxford University Press 1977*

British Library Cataloguing in Publication Data
Sturrock, John
  Paper tigers.
  1. Borges, Jorge Luis – Criticism and interpretation
  I. Title
  863   PQ7797.B635Z/

  ISBN 0-19-815746-0

*Printed in Great Britain
by Cox & Wyman Ltd
London, Fakenham and Reading*

For
Nicholas

The writer who by a disquieting mission
finds himself obliged to construct the
rigours of fiction with the facilities of
prose . . .

Maurice Blanchot, *Faux-pas*

CONTENTS

INTRODUCTION

Jorge Luis Borges is the one Latin American writer to have made a permanent mark in the literary world as a whole. For English-speaking readers, at least, that mark was not made as promptly as it should have been, given what a remarkable writer and literary thinker Borges is. He began to publish books—poetry and literary and philosophical essays—in his native Buenos Aires in the 1920s, and the majestically cryptic stories of *Ficciones* (*Fictions*) and *El Aleph* (*The Aleph*), which are the best of Borges and the subject of the present book, were themselves written in the late 1930s and 1940s. The first recorded English edition of them did not appear until 1962.

Borges, therefore, was in his sixties before he established himself at all thoroughly outside his own subcontinent. Since then he has been lionized, especially in the United States, to an extent that will have amazed but gratified him. He has been taken up both by publishers and by universities; his books have been widely translated, and he has been invited to travel to give lectures and seminars. He has been copiously written about in learned, and not-so-learned journals, and has given more than his share of interviews, where his answers to questions are in general as deceptive as they are courteous. Borges deserves the attention he now gets, ill-informed and irrational though some of it is. He has one of the sharpest, most exhaustive literary intelligences one will ever meet with; there is endless instruction as well as endless pleasure to be had from reading his work.

As a corrective perhaps to the publicity he has suffered in old age, Borges's own evaluation of himself as a literary man is that he is first a reader, next a poet, and only thirdly a writer of fiction. This evaluation many people will find perverse. As a reader, that is to say as a critic, of the work of other writers, Borges is admirably clear, vigilant, and self-effacing; as a poet, since he abandoned the 'baroque' (his own word) exuberances of the 1920s, when he could have been accounted a member of the Argentinian *avant-garde*, he is thoughtful, tight-lipped, and perhaps a little dull. For the mature Borges poetry differs from prose

mainly typographically: poetry disposes thoughts more formally
on the page and prepares its readers for a more intense, emotive
experience than prose does. Borges challenges us to read more of
himself into his poetry than into his prose.

But to me it is his stories which are by far the most memorable
and compelling part of his work. Indeed, given the extraordinary
care with which they are made, and their scrupulous artificiality,
one might even say they were the most poetic part of Borges's
work. There are not many of them: forty-four of them in all, if
my mathematics is right—though that leaves out the *Historia
universal de la infamia* of 1935, whose contents certainly count as
fiction, if not quite as 'stories'. It is with the earlier fiction that I
shall be chiefly concerned, because it is much more complicated
and 'Borgesian' than the later. For seventeen years, between 1953
and 1970, Borges published no fiction at all; when he returned to
it, with the collection called *El informe de Brodie*, and five years
later, with *El libro de arena*, his stories were altogether less enigmatic, even if they were still not as transparent as he made out
they were. Some of these later stories are analysed in the pages
which follow, but mainly it is the stories in *Ficciones* and *El Aleph*
which set the student of Borges the most, and the right, questions.

Ficciones was first published in 1944, though the first part of
the book, eight stories in all, had appeared a year or two earlier
under the title of one of the stories, 'El jardín de senderos que se
bifurcan' ('The Garden of Forking Paths'). The second part of
the book, which contains nine more stories, has the sub-title of
'Artificios' ('Artifices'). *El Aleph* first appeared in 1949, although
four of the stories which that collection now contains were not
added until the second edition of 1952–3. The title, *Ficciones*, and
the sub-title, 'Artificios', give a very good idea of what Borges
was about when he wrote these earlier stories. They are, in the
rather fusty jargon of scholasticism, universals applied to particulars. Borges's stories were displayed as specimens of the genre
to which all stories belong and as archetypes, representative of all
stories everywhere.[1]

There could be no better justification for studying them, when

[1] Borges was well ahead of fashion in this respect. Such is the nostalgia for
the Platonic Forms that one is quite accustomed nowadays to coming across
particular specimens bearing the generic name: dogs called 'Dog', tins labelled
'tin', and the like. The next step, perhaps, will be husbands and wives who, like
the husbands and wives in fairy-tales, address each other as 'husband' and 'wife'.

to study Borges's fictions is, in a large measure, to study fiction as a genre. These fictions are exemplary, not morally exemplary like the stories once written by Cervantes and others to teach improving lessons in human conduct, but technically exemplary in that they dramatize the rules and procedures of the narrative genre to which they belong. They are working models of narrative and to read them intelligently is to understand better than ever before the conventions on which narrative depends. They are as much critical as creative works, as much theoretical as circumstantial. They are also, to put it mildly, secretive: sequences of events the logic of whose articulation is very far from obvious. The highest satisfaction in reading Borges is to try and uncover that logic, and reconstruct the workings of the mind whose logic it is. Borges likens the making of a fiction to a game of chess, and it is to a game of chess that his fictions, once made, invite their readers. It is a game in which we are always on the defensive; the most we can hope to do is rationalize the moves Borges makes after he has made them.

Stories as rigorous and theoretically inclined as Borges's stand quite apart from the tradition of short-story writing in English. As exemplary narratives they are all plot and no psychology, and it is for the dissection of the psyche that most English readers suppose that the short story, with its strong unities of time and action, was invented. But Borges's fictions are 'think-pieces', they are stories about ideas instead of people. He is, we shall see, absolutely a Classicist in literature, and he knows very well that his view of narrative is that of Aristotle, one of whose foremost precepts was that the poet should bring in character for the sake of the action, rather than the other way round. We are predisposed to the opposite view, that action is determined by character and what happens in a story by the sort of people involved in that story. This is essentialism: we conclude that what people do is the result of what they are. As a writer of fiction—and I say nothing of his opinions as a man—Borges is existentialist: what his 'characters' are is the result of what they do. They are no more and no less than the sum of their actions. There is no incentive to try and 'understand' them because they are, patently, functions of the narrative in which they play a part. They are merely the actors without whose participation there could be no play.

In a quiet way, Borges has been a missionary for fiction in

which events predominate over persons. His method, a character-istically subtle one, is to concentrate on the priorities of the maker of the fiction, instead of the priorities of the reader. Thus he can even claim a writer as fastidiously 'mental' as Henry James as one of his own kind. In his preface to a translation into Spanish of a James story, 'The Abasement of the Northmores', he argues that 'Paradoxically, James is not a psychological novelist. In his books, the situations do not arise from the characters; the characters have been imagined to justify the situations.'[2] Here Borges stands alongside the author. First comes the plot; James knows what has to be made to happen and invents the psychology which makes it happen. He works backwards, from effect to cause. As readers we work forwards, from cause to effect, and argue very readily from the psychology we are presented with to what seems to be its public effect in the world.

Borges's distaste for 'psychology' is part and parcel of his extreme concern for the *art* of fiction. He believes that an artefact should be seen to be an artefact, and should not compromise with techniques indelibly tainted with realism. Psychological fiction is trapped within the confines of realism because it is not clear that there can be a fantastic or unreal psychology. Psychological laws are so lax, compared with physical laws, that it is very hard to infringe them. A fantastic psychology is never wholly incredible, because we believe that all things are possible in the mind.

It is in the invention and ordering of public events that a fiction, for Borges, consists. Here logic is at a premium; sequence is all. 'The adventure novel', he writes in the preface to a decidedly Borgesian novel by his friend and collaborator, Adolfo Bioy Casares, *La invención de Morel* (*The Invention of Morel*), 'does not offer itself as a transcription of reality, it is an artificial object which will not tolerate a single unjustified element.'[3] This old-fashioned belief in the power, and unreality, of narrative explains Borges's prejudice against whatever he feels to be formless. His own fictions are formal to a degree that no writer of fiction, surely, has ever surpassed. There is nothing in them for those whose tastes are moralistic, or sociological; everything in them for those whose tastes are literary.

It is right to try and analyse these fictions in the same spirit in

[2] J. L. Borges, *Prólogos*, Buenos Aires, 1975, p. 102.

[3] A. Bioy Casares, *La invención de Morel*, Madrid, 1968, p. 10.

which they were written, and to generalize from Borges's practice to the practice of fiction as a whole. This study, therefore, is meant firstly as a contribution to the literature on a particular author and secondly, more tentatively, as an introduction to some of the larger questions in the so-called Theory of Fiction. Some of the explanations it contains of particular Borges stories will seem contrived; I can only say that to me they seem, sadly, much less contrived than the stories they claim to explain. Borges's canonical stories are too dense and involved ever to be explained in full; he has hidden too many meanings in them, and hidden them too ingeniously, for each single movement of the plot to be elucidated. No one who analyses Borges could reasonably feel he had properly accounted for a single episode, let alone an entire fiction; many riddles remain and all one can do is indicate their existence. My own purpose is to show how alertly and attentively Borges ought to be read if we are to make the most of his few but exemplary fictions.

The first two chapters are introductory and set Borges's fictions in the context, firstly, of certain literary traditions of Argentina and, secondly, of some of the larger questions in Western philosophy with which Borges delights to engage both in his essays and, in dramatic form, in his stories. His highest originality, indeed, is to have made fascinating and ingenious fictions out of intractable and, some would suppose, arid problems in metaphysics. I have kept the chapter on the philosophical background to Borges (like the companion chapter on the Argentinian background) deliberately—I hope not dangerously—short, so as not to delay unnecessarily the main business of the book, which is the study of the stories themselves. There are a number of references back to these first two chapters later on in the book, but no lasting harm would come to anyone who decided to leave them out.

The translations from Borges's work in this book are my own. They stick as closely as possible to the original Spanish because they are intended to be illustrative rather than stylish. Where a Spanish word seems to me more ambiguous or meaningful than any single English equivalent— and this is quite often the case— I have given it in brackets after the word which translates it. The page references to the original are to Borges's *Obras completas*, published in Buenos Aires by Emecé in 1974 (referred to hereafter as *OC*). The bibliography of Borges, both in the Spanish-language editions of his works and in their English translations, is complicated, and it seemed sensible to rely for references on the one available and authoritative compendium. The *Obras completas* does not, however, contain the stories published in 1975 as *El libro de arena*, and my references to those stories are to the first Emecé edition.

I would like to thank my employers, Times Newspapers Limited, and the editor of the *Times Literary Supplement*, John Gross, for giving me the time off to write this book; the Librarian of King's College, London, for letting me use the library of the Modern Languages Faculty there; and Professor Jean Franco of Stanford University for vetting the opening chapter.

PART I

'. . . an Argentinian strayed into metaphysics . . .'

CHAPTER 1
THE ARGENTINIAN

THE circumstances of Borges's life intrude only in small ways on his fiction, and should not be dwelt on. Such accounts of himself as he has given are sparse and schematic, and refined to the point where they read more like a legend than a life-story. The details of Borges's biography corroborate his stories without doing much to explain them; as we have been given it, his life-story is that not of a man but of an author, very obviously fashioned to form an aesthetic whole with his published work. In Borges's case, that work might be held to explain his biography, rather than the other way round.

I shall not myself have much to say about Borges's life, then, when it would be even more mistaken and deceptive than usual to justify the fictions he has made by the facts he has experienced. Nevertheless, some things need to be said about Borges's cultural exchanges with his native traditions. He is the first South American writer to be seen, in Europe, as the equal of the best European ones, but then he is far from being what we, in our patronizing way, have generally thought of as a 'South American' writer. Borges, urban, reticent, and steeped in literature, contradicts our stereotypes of the culture to which he belongs.

Alien cultures are commonly prized, when they are prized at all, as a counter-work to our own. We appreciate them for their recognition of values long dead or in eclipse nearer home, and it is all the easier so to appreciate them when we really know very little about them. For all its historical and linguistic ties with Europe, South America is still an obscure continent and its culture (or cultures) the obscurest thing about it. Partial views of it are regularly and simply taken, and we misinterpret South America the better to protect certain prejudicial myths about it and its inhabitants: its political volatility is 'proof', for Anglo-Saxons, of how inferior Latins are at managing their affairs, and so on. In general, one might say that South America remains in our mythology what has been for four centuries, a basically primitive and so more 'natural' place than Europe.

This mythology invests Argentina all too readily. That large, rather empty country has traditionally been seen as South America's version of the North American West, and its uncharted pampas as the elemental stage on which cowboys alternately pluck guitars and take up their bolas to topple a steer. The books of W. H. Hudson and R. B. Cunningham Grahame are now not much read but their exaltation of Argentina's vast horizons and insistent hoof-beats conveys very well what has so often been asked of the country, which was to be a simplified place where men could be men, freed from the disabling presence of politics or history. South America as a whole, and Argentina in particular, offer the satisfactions of Hudson's 'purple land', an area insufficiently mapped which we can suppose to be strange, rudimentary, and, most important, therapeutic.

This craving for simplicity persists; South America is still, even in the age of the urban guerrilla, the place one goes to not to exchange one culture for another but to escape from culture altogether. Such nostalgia, I take it, explains the remarkable success in English translation of Alejo Carpentier's novel of *Los pasos perdidos* (*The Lost Steps*) when it was first published in the late 1950s. Carpentier, a Cuban long exiled for political reasons in Europe between the wars, is concerned in this book to establish the claims of indigenous South American cultures to a hearing in the art produced by South Americans. The main theme of the novel is the retreat from a false cosmopolitanism to a more authentic synthesis of European with native culture. The hero, a refugee from the sophisticated world in which 'native' artefacts are good only as quaint, barbarous exhibits in museums, sets off into a steamily symbolic jungle in search of a truly primeval musical instrument, which itself symbolizes the source of music and human speech as a whole.

The Lost Steps was successful because it was so crassly misunderstood. Sophisticated readers in Europe identified its hero's quest, to gratify themselves, as a definitive turning of the back on civilization and a recommendation by Carpentier of the truer, deeper forces of the 'interior'. The novel seemed to be confirming, and from a South American point of view, the accepted mythology of South America, to be reviving, if in a more advanced form, the picturesque searches of Conan Doyle's Professor Challenger for the anachronistic fauna of *The Lost World*. Carpentier was admired for advocating the very thing he was set on destroying: the primitivism which is the shallow but tenacious corollary of Western sophistication. *The Lost Steps*, like all his novels, aims at an equilibrium, in cultural terms, between Europe and South America, never at the irrational substitution of the first by the second.

Carpentier is perhaps the supreme example of a South American writer troubled by his double allegiance, to a local culture—more easily identified in Cuba, with its Negro and Indian populations—and a European one. He is at one with contemporary anthropologists in asking that we see local cultures *as* cultures, as intelligible wholes, and no longer as random collections of alien facts, to be appreciated only in isolation from one another. The quest for the musical instrument in *The Lost Steps* is a quest for the social function of music; the instrument's 'meaning' will be fixed by discovering how music is used in the culture which produced it. Like Claude Lévi-Strauss, so much of whose field-work was in fact done in South America, Carpentier is arguing that we must understand other cultures structurally, from within, not dismember them to please ourselves. The word he most objects to is 'barbarous', for the good reason that whatever is barbarous is so only because we do not know the 'language' to which it belongs; it is barbarous because we misappropriate it and insert it into our own 'language'. *The Lost Steps* is an attack on our deep-rooted cultural colonialism.

Carpentier, whose case is exemplary, has 'called the New World into existence, to redress the balance of the Old'. Traditionally, in South America, these two worlds have been taken to be incompatible; either you were for Europe, with its social and intellectual graces, or you were against it, and for the *criollo* virtues supposedly born of the South American landscape itself. The incompatibility is between town and country, intellect and muscle. In the most positive and influential book in the whole of Argentinian literature, Sarmiento's *Facundo*, it is between, as the sub-title has it, 'Civilization and Barbarism'. Sarmiento, a journalist who later became President of the Republic, stands for the enlightened, liberal, urbane values of Europe. Juan Facundo Quiroga, the brutish subject of his book and a *caudillo* who terrorized large tracts of provincial Argentina in the late 1820s and early 1830s, stands for savagery, ignorance, and tyranny. But Sarmiento, writing in exile in Chile, had as his real target not the dead Facundo but the living Rosas, the contemporary dictator of Argentina, whom he damns as the uncouth, bloodthirsty manifestation of the gaucho mentality and as the scourge of everyone and every institution most progressively European.

The issues so bitterly exposed in *Facundo* are not dead either socially or culturally in Argentina. There are still those who flaunt their European manners and metropolitan tastes, and others who resent them. There are still cosmopolitans and nationalists. Borges is absolutely, it is tempting to say aggressively, cosmopolitan. His cultural universe is large and the national frontiers within it are so faintly drawn in as to be sometimes imperceptible. He is not ignorant or contemptuous of the literature of his own country; on the contrary, he is a mature and scrupulous judge of it. But the history of Argentinian literature could never be written so as to explain Borges, he could never be mistaken, as a writer, for a local product.

Borges was born in Buenos Aires in 1899 and has lived most of his life there. Between 1914 and 1921 he lived with his family in Europe, in Switzerland throughout the Great War and mostly in Spain afterwards. It was not this experience which made him, culturally speaking, a European, because it was an experience he would not have had if his family had not already been, culturally speaking, European. He was born into that section of the middle class of Buenos Aires which had the education to admire Europe and the money to travel there. More particularly, he was born into a family which read books, above all English books, as his grandmother was English. From the start Borges has been someone for whom any sort of cultural chauvinism was petty.

As a writer, Borges is the creature of wide and vigilant reading in English (and American), German, French, and, in the later part of his life, Old English. This great eclecticism he goes so far as to offer as a sensible Argentinian's answer to the question, What is the Argentinian tradition?:

I believe that our tradition is the whole of Western culture, and I also believe that we have a right to that tradition, a greater right it may be than the inhabitants of any one particular Western nation.[1]

---

[1] 'El escritor argentino y la tradición', *OC*, p. 272.

There is not much to be gained from listing the authors in other languages whom Borges has read and written about. They tend to be from the nineteenth or early twentieth century and to make, these days, a rather eccentric collection; but then Borges likes to quicken what we might otherwise disregard as now inanimate texts by exhibiting their modernity. As an essay-writer it serves his purpose well to analyse and cite such sources as De Quincey, Emerson, Chesterton, Carlyle, Stevenson, H. G. Wells, and the like. Borges's preferences are not those of a contemporary literary intellectual but of a leisured bookman of, say, the 1920s, but the literary arguments which he advances on the strength of his reading are well worth the attention of any literary intellectual.

Borges's cosmopolitanism is extreme, and genuine, but not all Argentinians would allow that it is, as he pretends, traditional. The nationalists must always have their say, and Borges, like other europeanizing writers in South America, has been often enough criticized for his aloofness from local concerns, and for his cultural and political élitism. His independence, both in his theory and his practice of literature, has not saved him from being identified with what one might call the 'boss class' in Argentinian culture.

In Buenos Aires, as in Paris or metropolitan Spain, literary life has historically been organized round compact groups of the like-minded, preferably with a tame magazine in which to publish their work. The effects of such a nuclear organization of literature can be good or bad: good when they lead to a general fortification of intellectual life, bad when they are merely doctrinaire. Seen from within, a literary *cénacle* is the custodian of certain admirable truths, seen from without it is snobbish and pernicious, setting social above intellectual values and fostering allusiveness in writing.

In the 1920s Borges was associated with at least three short-lived but aggressive literary magazines in Buenos Aires: *Martín Fierro*, *Prisma*, and *Proa*. In local terms these were *avant-garde* publications, and cosmopolitan ones, conscious of how backward and narrow-minded Argentinian intellectual life was. Fresh from Europe, Borges campaigned with others to educate and enliven the locals, and to introduce them to the twentieth century. The campaign was vigorous but not solemn. The writers of *Martín Fierro*, says Jean Franco, made fun of the older generation, and satirized the establishment mercilessly, as if determined to shatter for ever the old image of Argentina. And this, in fact, was their intention. For them, a big modern city like Buenos Aires should take its place in the literary *avant-garde*; its writers should proclaim their modernity and identify themselves with the new and create new values.[2]

Subsequently, Borges disowned a good deal of what he thought and wrote in these early, experimental years. But he has never disowned the cultural eclecticism which he saw as one of the advantages of being born an Argentinian, nor, unlike other lapsed members of the *avant-garde*, has he lost the spirit of irreverence. In the 1930s he began a more placid, permanent association with a literary magazine, *Sur*, started in 1931 by Victoria Ocampo and still in existence today. *Sur*, in its much quieter way, was also on the side of the advanced and the European where the arts were concerned, but socially it was decidedly élitist. 'The European salons of Señora Ocampo' were a major grievance against life in Buenos Aires of the exiled Polish writer, Witold Gombrowicz, who likes to present himself in his aristocratic way as being made of far coarser stuff than the patricians of *Sur* could tolerate.[3]

The cosmopolitanism for which Borges stands may once have seemed a very radical thing to stand for in Argentina, but it is also politically conservative. Left-wing critics of Borges's work either dismiss it out of hand or admire his writing and deplore his politics. He is a profound sceptic who does not believe that writers should or can do anything to improve the institutions of their country. He has become, in old age, pessimistic about the future of his own detached, civilized values. In his most recent collection of stories, *El libro de arena* (*The Book of Sand*), published in 1975, he permits himself one or two melancholy comments on the cultural state of Argentina. These comments would have been unthinkable in his earlier fiction, not because he did not then hold the views he holds today but because such seemingly direct interventions in a fictional text would have belied the rigour of its construction. The first story, 'El otro' ('The Other'), confronts two Borgeses, the elderly one of 1969 and the young one of 1918. The 1969 Borges is disgusted by the philistine nationalism

[2] J. Franco, *The Modern Culture of Latin America*, Harmondsworth, 1970, p. 107.

[3] W. Gombrowicz, *Journal Paris Berlin*, Paris, 1968, p. 17.

which would like to cut Argentina off culturally from Europe: 'With each day that passes our country is more provincial. More provincial and more conceited, as if it had its eyes shut. It would not surprise me were the teaching of Latin to be replaced by that of Guaraní.'⁴ This complaint, it seems to me, is made to us and not to Borges's younger self. The story, admittedly, is a dialectical one, but the Borges of 1918 is not at all interested in the grievances of the older one. He does not quarrel with them, or put forward the view that Guaraní, the language of an aboriginal, repressed population, has every right to replace Latin, the dead, emblematic tongue of the clerisy. The dialogue here is not between Borges and his callower self but between Borges and some of his fiery young contemporaries, set, as he sees it, on reverting from civilization to barbarism, with the difference that this time, unlike in the days of Rosas and Facundo, it is the Indian instead of the gaucho who is to be seen as the true expression of the indigenous spirit. Borges himself has been a cosmopolitan all his life, he does not write as a reformed primitivist.

But neither is he *of* the literary salons. He has never been in danger of corruption from the bigotry and affectation which cliquishness breeds. Indeed, that is a form of corruption of which he makes fun, not in his own stories but in those he has written with another *Sur* writer, Adolfo Bioy Casares. These make great if, to an outsider, obscure play with the forms of literary pretentiousness which one imagines Borges and Bioy to have suffered in their time in Buenos Aires. The stories of *Seis problemas para don Isidro Parodi*, and the brief satirical exercises of the *Crónicas de Bustos Domecq*, which are the most substantial of the books they have written together, constantly guy the styles and attitudes of would-be sophisticates. The falsely cosmopolitan are every bit as contemptible for Borges as the opportunistically primitive.

In only one of his own, canonical stories does he make the same fun of the *salon* mentality; in one of the earliest of them: 'Pierre Menard, autor del Quijote' ('Pierre Menard, author of Don Quijote'), the provocative history of a very minor littérateur indeed who ends up writing two chapters and a bit of a book which already exists, *Don Quijote*. I shall have more to say about this supreme fantasy later on, but it is unusual in Borges's work for

⁴ *El libro de arena*, Buenos Aires, 1975, p. 14. Guaraní is a South American Indian language, spoken in the south of Brazil and in Paraguay.

the satire it makes of cultural presumption. The narrator of the story is keen to save Menard, now dead, from misrepresentation, a 'fallacious catalogue' of his œuvre having been published in a 'protestant' newspaper, a 'deplorable' organ whose readers are envisaged as being 'few and calvinist, if not freemasons and the circumcised'. The narrator then switches from his backbiting to stilted, neo-symbolist pieties towards the dead author, whose tomb he periphrases as 'the final marble' set amidst 'unhappy cypresses'. Finally, he invokes such important ladies as the Countess of Bagnoregio and the Baroness of Bacourt—'at whose unforgettable *fridays* I had the honour of meeting the late lamented poet'.[5]

This spiteful and ornate narrative persona is not one Borges has ever resumed, nor does it survive throughout the daunting ingenuities of the story it introduces. Moreover, in 'Pierre Menard', Borges is not being *merely* satirical in employing it because, as I will show, the mannerisms of his narrator have their function in the narrative of the story as well. It does seem to be the case, though, that they are *also* satirical.

Borges, then, has no more taste for literary politics than for the real kind; he has a taste only for literature. He is conspicuous in Argentinian literature, as he would be conspicuous in any other literature, for putting the reading and writing of books before more obviously active ways of living. He harps on how sedentary a life he has led and, on occasions, on the nostalgia he feels for the military glory that some of his ancestors won during the turbulent years of the nineteenth century. In Argentina, moreover, as in Golden Age Spain, a number of the most celebrated writers in the last century were also soldiers: Ascasubi, Estanislao del Campo, and José Hernández, author of the gaucho epic *Martín Fierro*, all fought in the country's civil or other wars. It is from this tradition that Borges is taking his distance when he deplores his own extreme bookishness.

This he traces back to his earliest memories—or the earliest ones he cares to make public. The definitive résumé of his childhood is surely the one he gives in his preface to *Evaristo Carriego*, a book of essays on the Buenos Aires poet of that name and on other Argentinian themes: 'For years I believed I had been brought up in a suburb of Buenos Aires, a suburb of dangerous

[5] *OC*, p. 444.

streets and conspicuous sunsets. What is certain is that I was brought up in a garden, behind lanceolate iron railings, and in a library of unlimited English books.'[6] Borges was brought up in a Buenos Aires suburb, no one doubts that, but the 'dangerous streets' and perhaps the 'conspicuous sunsets' too mark the first intrusion of romance, if not into his life then into his account of his life. They are characteristics not of the real Palermo where he lived, but of the legendary one, the 'Palermo of the knife and guitar' as he goes on to call it. In his earlier days as a writer, in the 1920s, in the uninhibited and florid poetry he produced about his native city, Borges was still a realist, capturing as he thought its transient charms in his distinctive tropes. That poetry, distastefully metaphorical as it came to seem to the mature Borges, suffers from the belief that it is in immediate communication with the real city of Buenos Aires. In Borges's fictions that belief is scrupulously excluded, and the mediate nature of language kept always in view.

Borges's bookishness is comprehensive; the lances of the iron railings round the garden are a meek substitute for the lances his more warlike forebears had to face. Borges has lived with books and worked with them; when he had to get a job he became a librarian, ending up at the Biblioteca Nacional in Buenos Aires. And he writes as bookishly as he has lived, refusing to play the game which writers of fiction habitually play of making us think they write not out of books but out of their deep, direct experience of human life. They forget to what a high degree their experience of life is interpreted for them by their experience of reading.

Borges has no time for the naïveties of 'realism'. 'Borges, what can you know about bad men?' the narrator is asked contemptuously in the story of 'Juan Muraña', which is about one of Borges's favourite cultural stereotypes, the knife-fighter. The nervous, ostensibly inadequate answer is: 'I have documented myself.'[7] This will not do for the interlocutor, who shoulders Borges aside and tells a 'real' first-hand story himself about a bad man. The story is totally implausible: the supersession of the diffident Borges by his more wilful friend has done nothing to bring about a 'realistic' narrative. Fiction, clearly, is not the place where intelligent people will look to find the real Buenos Aires.

The narrator's feeble excuse, that he has 'documented' himself

[6] *OC*, p. 101.   [7] *OC*, p. 1044.

on the local ruffians, is rather damaging, as it happens, to the prestige of that 'documentary' mode of realism to which we are now so accustomed. Documentary realism is supposedly the most direct form of representation we have; the one thing it is not supposed to be is based on documents, or second-hand evidence. But how direct is it? Even in the cinema, or television, which is where the term belongs, if anywhere, the maker of a documentary sees it as necessary to his job to document himself on his subject before he films it. In this sense the immediacy of his film is a sham, since his understanding and presentation of what he has seen have been conditioned by his rapid acquisition of second-hand evidence. It is a sham additionally in that the maker of a documentary film knows very well what is expected of documentary films and the form they must take to be recognizably of that genre. Borges's aside cuts deep into the abuse of the term.

He will allow no such easy appropriation of the real by the literary and it is this which, in the end, disqualifies him from membership of any particular literature in so far as that literature is *about* as well as *of* its country of origin. As an Argentinian, Borges saw long ago that to establish his own more accurate and sophisticated view of literature he needed to instruct his compatriots in the artificiality of the most 'realistic', that is to say the most distinctively Argentinian, literary genre available to them: the *gauchesco* prose and poetry whose subject-matter is the agrarian life of the plains. This is the one heroic tradition of Argentinian writing, and culminates in the vast poem of *Martín Fierro*. Martín Fierro is an outlaw and the tough, solitary product of an atomistic society. His cult is a reaction against the crusading urbanity of such as Sarmiento.

Borges does not for one moment belittle the *gauchesco* tradition and the cult of simple virility which goes with it; he wants only to show how thoroughly literary they are. His argument is simple: that *gauchesco* writing is writing *about* gauchos, not writing *by* gauchos. It is, in fact, writing by literary men. The *Martín Fierro*, as Borges likes to recall, was not written down out on the plains, amidst the life it claims to portray, but in Buenos Aires, in a hotel room (there seems to be some dispute about this nowadays, but Borges's point stands whether or not experts agree on the exact spot where José Hernández did his writing). Real gauchos, or those of them who could read, would not, Borges suggests, have appreciated the *Martín Fierro* because it is not at all the kind of literary work they were used to. Borges compares the work of real gauchos with the products of the urban *gauchesco* tradition, and finds them more or less irreconcilable. The first deals in abstract, universal topics—love, death, and so on—in an abstract, standardized language; the second is strenuously circumstantial, full of local colour and the idiolect of the plainsmen. Local colour, for Borges, is proof that *gauchesco* writing is not the work of gauchos, but of town-dwellers writing for other town-dwellers. It proves the inauthenticity of the tradition, its fundamentally literary nature. Borges, who is nothing if not paradoxical, argues the exactly opposite case, that authenticity is proved by the absence of local colour. He quotes an observation by Gibbon, in the *Decline and Fall*, that there are no camels in the Koran—the implication being, I imagine, that for Gibbon this casts doubt on the reputability of the sacred text. Borges, a greater sceptic even than Gibbon, takes the lack of camels as a decisive argument in favour of the Koran, because Mahomet, an Arab to whom camels were absolutely commonplace, could never have understood that they were not common to every place. The use of local colour alienates a writer from the milieu he is writing about and gives him the perspective of a stranger.[8]

Borges, then, is the last person Europeans should read if they want information about South America, because Borges will give them information only about Borges, who is perhaps most truly Argentinian in having no deep cultural roots in that country. As an author, Borges belongs to a far wider, ideal world, where frontiers and nationalities matter not at all. He is fascinated, above all, by artifice, and it is an excellent thing that so resolute and enterprising an artificer should come from a part of the Western world all too often imagined to be quite essentially natural.

[8] 'El escritor argentino y la tradición', p. 270.

CHAPTER 2

THE METAPHYSICIAN

PERHAPS we no longer expect all Argentinians to be horsemen, but we do not yet expect them to be philosophers. Not even Argentinians, it seems, expect their fellow countrymen to be that. In a brief preface to his essay 'Nueva refutación del tiempo' ('New Refutation of Time') Borges calls it, with his usual mock modesty, 'the feeble artifice of an Argentinian strayed into metaphysics'.[1] Philosophy, more than any other form of mental activity, is European; there have been no serious local contributions to its development from South America. What call, therefore, has an Argentinian to be bothering himself with this alien discipline? Metaphysics, the most radical and portentous branch of philosophy, was not designed for naïve, provincial minds and Borges must apologize for taking so much interest in it. He recalls what happened to his ancestor, Juan Crisóstomo Lafinur, who tried to reform the teaching of philosophy in the early days of the Argentine Republic and free it from the grip of the Church, by expounding 'the principles of Locke and Condillac'. In a typical parataxis, Borges adds: 'Lafinur died in exile; there fell to him, as to all men, bad times in which to live.'[2]

Lafinur, a free thinker in an age of institutionalized bigotry, is an ancestor for Borges to be proud of. Borges would say that 'free' thought is really a pleonasm, since thought which is not free is not thought. He would defend free thought less as a right than as a pleasure. It is the model for all our intellectual operations: we discover what has been thought already and rethink it slightly differently. The free thinker is free, therefore, not necessarily in respect of some repressive orthodoxy, but of his chosen model, the particular thought from which he has distinguished himself by departing. In Borges's system the thinkable is conditioned only by the already thought.

He takes advantage of his Argentinian birth to approach philosophy as a complete outsider. He approaches it as a reader of

[1] *OC*, p. 757.

[2] *OC*, p. 758.

philosophy, not as a philosopher. In Oxford, at one time, it was common to hear distinctions being superciliously drawn between those who 'read' philosophy and those who 'did' it. Mere readers of philosophy were those who could at best understand the thoughts philosophers have had without having fresh philosophical thoughts of their own; doers of philosophy went one better and advanced the discipline at the same time as they studied it. Borges would never claim to be a doer, nor to have advanced the study of philosophy at all. Rather the reverse: such is his benign incredulity that he shows traditional philosophy to have been travelling earnestly in circles, getting nowhere.

Borges enjoys metaphysics for what it offers him as a writer of fiction. He appreciates speculative styles of philosophy for the very reasons that most practising philosophers in the West despair of them, as offering unfounded, contradictory, and frequently incredible representations of the cosmos. Borges is not in the least sceptical of the human mind, only of its medium, language, whose co-ordination with reality, which is not verbal, he rightly finds unconvincing. Metaphysics to him is an art form, one way of producing what art produces, which is 'visible unrealities'. He works the history of metaphysical thought, therefore, to his own great advantage and to the great disadvantage of the reputation of metaphysical thought. His fancy is caught by the great many repetitions within that history, by the way particular metaphysical positions are taken up again and again by thinkers refining, whether consciously or not, on the ideas of their predecessors. The pattern is one of recurrence and disagreement. This pattern is just what the sceptic likes, because it demonstrates the ultimately gratuitous nature of metaphysics and its autonomy from the normal verificationist procedures of empiricism. Borges admires it for its freedom and its irresponsibility.

Metaphysics, in contemporary Anglo-Saxon philosophy, is not what it was. It was never quite strangled by the positivists but it now seems to take infinitely more cautious forms than it did before they tried to banish it. Professional philosophers these days care more than they once did that their philosophy should be true. After two thousand years of unsuccessful system-mongering they are anxious to establish incontrovertible laws of thought. The paradigm of modern philosophy is surely symbolic logic, which can be manipulated in complete security by those who have learnt its notation even if the results of its operations turn out to be elaborate tautologies. The wish for certainty makes for dullness and for secrecy. There is nothing, except for its often exquisite detachment from reality, which might stir Borges's enthusiasm for such die-hard empiricism.

He values philosophy for something quite other than its likely truth or falsehood: for its power to attract or astonish, and there is all too little to attract or astonish in the work of contemporary logicians. Borges can deal aesthetically with metaphysics because he disbelieves the justifications traditionally made of it. He is the freest of all free thinkers in the sense that he sees no need to refer metaphysical thoughts to reality in order to establish some degree of correspondence with the facts.

Borges's main concern as a reader of philosophy is with the most fundamental of all topics: ontology; with 'what there is', in the no-nonsense formulation of Professor W. V. Quine. 'A curious thing about the ontological problem is its simplicity', starts Quine, before setting out to deny is-ness to such fictive entities as winged horses and round, square cupolas.[3] A simple and a recurrent problem, with whose historical solutions Borges loves to engage. Quine the philosopher is very hard on fictions and on their deluded proponents; he is an unforgiving Realist. Borges the author admires fictions because they are departures from fact; he is the complete Idealist.

Realism, the common-sense doctrine that real things exist independently of the mind, offers Borges, as a maker of fictions, nothing. Idealism, which holds that mental phenomena are all we can ever know of reality since whatever lies beyond them is by definition unknowable, offers him, on the contrary, everything. Borges has always approached philosophy, so far as one can tell, in the intention not so much of learning from it as of making use of it. In a book of interviews with Jean de Milleret, which are the most intelligently conducted of all the many interviews he has given, Borges says:

... I thought above all of the literary possibilities of Idealist philosophy, let's say, rather than its intrinsic merits (*son bien-fondé*). This does not mean necessarily that I believe in the philosophy of Berkeley or Schopenhauer ... I believe I was thinking rather of the alchemy or unreality of the material world as subjects usable by literature.[4]

[3] W. V. Quine, *From a Logical Point of View*, New York, 1961, p. 1.

[4] Jean de Milleret, *Entretiens avec Jorge Luis Borges*, Paris, 1967, p. 72.

Thus Borges is an Idealist in philosophy only when he writes; his subscription to the ideas of Berkeley and Schopenhauer begins and ends with the making of his fictions. These are ideas to play with, not ones to live by. Their literary possibilities are straightforward. The Idealism of Berkeley and Schopenhauer is seamless; it is a pure mentalism. Whatever may or may not lie outside the limits of consciousness, the troublesome Thing-in-Itself is left to itself. In Schopenhauer the Real is reintroduced not in the service of some hypothetical matter but as the inconceivable noumenon or Will, of which all that we can perceive is the objectification. In Berkeley, too, the Will is the active principle, referred to more often as the Spirit and visible only in its effects. Schopenhauer's system, in which Will is a universal principle, requires no God; Berkeley's, being the system of an Anglican bishop keen above all to demolish atheism, does—according to him whatever we perceive that we have not willed ourselves has been willed by God.

Such philosophies of *esse est percipi* are perfectly applicable to fictions. The 'world' which a fiction creates is an ideal one, on which matter cannot intrude. Matter is present only in the wholly trivial form of paper and printing-inks. Nothing lies beyond the fictive world; it need not even claim to be a reproduction of the real world. What we perceive, therefore, as readers is all there is. It is subtended by an agent, the author, who, try as he may, must himself remain immaterial, visible only in his effects. An author can no more appear in person in his fictions than Berkeley's Spirit or Schopenhauer's Will can be captured by the human senses. Rather the reader is given the effects of the author's Will in just the same way as the scientist, for Berkeley, is given the effects of God's Will—Berkeley, naturally enough, refers to God as the Author of nature and to natural phenomena as a language which the student of nature is called on to decipher. Such a metaphysic turns reality itself into a divine fiction, reminding one of E. M. Forster's casual insight that 'If God could tell the story of the universe, the universe would become fictitious.'[5]

The particular ways in which Borges dramatizes the Idealism of Berkeley and Schopenhauer will, I hope, become apparent in the later chapters of this book. But quite apart from its particular uses, Idealism is, self-evidently, the one philosophy which helps to define the specific fictiveness of fiction. We are being asked to

[5] E. M. Forster, *Aspects of the Novel*, London, 1927, p. 79.

read all fiction, but especially Borges's own fiction, just as if we were Berkeley or Schopenhauer 'reading' the world. As readers we have the advantage, over even the most optimistic of Idealist philosophers, of knowing for a fact that the reality which confronts us is commensurate with our powers of comprehension, since it has been constructed by a mind no different in kind from our own. As an author, Borges gladly and logically affiliates himself to the Idealists because he wishes to demonstrate the true nature of fiction: the immateriality of fictional objects, the distinction between succession and causation, the juxtaposition on an equal footing of the possible with the impossible, and the provisional but complete authority of the fiction-maker over the fictions he makes.

Apart from Idealism there are two other philosophical topics it is as well to summarize before analysing Borges's stories. The first is the age-old, which is again to say recurrent, quarrel between Realism and Nominalism. The Realism involved in this case is of a quite different kind from the Realism involved in the simple problem of ontology. It holds, against Nominalism, that general terms have reality and are not merely convenient abstractions from particulars. This of course is Platonism, in that the general is also the eternal, the enduring form of which particulars are fugitive tokens. Nominalism, on the other hand, holds that general terms have no reality, that they are simply terms or forms of words. For the Nominalist, reality is all particulars.

This argument was, most of us would assume, settled long ago. Realism, in this other, medieval use of the word, now seems absurd or, worse still, incomprehensible. Borges, after recording the various related arguments put forward at one time or another in its support, cheerfully admits that it is now so far removed from us that he disbelieves all interpretations of it, including his own: 'Nowadays, like the spontaneous and simple-minded proser in the play, we are all unwitting nominalists; it is like a general premiss of our thinking, an acquired axiom. Hence the futility (*lo inútil*) of commenting on it.'[6] This may sound as if Borges were dismissing Realism once and for all; and, as a man, he would no doubt be perfectly prepared to do so. For an author, however, it is not quite so easy. It is striking that, in writing about the particularist doctrine of Nominalism, Borges should claim it as a

[6] *OC*, p. 364.

'general' premiss of contemporary thought, thereby recognizing Nominalism itself to be a general term. Nor should one get the idea that what is futile, or *inútil*, for Borges is without value; on the contrary, it has a very high value indeed: it is a fiction. Realism or, more generally, the Platonic theory of archetypes, is a second philosophical fiction to which Borges is devoted.

The disagreement between Realism and Nominalism does not concern the use of general terms but their ontological status. The excuse for Realism, as Nominalists must acknowledge, is that language itself is Realist, being a system of general terms constantly employed to refer to particulars. Language represents a first, gross abstraction from the uniqueness of every real experience because without that abstraction meaningful communication about the world would be impossible between one person and another. 'It is not enough,' says Locke, 'for the perfection of language, that sounds can be made signs of ideas, unless those signs can be so made use of as to comprehend several particular things: for the multiplication of words would have perplexed their use, had every particular thing need of a distinct name to be signified by.'[7]

This much is, necessarily, common ground between the parties. Contention starts when general terms are treated as hypostases and held to refer to real entities; in the classic example 'redness', from being a quality predicated of two red objects, becomes a third object of its own. Realism thus denies the abstraction which Nominalism depends on and opens up what to most of us today seem whimsical perspectives of identification between particular specimens of reality and the class of thing to which they belong. The English, as Borges notes in his essay on 'El ruiseñor de Keats' ('Keats's Nightingale'), are constitutionally incapable of accepting any such notion: we are the most stubborn of Nominalists. Borges's considerable Anglophilia makes him go further, indeed, and suggest that our Nominalism is ethical rather than philosophical, that it is part and parcel of the high respect we feel for individuals. The Germans, on the other hand, the great abstractors of modern philosophy, are the heirs of Platonism and of medieval Realism. Hence it is his favourite Schopenhauer whom Borges calls in to explain the nightingale in Keats's ode, that undying example of its class which is absolved from death by what we

[7] John Locke, *An Essay Concerning Human Understanding*, III, 1, 3.

incorrigible Nominalists tend to condemn as a philosophical trick. Schopenhauer, like, if Borges is right, the not-very-philosophical Keats, identifies the particular birds and animals of his experience with their species, so removing them from the real world of time and decadence into the ideal world of eternity.

This magical transposition is achieved simply enough by naming a real thing, by exchanging objects for words. To name something is to fictionalize it, or make it unreal; apart from those quite rare occasions when we use language ostensively, and invoke existing particulars as it were to check the tendency to abstraction, words replace things. Such is the process of fiction, to substitute language for the world. Borges, the archetypal writer of fiction if ever there was one, is in this respect the complete Realist, deeply gratified by the way in which language abstracts from existences to essences. One of the less obvious but most pertinent philosophical themes in his work is the acquisition of a name, because to acquire a name is to acquire an enduring essence, to go from being that particular, short-lived nightingale in that particular Hampstead garden to being the specific, deathless nightingale in an ode. It is Borges's appreciation of this power in language which has surely given him his interest in such linguistic speculations as those of the seventeenth-century English bishop, John Wilkins. Wilkins tried to devise a universal language in which the names of things were determined by the nature of the things of which they were the names; his aim was to lift the curse, if it is a curse, of what is often called 'the arbitrariness of the sign', or the fact that the names of things are only conventionally related to those things. Poetry too, and the whole of literature, might equally be seen as a protest against this same unfortunate fact. The truly literary person, suggests Borges, will overlook the arbitrariness of the sign and speculate with Plato:

> If (as the Greek declares in the *Cratylus*)
> The name is archetype of the thing,
> In the letters of *rose* is the rose
> And all the Nile in the word *Nile*.[8]

As an author, therefore, Borges takes a name to be the 'cipher' (*cifra*) of the thing, a term he uses again and again in this precise, characteristic sense. The 'cipher' is eternal and essential even

[8] 'El Golem', *OC*, p. 885.

though the thing is not; but the 'cipher' is also a zero, a non-entity—it is a convenient fiction. Borges, as a good Nominalist, knows that fictions must end and that their identification of the particular with the universal is a temporary alleviation at best of the ephemerality of life. The fiction over, we are returned to a perishable world in which only particulars have real existence; the nightingale to which Keats actually listened is long since dead. This does not mean that those plodding English Nominalists— Robert Bridges, Sidney Colvin, H. W. Garrod, F. R. Leavis— whom Borges singles out as having misunderstood the poem, were justified. They failed or refused to grasp that such is the nature of poetry that Keats was bound to conflate the one nightingale with the many.

The only error is to extend this conflation from literature and language into life. We write as Realists and live as Nominalists. Borges, quoting Coleridge, divides people into born Aristotelians and born Platonists:

The latter feel that classes, orders, genera, are realities; the former that they are generalizations; for the first language is nothing more than an approximate game with symbols; for the second it is a map of the universe. The Platonist knows that the universe is somehow a cosmos, an order; for the Aristotelian, this order may be an error or a figment of our partial knowledge.[9]

One would be hard pressed today to find any avowed Platonists. Borges, a born Aristotelian, is intrigued by the long history of Platonism and its offshoots because Platonism, for him, is specifically fictional. Fiction, as he practises it himself, is a very evident exercise in generalization and so reinforces the power of language to dissociate us from reality.

Borges's reading of philosophy is unfashionable but purposeful and contributes in central ways to his understanding of literature. There is a third topic we need to look at before this summary is complete: infinity. Metaphysics, with Borges, is agreeably escapist —abstraction is also distraction. Platonism serves very well to counteract mutability and make eternity thinkable if hardly plausible. Infinity can do the same; the idea of endlessness diverting us for a while from the inevitability of our end. Borges's chosen source of speculation into the infinite is the second paradox of the

[9] *OC*, p. 718.

Eleatic Zeno, which sets Achilles racing against the tortoise. The form of the paradox is well known: Achilles can run ten times faster than the tortoise and gives him ten yards' start. He never catches the tortoise up, for by the time he has run the ten yards the tortoise has advanced by another one, by the time he has covered that yard the tortoise has run another tenth of a yard, and so on, *ad infinitum*. This paradox, and the good many others like it, intrigue us because they are an affront to our common-sense understanding of natural laws. We know very well that the result of Achilles' race conflicts with natural laws and that we should be able to explain the errors in its formulation. They are very Borgesian, demanding as they do a temporary disconnection from the real world while we attend to their logic. They are, in short, fictions.

They are not, or are no longer, serious philosophical problems, even though a number of serious philosophers have given solutions of them. What Borges takes from the paradox is the idea of infinite divisibility and that is an idea which depends, for the sake of the argument, on arresting the flow of time. The real continuity of movement of both Achilles and the tortoise is repeatedly and artificially broken, since to admit it would be to ruin the paradox at the outset. The paradox is, where Borges is concerned, an ideal fiction because it is so obviously a fiction; the reality which Zeno's ingenuity keeps at bay is an implicit presence and the figure we have in our minds is, in the words of Paul Valéry, 'Achille immobile à grands pas', a figure frozen in the act of moving.

Infinite divisibility is a very literary model of infinity. If we take a narrative to be a certain extension of time, then its author is free in theory to divide that extension up infinitely. The beginning and the end of the narrative are fixed points between which an infinite number of peripeteias may be interpolated. A narrative, just like a sentence in Chomskyan grammar, is infinitely recursive: there are no restrictions on the number of episodes or, in the case of a sentence, clauses, which can be embedded in it, so delaying its conclusion. The ideal narrative, from this point of view, is that of *Tristram Shandy*, which is so endearingly digressive that it fails to reach the point at which, in all logic, it should have begun, the hero's birth. Alternatively, there is the interminably recursive narrative which Borges alludes to on a number of occasions: that of Scheherazade in *The Thousand and One Nights* when she threatens to tell a story reintroducing all the six hundred-odd stories she has told already, thereby inaugurating an infinite and circular narration whose end would also be a new beginning. These forms of infinity are nice ideas, made possible for us by our ability to treat time as if it were space. Infinite recursiveness and infinite regressions appeal to us because they set the mind free, and satisfy perhaps our liking for what Roger Caillois calls the *ilinx*, or that 'poursuite du vertige' which he sees as distinguishing a particular class of ludic activities practised around the world.[10] They are games, and it is as games that they are dismissed by Bishop Berkeley: 'The *infinite* divisibility of *finite* extension . . . the source from whence do spring all those amusing geometrical paradoxes, which have such a direct repugnance to the plain common sense of mankind, and are admitted with so much reluctance into a mind not yet debauched by learning . . .'[11] Such intellectual amusements offend by ignoring Berkeley's strict criterion of the *minimum sensibile*, according to which the limits of the actual are the limits of the perceptible. Infinite divisibility is not realizable because the human eye, however powerful the instruments it calls in to help it, will eventually be defeated. It perceives smaller and smaller divisions of space, but not infinitely small ones. Similarly, there are limits on the subtlety with which we can measure time.

Scheherazade's infinite narration is a vertiginous, unrealizable fantasy, like the book of sand in the title-story of the collection, *El libro de arena*, which has, quite simply, innumerable pages, because there is no number which cannot be made larger by adding 1 to it. Scheherazade, we should remember, was the inspired girl who kept herself alive by telling stories. Threatened with execution should she fall silent, she is the very model of a narrator, perfectly coextensive with her narration. But even she could not have expected the immortality she would have needed to go on narrating for ever, for at some sadly arbitrary moment in the sequence she would have dropped dead. As it is, she is released from her commitments by the Caliph's decision to marry her.

Borges allows us no such comfortable conclusions. For him, once the illusion of an infinite divisibility is over, it must be seen to be over. Time, which has been arrested, must be restarted. At the

---

[10] Roger Caillois, *Les Jeux et les hommes*, Paris, 1967, pp. 67–74.

[11] *Principles of Human Knowledge*, CXXIII.

end of one of his most densely contrived stories, 'La Muerte y la brújula' ('Death and the Compass'), Borges introduces the notion of a labyrinth (or a narrative) made up of a single straight line; as a tribute presumably to the paradoxical Zeno, it is described as 'a Greek labyrinth'. The suggestion, put forward by the detective-cum-hero of the story just as he is about to be executed by the criminal-cum-hero, is that his executioner should commit a first crime at a given point A, a second crime at a point B, eight kilometres from A, a third crime at a point C, equidistant from A and B on the straight line joining them, and then finally wait for the pursuing detective to catch up with him at a fourth point D, equidistant between A and C. At D the criminal will execute the detective. 'The next time I kill you,' he says, 'I promise you this labyrinth, which consists of a single straight line and which is invisible, unceasing.'[12] This rectilinear labyrinth, which is a simplification of the geometry of the crimes committed in the story, is a reminder that the spatial games of fiction are themselves played in time. With the death of the detective, his purpose now fulfilled, we are returned to the indivisible continuum of real time. The author of a fiction may pretend to control time by disguising its passage as a chronology but he should not pretend to defeat time. It is characteristic of Borges that he should have written, *in* his time, not one but two 'refutations' of time; they are not indentical and their separate existence, as two particulars, refutes the hypothetical eternity they each propose. Borges is never to be accused of taking his philosophy too seriously.

[12] *OC*, p. 507.

PART II

'. . . in the Pavilion of Limpid Solitude'

CHAPTER 1

ISOLATION

ALL Borges's fictions dramatize, in some measure, the life-cycle of a fiction: its birth, as a wilful departure from fact, its life, as a succession of choices made by its author, and its death, which is marked by a return to the world as it is, and no longer as we might like it to be. Borges has now and again asked to be taken as a realist, while knowing full well that it is very difficult for us to take him as anything of the kind. His realism, if it is realism, is of an etiolated kind: it is mimetic not of the happenings of the real world but of the activity of mimesis itself. Borges holds the mirror up to art, not to nature. Realism of this secondary sort I suspect contradicts rather than extends the realism we are used to. It involves, for Borges, fidelity not to the outside world but to the situation within that world of the maker of fictions; both his physical situation and his mental situation. The proper place to begin an analysis of Borges's fictions is with the special conditions which make fiction possible.

These conditions are special, and temporary. Once he ceases from being an author and reverts to being a man, the peculiar physical and mental state which authorship requires is suspended. That state is one of voluntary isolation. The author is withdrawn from his full involvement in the world and with other people. He takes steps to protect himself from contingencies, from any Persons from Porlock who might reclaim him for reality. He cannot, of course, suppress the real world altogether; he still has to occupy a point in space and time, and to have around him a number of material objects, notably the instruments of his profession. But his field of vision, like his field of action, is much reduced. An author may be praised for his 'powers of observation' but he is unlikely to be able to make much use of them while he is actually writing. He must work from memory and from such documents, written or pictorial, as lie to hand. The author, in short, willingly gives up for a time all immediate reference to the world outside his work-room.

Physical isolation comes repeatedly into Borges's stories as the necessary condition of authorship. It comes into one of his earliest inventions, a brief tale loosely derived from the Arabic called 'El brujo postergado' ('The Sorcerer Postponed') in the *Historia universal de la infamia* (*Universal History of Infamy*). The story concerns a dean of Santiago in Spain who is keen to learn the art of magic and who travels to Toledo because he has heard that one Don Illán of that city is a great magician. Don Illán, a decidedly literary man, is discovered reading in 'a room apart'. There is a first postponement: Don Illán tells his visitor that food comes before magic, that they will eat before they get down to business. They eat, the visitor promises the sorcerer, who is afraid of ingratitude, that he will never forget him but remain always at his command, and Don Illán explains that the magic arts can be imparted only in 'a place apart'. He raises an iron ring in the floor and leads his pupil down a 'well-worked' staircase: 'At the foot of the staircase there was a cell and then a library and then a sort of study with magic instruments.'[1] The two of them are examining the magician's books when two men suddenly enter with a letter for the dean and a rapid chain of events is set in motion which has the dean promoted to bishop to cardinal to pope. At each successive promotion he ungratefully refuses Don Illán his patronage. The end of the story is no surprise: the spell is broken, the dean finds himself back in the underground cell in Toledo, the angry magician expels him from his house. The dean leaves without being allowed to share the grouse Don Illán had ordered to be prepared for their supper.

This ingenious, mock Arabian Nights tale embodies all the stages of a fiction. The magic art in which Don Illán is so well versed is the art of fiction, of whose magical properties Borges has written in his essays and to which I shall come back in due course. Don Illán makes a habit of seclusion; he is first discovered in 'a room apart' and then takes his pupil to 'a place apart'. On the first occasion he is discovered reading, on the second he and the dean are interrupted as they examine his books. These symmetrical interruptions mark the points at which fiction intrudes on fact; the first interruption is followed by a meal and by a postponement of any instruction in magic, the second interruption (caused this time by two men instead of one) by the incredible, magical satisfaction of the dean's ambition and then by the refusal of a meal.

[1] *OC*, p. 339.

There are thus two, symmetrical stories in 'El brujo postergado', the first taking us from the first interruption of Don Illán's solitary reading to the second, no longer solitary reading, the second story from that interruption to the end. The second story is the transformation of the first, with magic instead of a meal, or emotional instead of biological satisfaction. The form the second story takes, of the amazing *a*scent of the dean, is prefigured in the first story by his *de*scent into the underground room; the 'well-worked' staircase wrought by the magic of Don Illán naturally serves to carry people up as well as down.

That magic originates in the act of reading, and the 'magic instruments' to be found in Don Illán's hide-away surely include books—the realization of other men's magic. Borges, as I have said, wishes to show fictions at their point of departure from facts, but the facts he shows them as departing from are literary facts: the stock of existing fictions which the new maker of fictions takes as his models. The second time Don Illán is interrupted, in the company of the dean, they are said to be 'revising' the books on his shelves—*revisaron los libros* in the Spanish. This is the selfsame activity which Borges himself claims to be engaged on in the book of which 'El brujo postergado' forms part, whose contents are offered as the author's own modifications of stories he has read elsewhere, even if it is perfectly plain that some of those modifications are excessive and that some of the pieces in the book are Borges's from start to finish. What is more, the conspicuously magical part of 'El brujo postergado', which is the dean's promotion, might be said to start with him reading the letter, brought by the two messengers who have so mysteriously appeared in Don Illán's underground room, announcing that his uncle the bishop is sick. The dean prefers to pursue his study of magic rather than go straight away to his uncle's house—which is another act of postponement. The gratifications that ensue have been inspired by his reading of the letter; Don Illán, in the succinct words of Jean Ricardou, has chosen 'the sorcery which emanates from the text'.[2]

[2] Jean Ricardou, 'Réalités variables, variantes réelles', in *Problèmes du nouveau roman*, Paris, 1967, p. 43. Ricardou, the most acute and helpful critic the French New Novel has so far had, was quick to see, as other French writers have seen, how very closely Borges's views on fiction match those of Robbe-Grillet and others. Borges, of course, came first and has almost certainly never read a *nouveau roman* in his life. His own fictions regularly converge on those of

The admirable complications of 'El brujo postergado' have themselves led us away from the place where we, and it, began: the
magician's 'room apart'. In its second manifestation this privileged place becomes a 'cell' (*celda*), to reach which Don Illán has
first to raise an iron ring in the floor. To isolation is added the idea
of incarceration, which is perhaps Borges pretending that the
author's lot is a sad one and the solitude he needs in order to do
his work a punishment.

In others of his fictions he makes no bones about it: the place
into which his makers of fictions are withdrawn *is* a prison-cell.
Such is the case with the remarkable detective whom Borges
invented with Bioy Casares, Don Isidro Parodi. Parodi's given
name is a hint that he could turn out to be the detective to end all
detectives, a *reductio ad absurdum* of his profession. And so in a
sense he is. The line of fictional detectives to which he belongs is
that of the pure reasoner, the line inaugurated by Poe's Auguste
Dupin. In this tradition the direct involvement of the detective
with the crimes he is asked to solve is small. These immaculate
thinkers receive accounts of unsolved crimes from third parties
and then apply their minds to the rationalization of the events
recounted. In order to succeed they must show that what seemed,
to the benighted and inadequate mind of the recounter, a string
of random contingencies, is really, 'read' by their own superior
minds, a coherent narrative. The reasoner's job is to make sense
of what he is told and to pass from an account *of* the crime to
accounting *for* the crime.

Don Isidro Parodi pushes the possibilities of the pure reasoner
to the limit. He is in prison, in cell number 273 of the Penitencería,
to which, in defiance of all verisimilitude, his clients come in
droves to consult him. Each visitor contributes a share of the
narrative of the crime, often in an idiom well-nigh impenetrable
to those of us ignorant of the rarer ins and outs of Argentinian
usage, since in the *Seis problemas para don Isidro Parodi* Borges
and Bioy freely satirize some of the more offensive styles of local
speech or writing. Once the narrative is complete and his last
visitor has gone, Parodi sits alone in his cell for a few days and
then eventually comes up with the solution. One or other of his

---

certain *nouveaux romanciers* because he, like they, believes it is the duty of
any particular fiction to illustrate the methods of the genre as a whole.

previous callers returns, preferably a suspect, and Parodi then *re*-tells the story that has been told to him. In the re-telling the logic of the narrative is made clear; what before had seemed to be mere contingencies are now seen to be elements of a plot. The crime is explained, and Parodi has further justified his name, since his more summary and less grandiloquent versions of the stories he has heard are essentially parodies of those stories. The origins of his own narration lie in the narrations of others. Parodi in his prison-cell—he is a barber (for some reason) who has been sentenced to twenty-one years of 'reclusion' after being framed—is also the writer in his place of work. The chicanery which has put him in prison, and the very literary affectations of the harassed citizens who visit him there, partake far more of literature of (bad) literature than of life. Parodi is fully insulated against the intrusions of reality.

Seis problemas para don Isidro Parodi begins with a somewhat arch 'Liminal Word' in which the two authors trace the antecedents in literature of their own detective. These include Dupin, Prince Zaleski, who solves the enigmas of London from a 'remote palace', and Max Carradus, who 'everywhere carries with him the portable prison of blindness'. All three are prevented, by temperament or by physical handicap, from gross interference in the mysteries they resolve; by which I mean that their temperament or handicap is in fact dictated by the role they are given in the narrative. Max Carradus is not a blind man who is a detective, he is a detective and therefore blind, since there is no compelling reason why a 'pure' detective should need to see; provided he can think he is quite able to solve the puzzles presented to him. In just the same way, Borges has never shrunk from treating his own near-blindness as an affliction appropriate to the maker of fictions, who needs memory and intelligence but not eyesight—except to be able to read. The most archetypal of writers for Borges, apart from Shakespeare who is a case apart, are Homer and Milton, the great sightless poets.

Borges and Bioy are anxious that their readers should understand their intentions in respect of Parodi. They end their brief literary genealogy of him:

Such ecstatic investigators, such inquisitive *voyageurs autour de la chambre*, presage, if only partially, our Parodi: a figure inevitable perhaps in the course of detective literature. Parodi's immobility is an intellectual symbol in itself and represents the roundest of denials to the vain and feverish agitation of North America . . .[3]

Parodi belongs at the end of the line. He is to be appreciated for bringing that particular line to a logical conclusion, since it is hard to see how any detective could actually outdo him in in-activity, and at the same time for distinguishing that line from other, comparable lines. Not all detectives are reasoners; indeed, one would have thought that reasoners are the exception, having become less and less fashionable in the present century. The line that descends from Poe and Auguste Dupin is crossed by the other line, descending from who knows whom (Wilkie Collins?), of detectives (or policemen) who are as much doers as thinkers and whose periods of reclusion are both short and often violently interrupted. Under the influence of writers like Dashiell Hammett the old paragons of intellectuality have been supplanted by men bearing more dynamic labels: instead of being called detectives they may be called 'agents' or 'operatives', as if in criticism of the cushioned life led by their literary predecessors. The great argu-ment against the reasoners—it is the argument of Raymond Chandler's caustic essay on 'The Simple Art of Murder' (whose title was, one hopes, a tribute to one of Borges's favourite English writers, De Quincey, the author of 'Murder as a Fine Art'—was the naïve but inevitable one that they lacked realism, that the crimes they investigated and the solutions they produced were too glibly isolated from everyday contingency to serve as models for crimes and their detection in real life. It is odd, now that the conventions of the genre have changed further, to think that Chandler's own strikingly artificial stories and stylish hero, Philip Marlowe, were invented for the sake of realism.

The exploits of Don Isidro Parodi were invented for the exactly contrary reason: to display the conventionality of detective fiction and, by extension, all fiction. One of the nicest aspects of Parodi's immobility is that, although he never moves himself, he unfailingly discovers what makes other people move: he is skilled, that is to say, in the detection of motive. The establishment of a motive in the investigation of a crime is a paradigm of the causal process in narrative generally. It is to work backwards from effect to cause,

---

[3] H. Bustos Domecq, *Seis problemas para don Isidro Parodi*, Buenos Aires, 1942, p. 13.

since there can be no talk of motive until a crime has been committed; in stories, if not in life, it is the crime which justifies the motive, never the other way round (I am taking here the author's, not the reader's, standpoint). If a crime were not motivated at all, it would be not a crime but an accident; the supposedly 'unmotivated' crime or *acte gratuit is* motivated, by the wish to commit an unmotivated crime, and the detective called on to investigate one need only look for a particularly literary style of criminal, with a strong interest in narrative causality.

A mobile mind in a stationary body: such is the specification of the writer. Parodi, like the earlier detectives whom Borges and Bioy list, is explicitly granted the power of mental displacement, he is capable of ecstasy, or, since that word has now pretty well lost its original meaning, ec-stasis. Parodi is an ecstatic who can stand 'outside' himself. The writer's first act is to isolate himself, his second, as one sees with Don Illán, to duplicate himself, to be in two places and to be two people at once. He withdraws, as we shall see, into a peculiar and imaginative state of mind.

Parodi is an intentionally comic representative of his, and Borges's, profession. In the stories which Borges has written on his own such representations of the author are sometimes quite grim. Take the case of Jaromir Hladík in the story of 'El milagro secreto' ('The Secret Miracle'). Hladík is a literary man: 'Apart from a few friendships and many customs, the problematical exercise of literature constituted his life; like every writer, he measured the virtues of others by what they had executed and asked that others should measure him by what he conjectured (*vislumbraba*) or was planning.'[4] The word 'executed' has a sinister ambiguity. Hladík, a Jew living in Prague, has been arrested by the Nazis and sentenced to death. He is not merely in a prison-cell but in the condemned cell, with ten days to live. These ten days represent the postponement of his execution and an interval in which his magic, like that of Don Illán, can become effective. The imminence of his death is a powerful summons to his imagination; it is the preordained end which he will try and keep at bay. He imagines over and over again the circumstances of his execution, each scenario being slightly different from the others, as if to exhaust all the possible combinations and to conjure the eventual reality by imagining it beforehand. This 'feeble magic' does not

[4] *OC*, p. 509.

satisfy him. The night before he is to be shot Hladík turns instead to his unfinished verse tragedy of *Los enemigos* (*The Enemies*), which still lacks two acts. He asks God for one year in which to finish the work, which is to be the 'justification' of his life. The next morning, as the guns of the Nazi firing-squad are raised to execute him, the miracle happens (it has been prefigured in a dream during the night, with the help of a blind librarian!). Everything around him is immobilized but his mind is left free to think. For the second time in the story Hladík has been given a postponement of his execution, and his situation now is symmetrical with his situation before, when he had been in his cell. Again, some magic is called for: he can add the two missing acts to his tragedy just as two acts have been added to his own story:

> The only document he had was his memory; the apprenticeship of each hexameter he added imposed on him a fortunate rigour not suspected by those who venture and forget vague and temporary paragraphs . . . Meticulous (*minucioso*), unmoving, secret, he wove in time his tall, invisible labyrinth . . . Not a single circumstance importuned him.[5]

Hladík completes, in imagination, his tragedy; the last epithet is decided and time restarts: his execution is complete. The 'year' he has been miraculously granted has to be fitted in to the least interstice in the public events of the story, between the giving of the order to the firing-squad to fire and the discharge of their guns. Hladík's fate was originally sealed by an invasion—the invasion of Czechoslovakia by German troops in 1939, a historical event, duly dated—and he dies from another invasion, this time of his body, by four German bullets. Between these, as ever, symmetrical limits, his privacy has been maintained and circumstances have been rendered harmless. Free from disruption as he is, as he stands paralysed in the prison-yard, Hladík can indeed take advantage of circumstances. He can refer to his memory for documentation and also to the scene around him, which survives for a year like a snapshot—there has, as it happens, been an almost imperceptible hitch in the proceedings of the execution when Hladík, already anticipating the firing of the rifles, is moved away from the wall against which he has been put, for fear he will splash it with his blood; 'absurdly', this puts him in mind of the 'preliminary vacillations of photographers'. The photographer is

[5] *OC*, pp. 512–13.

himself. During the course of his labours over his unfinished tragedy he is able to make use of one of the faces he can see, which modifies 'his conception of the character of Roemerstadt'. The few images he can see are thus a source of improvisation. It may well be asked how the sight of a face can modify the conception of a character, but that is a question to which I shall revert in a more appropriate chapter of this book.

Isolation and immobility, then, are the two conditions the imagination requires if it is to be preserved from the ruinous distractions or 'invasions' of reality. The author must not be importuned. Roemerstadt, the protagonist of Hladík's tragedy of *The Enemies*, is importuned repeatedly throughout its first act, by strangers whom he comes to recognize, along with the audience, as 'secret enemies sworn to destroy him'. Roemerstadt 'succeeds in arresting (*detener*) or foiling their complex intrigues'. There is mention too of his fiancée and of one Jaroslav Kubin 'who once importuned her with his love'. Kubin has since gone mad and now 'believes he is Roemerstadt'. In the third act *The Enemies* begins over again, with an exact repetition of the opening scene, in which Roemerstadt is visited, at sunset, in his library, on one of the last evenings of the nineteenth century, by a stranger: 'Roemerstadt speaks to him unamazed; the spectator realizes that Roemerstadt is the wretched Jaroslav Kubin. The drama has not occurred: it is the circular delirium which Kubin lives and relives interminably.'[6] But a 'circular delirium' can still be a drama once it is made, as Hladík and Borges make it, into the subject of their narratives. Between the first and third acts of *The Enemies* there has been a transformation; in the third act, where the protagonist is at last identified with the author, importunity is no longer possible and Roemerstadt responds differently to the intrusion on his solitude. The author is the man who bests the invader by incorporating him into his schemes. His privacy is intact.

None of Borges's author-figures, if I may call them that, ever writes anything down. Hladík is typical, he projects the completion of his drama without entering on to the labour of transcribing it on paper. Borges is content to symbolize the conditions of authorship because to go further, and show it as a particular form of bodily activity, would be a dangerous concession to realism. The author, for Borges, remains someone whose body is useless.

[6] *OC*, p. 510.

This is the case with the storekeeper or publican, Recabarren, in 'El fin' ('The End'), one of the slighter, and shorter *Ficciones*. Recabarren owns a *pulpería*, a sort of general store cum bar. Such locales crop up regularly, and systematically, in Borges's stories, as offering refreshment or, more potently, intoxication. Now intoxication, as we shall see, is a state akin to inspiration, symbolic of the altered state of consciousness entailed in author-ship. The *pulpería* is just the sort of place where one would expect stories to be born or, more precisely, retailed, since with Borges new stories are no more than modest revampings of old ones. Recabarren, too, is a kind of librarian, the guardian of a place where literary inspiration may strike the tongue-tied author.

Recabarren, in fact, is paralysed and has lost the power of speech. He is the silent witness of what happens within eyeshot. His name is a strong clue that whatever does happen within eye-shot has been willed by himself. *Recabar* is a Spanish verb meaning 'to achieve one's desire', though its usual meaning in Argentinian Spanish seems to be rather weaker, and to be 'to ask for' or 'solicit'. Whether one takes the word in its stronger or its weaker sense, it characterizes the bed-ridden storekeeper definitively as a pre-destined maker of fictions.

He has suffered his paralysis very suddenly, ostensibly while stacking away a load of maté or tea. He is not completely paralysed only 'his right side had died suddenly'. The real cause of the paralysis, as always with Borges, is what immediately precedes it in the story, even if the two events seem to have no serious con-nection at all. The day before he is struck down Recabarren has witnessed in the *pulpería* a lengthy, contrapuntal *payada*—which is an improvised poetic dialogue, accompanied on guitars, tradi-tional in rural Argentina. This particular *payada* has been a con-test between a Negro and a white stranger. The stranger has won and has ridden off, leaving the Negro to meditate his revenge at the *pulpería*. The very next day Recabarren becomes paralysed.

One does not need to read very far into 'El fin' before suspecting that this story will be one of Borges's characteristic footnotes to literature. There is a famous *payada* in Argentinian literature, near the end of José Hernández's epic, *Martín Fierro*. The con-testants are Martín Fierro himself and an anonymous Negro. The Negro is the brother of another Negro whom Fierro has killed in a knife-fight earlier in the poem. The musical encounter, therefore, is a sublimated replay of the first, lethal encounter. Borges's, or Recabarren's, story reverses this pattern; it provides the counterpoint to Hernández (and I am sure Borges will have enjoyed introducing the notion of counter*point* into a story centred on a knife-fight). The real-life contestants in the *payada*, therefore, are a nineteenth-century poet and a twentieth-century prose-writer, who has set out to correct something of which he perhaps does not approve in the other's work. In 'El fin' the white stranger returns to the *pulpería*, is challenged by the Negro to a replay, only this time with knives instead of guitars, and is killed, being named as Fierro only once he is dead. The paralysed Recabarren witnesses the end of Argentina's greatest literary hero who, at the end of Hernández's poem, had in fact been allowed to ride off into the darkness 'to begin a new life'.[7]

So the wish which Recabarren fulfils is, predictably, the wish of a literary man. The *payada* he has conducted with the *Martín Fierro* is figured in the form of his paralysis: the 'death' of one side of his body parallels the 'death' which he later observes of Martín Fierro. It is the 'right' side which dies in each case and the left, or 'wrong', side (the sinister side one might say) which triumphs. Recabarren has contradicted the facts of Hernández's poem and offended against its morality. But then he is a pitiless man, as we have already been told:

By dint of feeling sorry for the misfortunes of the heroes of novels, we end up feeling excessively sorry for our own misfortunes; this was not the case with the afflicted Recabarren, who accepted paralysis as he had earlier accepted the rigour and solitudes of America.[8]

Unimpeded by any ethical or emotional restrictions, Recabarren is free to rearrange the stock elements of the story as he wants; he is, like all makers of fiction in Borges, an engineer or pure artificer. There is only the pretence of evil about 'El fin', a playful consorting with the powers of darkness which lead us to want literary heroes to suffer the ultimate misfortune. At the end of the story Recabarren, having disposed of one part in his inward dialogue, seems to reabsorb the other. The Negro considers his victim: 'Unmoving, the Negro seemed to be watching over his laborious agony . . . His judiciary task fulfilled, now he was nobody.

[7] *La vuelta de Martín Fierro*, ll 4583–94.
[8] *OC*, p. 519.

Or rather he was the other: he had no destiny on earth and had killed a man.'[9] This may be understood as an author's farewell. It is Recabarren who is unmoving, and who has just undergone a 'laborious agony': the construction of a perfectly agonistic narrative. And it is Recabarren now whose job or destiny is finished, having reached his predetermined end ('El fin' in fact). It is Recabarren, finally, who has killed a man, because he has, in his high-handed way, killed another writer's hero. He has put his paralysis to excellent use.

There are other variants of the author in Borges's stories, but it would add little to introduce or examine them here. The indices of authorship are now I hope recognizable. Authors are to be found, in the very first instance, on their own, even if their solitude is quickly broken as the work of imagination involves them in the duplication of their selves. They may be found in towers, that long-established refuge of fictional and very occasionally (I am thinking of Montaigne) real authors, or more picturesquely, like Ts'ui Pên (a name doubly consonant with authorship, *pen* being both the English word for a writing instrument and the colloquial Chinese term for one of the stitched 'gatherings' of which books are made), in the willow-pattern elegance of a Pavilion of Limpid Solitude.[10]

Best of all they may be found in hotels, like the real-life José Hernández, hotels being the most provisional of residences and a holiday from everyday necessities. The finest specimen of a hotel in Borges is the Hôtel du Nord in the story of 'La muerte y la brújula' ('Death and the Compass'), which is also the scene of the first of the crimes in that exemplary detective story. The North, in Borges, is that frigid point of the compass from which the imagination customarily starts out to seek the warmth and consolation of the South. The Hôtel du Nord is 'that tall prism overlooking the estuary whose waters have the colour of the desert. At this tower (which very manifestly incorporates the abhorrent whiteness of a sanatorium, the numbered divisibility of a prison, and the general appearance of a house of ill-repute (*una casa mala*)) there arrived ...'[11] A strikingly adaptable building, then, Borges's hotel, with

---

[9] *OC*, p. 521.

[10] In the story of 'El jardín de senderos que se bifurcan' ('The Garden of Forking Paths'), *OC*, p. 476.

[11] *OC*, p. 499.

some valuable overtones. It is a place to make fictions in. It is a prism because a fiction reconstitutes the 'light' for us, that is to say it projects existing fictions in a different form (play is consistently made with certain colours in 'La muerte y la brújula', to symbolize the prismatic effect of an author's work); it is a sanatorium because the making of fiction is both a sickness and a cure (in a sense explained in the next chapter), and the 'abhorrent whiteness' might very well be the as yet empty sheets of paper which confront the author at the outset and which he must agonize to cover; it is a prison of 'numbered divisibility' because a fiction, as I have tried to show, is an artificial extension of time which can be divided and subdivided as many times as the author likes: once enclosed in his narrative he is the absolute master of its chronology and also, as Borges wryly indicates, its prisoner. I am less confident of interpreting the *casa mala*, unless it is there simply to reinforce the idea which Borges loves to give that the writing of fictions is a punishing business which the sensible person is well advised not to tackle. The word *casa*, like the word 'house' in English, has an astrological as well as an architectural meaning, and Borges often seems to use it in that sense, to symbolize the 'irrational' or anyway less than scientific causality on which fiction depends; the *casa mala* could therefore be that division of the zodiac which promises the author a troublesome time and his readers a series of particularly ominous events.

The Hôtel du Nord is, for all the differences of scale, style, and topography, a variant of Ts'ui Pên's Pavilion of Limpid Solitude, Recabarren's truckle-bed, Don Isidro Parodi's prison-cell, Don Illán's 'place apart'. The possible metaphors for the necessary isolation of the author are many, and Borges has not tried to exhaust them. Common to all of them is the fact that the maker of fictions is removed from *immediate* contact with reality. His reality is therefore mediate. It consists of whatever there is in his own head, or whatever is contained in the mediations of reality— the books or other documents—which surround him. Ultimately, the author looks for a creative reclusion to that place which is, for Borges, the *locus amœnus* above all others, the library.

CHAPTER 2

INSPIRATION

THE bodily requirement is now met: the author is removed from contingency.[1] The next requirement is a psychological one, and concerns the authorial state of mind. This state of mind has traditionally been recognized as distinct from our ordinary state of mind, and any over-all theory of literature should allow room for the concept of 'inspiration', for otherwise it will not adequately account for the divergence from fact which literature represents, or its wholesale eclipse of the reality principle.

It might be argued that, logically, inspiration comes before isolation, that the author first feels the urge to write and then shuts himself away in order to write. But for every author who sequesters himself because he has been inspired, there are likely to be a great many more who become inspired because they have first sequestered themselves. For them isolation is the spur to imagination, its necessary condition. It is the unnatural, anti-social confinement of the body which induces, for most of us, such abnormal activity of the mind as we are capable of. Confinement, rather obviously, lowers drastically the number and variety of stimuli the mind gets from the outside world. The author's physical environment offers him peculiarly little novelty, and if he relies on it, as many reluctant imaginers no doubt do, to spare him from the effort of imagination, he will usually be disappointed. The familiar offers scant purchase to his attention; if he tries to de-familiarize it, by attending to it with an extra intensity, he

---

[1] It is worth underlining that Borges never describes the author's temporary absence from reality, only symbolizes it. Authors really do withdraw to do their work but they seldom accomplish all their work at a single sitting. The writing of a fiction, however short, involves a whole series of withdrawals into privacy, and the author will not be exactly the same person on the second occasion he withdraws as he was on the first; he will have learnt new things, forgotten old ones, changed mentally in a number of small but significant ways. To this extent, contingency may seem not to be excluded quite as thoroughly as Borges's model implies. But the author-figure in Borges's stories is a Borges-like author, and Borges manifestly lays down such draconian rules for himself in the development of his stories that no interruption or interval of time spent away from his place of work could possibly affect his original scheme.

will find that nothing sets the mind adrift quicker than to try and stabilize it on a given point.

The author's isolation thus makes room—a spatial metaphor is most appropriate—for a higher level of mental activity than we can manage as we go about our daily business. The sequence of thoughts, or associations, which results is richer, freer, and probably stranger than any we could sustain moving open-eyed about the world. To close our eyes, figuratively speaking, is to solicit inspiration. The distraction against which the author must be protected is distraction only from outside; once he is safely cocooned in thought, the distractions come from within and whatever comes from within, from his memory, is worth his attention, provided he accepts, as most of us now do, that nothing comes to mind without having been, however obscurely, willed by us. The terminology of poetic inspiration is no longer what it was, and we have dispensed with Muses, frenziedly rolling eyes, and the afflatus. We have not dispensed with, nor is there any need to, the more humdrum belief that inspiration is a psychedelic state in which certain barriers are overthrown and inhibitions overcome. The Muses, after all, were once the divinities who presided over memory and the contemporary view of persons inspired is that they have access to a wider, more emotive range of recollections than the same persons uninspired.

To that extent, inspiration remains what it was, a Romantic idea. It is also a labour-saving idea. Inspiration is held to achieve artistic effects which might otherwise have had to be worked for. It tends to be synonymous with intuition, and the intuitive we see as the exact opposite of the intellectual. Intuition and intellection may produce an identical effect, but in the first case the process by which that effect has been produced is occult, in the second it is not. What charms some and repels others about the idea of inspiration is just this, that it economizes on the process of writing, achieving an estimable fluency with none of the self-doubts and hesitations which beset the uninspired.

Borges, whose writing is all intelligence and rigour, likes to present himself, and his representative authors in his stories, as men inspired. Partly this is a game: there is nothing at all wild or dishevelled even in the lyric poetry which Borges has written, no evidence at all that he has ever been carried away. Partly, however, it is more serious: a justification, in conventional terms, of the fact that those who write must have a reason for writing. Inspiration, in this sense, does not replace work, it precedes it: it is the excuse the author has for subjecting himself to a considerable intellectual ordeal. Borges's pose is to imply that inspiration lasts and is even coextensive with composition. In the preface to his third collection of stories, *El informe de Brodie* (*Brodie's Report*), he sides with the Romantics against the Classics: 'The exercise of literature is mysterious; our opinions are ephemeral and I opt for the Platonic theory of the Muse not for that of Poe, who reasoned, or pretended to reason, that the writing of a poem is an operation of the intelligence.'[2]

Poe's reasoning, or pretence of reasoning, is contained in his celebrated essay on 'The Philosophy of Composition' in which he sets out to rationalize, item by item, the writing of 'The Raven'. This would commonly be classified as a Romantic poem by a Romantic poet, a macabre, fatalistic affair typical of the dark imaginings of the age. It is quite legitimate to classify it thus, provided we do not go on to argue that such a poem is the inevitable effluent of Poe's dark, Romantic mind. The thrust of Poe's explanation of 'The Raven' is that it is a wholly conscious, deliberate performance, directed to a particular end; his 'philosophy of composition' is one which first posits an effect—the effect the poet wishes to procure in the sensibility of his readers—and then works out the most certain way to achieve it.

It pleases Borges that Poe, the Romantic, should put forward a theory of literary creation which is essentially Classical in the supreme value it sets on intelligence,[3] whereas Plato, the Classical philosopher, holds the opposite view and both exalts and diminishes the 'poet' by making him into the demented mouthpiece of forces greater than himself (Plato's ulterior motive being, though, to prove that poets were dangerous, anti-social people). 'The Philosophy of Composition' is a fascinating essay, even if it does not manage to deduce the actual poem of 'The Raven' quite as inexorably from its author's intentions as Poe might have liked. What it does do is to display the author as an actor, as someone who must work artfully to construct a public self:

---

[2] *OC*, p. 1021.

[3] It is Poe's rationalistic theory of literature which gave him such unexpected influence in France, not least with Mallarmé, who clearly learnt from Poe and who remains, in his gnomic way, the most profound and far-sighted of literary theorists.

Most writers—poets in especial—prefer having it understood that they compose by a species of fine frenzy—an ecstatic intuition—and would positively shudder at letting the public take a peep behind the scenes, at the elaborate and vacillating crudities of thought—at the true purposes seized only at the last moment—at the innumerable glimpses of ideas that arrived not at the maturity of full view . . . in a word, at the wheels and pinions—the tackle for scene-shifting—the step-ladders and demon traps—the cock's feathers, the red paint and the black patches, which, in ninety-nine cases out of the hundred, constitute the properties of the literary *histrio*.[4]

Poe thus introduces, or reintroduces, the work ethic into the business of writing. The difference between his theory and the Platonic is one of responsibility. Plato's poet is not to be held responsible for what he writes because he cannot help himself; Poe's poet, unwilling to surrender to the dictates of whatever power it be, the Muse, the id, or that most contemporary of divinities, language itself, can and does help himself. Once his work is published he stands by it; he is entitled to analyse it, as Poe analyses 'The Raven', so as to 'render it manifest that no one point in its composition is referable either to accident or intuition'.[5] Poe is not I think pretending that accident and intuition are not involved in literary composition, which would be a silly claim to make, but that when we are presented with the finished work we should treat each element of it as the voluntary product of its author. This is a precept for readers, and the full vindication of any poetic structure. The accidents or intuitions the writer may have had while he was writing are now taken in charge, they are a part of his structure. Their justification is their place in that structure, in which he will have related them to other elements, themselves it may be originally the product of accident or intuition. The question which Poe, or any structuralist critic, puts to the text is not Where from? but Why?

For Borges, Poe is a dissembler, an intuitive spirit disguising himself as a mathematician. Borges, whose philosophy of composition leaves very much less room for inspiration than Poe's did, is equally a dissembler: a mathematical spirit disguising himself as an intuitive one. It is 'intuition' which enables the mind to pass from the ordinary, everyday world of particulars to the

---

[4] E. A. Poe, *Essays and Stories*, London. 1914, p. 24,

[5] Ibid., p. 25.

linguistic, fictional world of universals. Intuition, that is, is the power by which we pass beyond existences to essences.

This power turns up in some unexpected places for Borges. The most unexpected is in the card-game of *truco*. Borges has written an essay about this game, and also a short poem; both of them early on in his career, the poem having been a part of his first published collection, the *Fervor de Buenos Aires* of 1923. It is clear both from the poem and from the later essay that *el truco* struck Borges as something much more interesting than a picturesque element of Buenos Aires life. He was susceptible enough to urban colour in those days but also capable of appreciating cultural phenomena which harmonized with his own nascent intellectual schemes.

Both the poem and the essay start more or less with the same words; in the poem 'Forty cards have displaced life', in the essay, more tentatively, 'Forty cards seek to displace life'. This is more than the commonplace suggestion that the playing of card-games is a distraction. In his essay particularly Borges presses larger, more ambitious claims for *el truco* in terms which make the playing of the game come increasingly to resemble the practice of literature. Rather than a trivial distraction from the real world the game is an alternative world of its own. It demands, at the outset, a distinct state of mind: 'The *trucada* is set up; the players, who are creoles all of a sudden, are lightened of their habitual selves. A distinct self, an almost ancestral, vernacular self weaves the designs of the game.'[6] To play the game of *truco* is to be identified with the earlier generations who have played it; the rules and procedures of the game are fixed, only the players can change. And so it is with literature for Borges, a man for whom the conventions which writers follow matter more than those writers' names. Each fresh game of *truco* realizes a doubtless unprecedented combination of the cards, but the number of possible combinations is finite: there are forty cards in the pack and starting from that it would be theoretically possible to compute the sum of the different ways in which they might fall. Again, Borges enjoys toying with the idea that literature, or rather language, is exhaustible, that the number

---

[6] 'El truco', *OC*, p. 145. The players become 'creoles' for the space of the game because the creoles are, in South America, the original European settlers of the continent and their descendants, to be distinguished from the truly indigenous populations and recent immigrants from Europe.

of its possible combinations is finite, that everything sayable will one day be said. The traditions of the game, which so far absorb the identities of its players as to make them indistinguishable from their predecessors, prove that an exact recurrence of events is possible, that time is therefore unreal, that a humble card-game can be an education in metaphysics. Similarly, in literature, when a writer repeats the words of a predecessor, time is abolished, and the person who quotes Shakespeare *is* Shakespeare.

One might extend the list of resemblances that exist for Borges between literature and *el truco*. The world of the card-players is a 'hallucinated little world' which verges on the real world but does not overlap with it—it is the 'place apart' of which I have spoken. There is a 'frontier' between hallucination and reality and whatever crosses that frontier constitutes an invasion of the author's autonomy: it is an enemy against which the author's one defence is to incorporate it into his fantasy. There are a fair number of references in Borges's stories to this *frontera* and to its negotiation by the true maker of fictions; Borges locates it—his geography is nothing if not systematic—between Argentina and Uruguay, the land which lies to the east. Just as he opposes North and South in his stories, so he opposes East and West, as the compass-points of disorder and order.

Where the practised *truco*-player is closest to the true maker of fictions is in his reliance on deception. As a deceiver he has more resources than the author because he can use his body as well as words: 'The style of his deception . . . is a mendacious action of the voice, of a face which is deemed to be a "semblance" and to be defending itself, of a wild, deceitful verbiage.'[7] The *truco*-player succeeds or not by the ambiguity of what he does and says. Like a good narrator he tells stories which may be true and may be false; the uncertainty is essential to the pleasure of his audience. He is not, strictly speaking, a liar, any more than the maker of fictions is a liar. The lie is a concept which should be confiscated at that clearly defined frontier between reality and hallucination. 'The poet never affirmeth' said Sir Philip Sidney and there could be no act more philistine than to try and smuggle truth-values into the consideration of fiction. Lies are answers made to questions which the answerer knows to be false; fictions are not written in answer to a question and do not, by definition, correspond with

[7] *OC*, p. 146.

particular states of affairs. The *truco*-player romances, as it were. The real scandal in his world would be for a player to step out of it for a moment and to ask him, on oath, whether he was telling the truth. Such spoil-sports, rightly, are not invited to play games they clearly do not understand; similarly, those who see fictions as lies should give up reading novels.

Granted that the *truco*-table is all these things, and a place where the temporal and moral laws are, by agreement, suspended, we have still not accounted for the force which turns people away from reality and towards hallucination. Why do they play *truco*,[8] compose fictions, or read fictions once other victims of hallucination have composed them? Borges, by his own account, turned to the making of stories in order to reassure himself that his brain had survived intact a serious illness. The composition of a truly rigorous narrative would be the ideal test for his possibly defective cerebral machinery. This account I am tempted to call a Poe-faced deception. Borges's illness happened at the end of 1938, three years after the first publication of the narratives of the *Historia universal de la infamia*. Those narratives are, admittedly, less obviously rigorous than the later ones of *Ficciones* or *El Aleph*, but they embody a great many of the fundamental principles of Borges's fiction. So does the story of 'El acercamiento a Almotásim' ('The Approach to Almotasim'), which has long formed part of the *Ficciones* but was first published in the *Historia de la eternidad* (*History of Eternity*) in 1936.

But there are more interesting reasons for distrusting Borges's own version of his original inspiration, above all its patently dialectical character. Borges's illness was septicaemia, and was associated with high fever and delirium; to find out whether his brain had recovered he chose to submit it to a severe test of its lucidity. The completed fiction was to be the proof that delirium had been defeated, it was the cleanest imaginable break with the mental disturbance he had endured. Indeed, there is no reason why Borges need have worried about the survival of his intelligence if his illness had not contained a factor he considered lastingly inimical to it. This factor was the temporary loss of control over

---

[8] It is likely that the name of this particular game attracted Borges because of its close resemblance to the French verb *truquer*, meaning 'to fake'. The *Nuevo Pequeño Larousse Ilustrado* gives the etymology of *truco* as being German, from *drücken*, 'to squeeze'; but this etymology only explains a second meaning of *truco*, as a game a little like billiards, played with balls and a table.

the workings of his mind, and his subsequent decision to write a fiction was the reassertion of his authority. In sickness, therefore, Borges had been exposed to the Romantic, Platonic theory of poetic inspiration; in health, he turned to the Classical, Edgar Allan Poe theory. Borges's account of this apparently crucial, formative episode in his life looks suspiciously like a brief fable on the nature of inspiration, a fable in which he affirms his own affiliation to the Classical doctrine. As a young writer, Borges had been something of a Romantic, with a Romantic belief in individualism, vivacious imagery, local colour, and all the rest of it; by the 1930s, when he first turned to publishing fictions, he was nothing at all of a Romantic, but a Classic who regretted his earlier misunderstanding, as he saw it, of the nature of language and of literature. So there was a 'conversion' in his career, even if it did not take place as neatly and dramatically as the account of his illness suggests.

The fever which so threatened to swamp his intelligence plays a decisive role in his fiction. Borges's authors are inspired in a robust, Romantic way. One of the most blatant and therefore most instructive of all his fiction-mongers is an early creation: the Negro Ebenezer Bogle, the *éminence noire* of the second story in the *Historia universal de la infamia*, 'El impostor inverosímil Tom Castro' ('The Improbable Impostor Tom Castro'). This is a re-telling of the story of the Tichborne Claimant, the impostor who tried to swindle the Tichborne family in Victorian England by pretending to be the long-lost heir to its fortune. In Borges's version, which is very much his own, Bogle master-minds the whole operation, and the impostor, Castro, is his compliant creature. Bogle is a Negro whose 'ancient African appetites [had been] much amended by the use and abuse of Calvinism', a temperamental confluence which bears, I think, an interesting resemblance to the dialectic between instinct and inhibition in Borges's account of his septicaemia. It bears an interesting resemblance too to the confluence within Borges's own ancestry, a confluence much remarked on by him, between the warlike and the ecclesiastical: the soldiers in his lineage are the South American or native branch, the Protestant pastors the European branch. Bogle is Borges's surrogate.

The name is not, it seems, Borges's own invention. It occurs, according to the very thorough Ronald Christ, in the version of the Tichborne story on which Borges claims to have based his own, the version given in Philip Gosse's *History of Piracy* (and where better to pirate one's own stories than a history of piracy!). In Gosse's version, according to Christ—and I make no apology for constructing this chain of allusion, since it's just the sort of construction Borges himself is a master at, even if in his case many of the links turn out, on inspection, to be forgeries—Bogle is a very minor personage, one of the victims of the trickster Orton.[9] His name looks quite like Borges's own, which may well have something to do with Borges's decision to promote him from victim to evil genius. An additional, even better reason is that a *bogle* is, in English, a 'goblin' or 'bugbear': an agency fit to rank with the 'backyard sorcerers and suburban wizards' to whose agency Borges ascribes the 'inventive and diabolical' ambitions of the game of *truco*.[10] The name of Bogle was indeed a happy accident for Borges.

In the Borges story Bogle meets Orton, 'a person of unruffled idiocy' and 'infinite docility', in Australia. Up until this meeting Bogle has been a servant; abruptly he is transformed into the master. Bogle has two abnormalities: his fear of crossing the road and of 'the violent vehicle which would put an end to his days', and 'the visits of the god'. Orton helps Bogle safely across the road in Sydney and their alliance is thereby formed. This road is surely the frontier between reality and fantasy, or fact and fiction. Bogle hesitates to cross it because he is 'fearful of the East, the West, the South and the North',[11] which is rather overdoing things in an operation as seemingly banal as getting from one pavement to the other. The fear of all four points of the compass at once implies a fear not of a single linear obstacle like a road but of a world. Bogle is fearful of entering the alternative world of fiction; it is Orton who introduces him to it because Orton is henceforward his subject, the nonentity whom Bogle will transform into a fictive entity. The aim of Bogle's diabolical scheme will be to impose Orton as Tichborne: to establish him in a different *name*.[12] His

[9] Ronald Christ, *The Narrow Act: Borges's Art of Allusion*, New York, 1969, p. 35.

[10] *OC*, p. 146.   [11] *OC*, p. 301.

[12] The impostor, born Arthur Orton, has taken the name Tom Castro from a certain family that had befriended him in Chile. 'No traces remain', Borges assures us, 'of this South American episode.' The 'South American episode', needless to say, is Borges's own version of the Tichborne story, which he offers,

cue is given to him by the death—the assumed death—of the real Roger Tichborne, a real accident which Bogle now intends to transform to his own advantage by using it to inaugurate a fiction. The birth of a fiction entails the death of a fact: as one can see in another of Borges's apprentice fictions, 'Hombre de la esquina rosada' ('Man of the Rose-Coloured Corner'), where the victim of the *cuchillero*'s knife is one Francisco *Real* (my italics).

The 'visits of the god' are those moments in his story when Bogle seeks inspiration, those moments when contingency threatens to wreck the structure he has been carefully erecting. For as long as Lady Tichborne is alive, for example, Bogle's scheme works well; the imposture is successful. Her death, however, like the original death of her son, presents Bogle with a challenge. The other members of the family do not believe in Orton and bring a lawsuit against him. Bogle at once goes out 'to seek inspiration in the decorous streets of London. It was dusk; Bogle wandered about until a honey-coloured moon was duplicated in the rectangular water of the public fountains (*fuentes*). The god visited him.'[13] Dusk is the appropriate time for inspiration to strike for Borges, for the good reason that it is the time when daylight gives way to darkness, sun to moon, and, symbolically at least, waking life to dream life. Borges's stories are predominantly nocturnal. They are also inspired, as we know, by literature, not directly by life: the 'rectangular' *fuentes* are more helpfully translated into English as the public 'sources' of Bogle's (and Borges's) inspiration, those available fictions or narratives from which their own depart. As for the 'honey-coloured' moon, that might be explained by the fact that the word *castro*, in addition to denoting a children's game, also means to remove the honey from a beehive. Tom Castro, who is Bogle's satellite or moon, is the creature who works for the gratification of the master apiarist.

The inspiration which Bogle gets is to have letters published in *The Times* denouncing Orton as an impostor. These letters are to be signed by prominent Papists, starting with Father Goudron of the Society of Jesus. This ingenious popish plot succeeds in

[13] *OC*, p. 304.

---

as he offers all his fictions, as a perfectly 'useless' (*inútil*) interpolation of which history has no need. The word *castro* in Spanish has as its chief meaning a game, not unlike hopscotch, played by children. Bogle's attempt to 'rename' Orton is preceded by Borges's playful attempt to turn Orton into Castro.

convincing right-minded Protestants that Orton is genuine. Bogle has pulled off a *coup* worthy of the *truco*-table; a true statement has been made in circumstances which imply its falsity or, better, a fiction has been imposed through the assertion of its fictiveness by an untrustworthy source. This is jesuitical indeed and it is small wonder that the first letter in *The Times* should be signed by Father Goudron. *Goudron* is the French word for tar, and tar, like the diabolical Bogle, is black. *Tar* is also the English word for a sailor, and Arthur Orton was a sailor before he fell into the clutches of Bogle. Roger Tichborne, the sophisticated young man whom the uncouth Orton has been impersonating, has already been described as 'Frenchified'. Thus the impersonation can be understood as the turning of the English *tar* into the Frenchified *goudron*. This bilingual punning, in a story itself of course written in a third language altogether, is a fearsome proof of how intricate and rigorous a writer Borges can be—where an apparently random name turns out to embody the essential plot of the story—and of how alert his readers need to be if they are to take anything like his full measure.

It is on a subsequent visit to the London streets that Bogle finds, instead of further inspiration, a violent death from 'the terrible vehicle which had been pursuing him from the depths of time'.[14] Contingency finally intrudes in a form against which there is no appeal. Bogle's function is over, his interval of mastery and authorship is done. Castro survives and goes to gaol, even though, when he is told his creator is dead, the news 'annihilates' him. The imposture is not sustained because it dies with Bogle. Orton continues to lie, but contradictorily now—without the rigour which a true fiction requires—and with 'scant enthusiasm'. Even this last word Borges does not use carelessly, because elsewhere in his work he stresses its original meaning of 'a god-inspired zeal'. It is Bogle, the god, who has supplied the enthusiasm; without Bogle, Orton, like the paralysed Recabarren, is only half a man.

I have lingered over 'El impostor inverosímil Tom Castro' because it is an early story, predating Borges's famous 'accident' and consequent illness, and a far less innocent story than it might at first appear. It serves excellently as the prototype of the later, even more meticulously contrived stories, where Borges is not hampered at all by the data of an existing version of the 'same'

[14] *OC*, p. 304.

narrative. It is also a splendidly wrought story in its own right, equivocal enough to act as a reminder that the English verb *to boggle* originally meant to hesitate 'as if at a bogle'.

Bogle is unique in Borges for finding inspiration somewhere as public as the streets of London; Borges's inspired inventors are more commonly to be found in the ultimate privacy of their beds, and in the unwelcome grip of fever. The most conspicuously feverish of all of them is Juan Dahlmann, the protagonist of the story Borges once called 'perhaps' his best: 'El Sur' ('The South'). Dahlmann, whose lineage, like Bogle's, displays a confluence of the martial or wild and the clerical or peaceable, suffers an accident remarkably similar to the one Borges has said he suffered himself. It happens on the day he buys an imperfect copy of *The Thousand and One Nights*. Hurrying upstairs to examine this discovery (he usually takes the lift, a point I will come back to) Dahlmann feels something brush against his forehead: 'a bat, a bird?' asks the story, as if bats and birds were readily to be found in the stairwell of what one has supposed to be an apartment block in Buenos Aires. When the door is finally opened to him—by 'a woman', another tiny indication, since this is his own home, that some kind of alienation has already begun—he finds that his forehead is covered in blood. Or is it blood? He has walked into a newly painted door that someone had forgotten to close; there is the possibility that the blood is 'really' paint, while the two doors, the one which has been left open and his own which is closed, form a symmetry typical of the origins of a fiction with Borges.

The effects of Dahlmann's brush with the door are unexpectedly drastic: 'Dahlmann managed to get to sleep, but by dawn he was awake and from that time on the flavour of everything was atrocious. Fever consumed him and the illustrations from the Thousand and One Nights served to decorate nightmares.'[15] The friends and relatives who come to see the injured Dahlmann declare him to be 'very well', which could be kindness and could be the truth—they are invaders from across the frontier with reality who will not tolerate such fictions. The reality of the story, however, is that Dahlmann is 'in hell'. He is taken to a sanatorium to have an X-ray, after the doctor treating him, his usual doctor, has been duplicated by a second, unknown doctor: a duplication symmetrical once again with the duplication Dahlmann either

[15] *OC*, p. 525.

has undergone or is about to undergo. The treatment which Dahlmann receives in the sanatorium is straight out of a horror film and far from obviously relevant to his complaint: 'When he got there, they undressed him, shaved his head, bound him with metal to a small bed, shone lights at him until he was blinded and giddy, sounded his chest, and a masked man stuck a needle into his arm. He awoke with nausea, bandaged, in a cell (*celda*) rather like a well.'[16]

The sanatorium is a place of transition in 'El Sur'; Dahlmann is sick when he is carried into it, convalescent when he re-emerges and sets out on a long-meditated excursion to the South. The South, I have said, is the pole which attracts the imagination away from the stern necessities of the North. Dahlmann's sanatorium is located midway: in the Calle Ecuador, or Street of the Equator. But it is not the sanatorium which marks the break with reality in the story: it is a place of inspiration but not the source of inspiration. The source of inspiration is surely the copy of *The Thousand and One Nights*, a book. Dahlmann has bought, naturally, a translation of that work, and an incomplete (*descabalado*) copy at that, so that he is doubly removed from the 'original' reality of the text. Translation, for Borges, is also the model of creation; whoever creates a new narrative is in effect 'translating' an old one, changing it here and there to suit himself. Dahlmann, like Bogle communing with the reflection of the moon in the 'rectangular public *fuentes*', has been inspired to get in on the literary act, to join the creators. The translation he has bought being incomplete, there is a clear challenge to him to complete it, to add some fantastic makeweight of his own to the traditional corpus of unrealities. It is as a result of finding this book, and of his eagerness to examine it, that Dahlmann breaks with his routine—taking the stairs instead of the lift —and sets in motion the sequence of events which leads him inexorably and gratifyingly to a heroic death in the land of his dreams, the South. The incongruities in his story start before he enters the sanatorium. The sanatorium is thus the place where the fever of inspiration is both endured and resolved: an ambivalent place. That ambivalence is endemic to the making of fictions, which, Borges implies, is both an ordeal and a gratification.

I shall return to 'El Sur' later, because many of Borges's most persistent themes are dramatized in it. For now, there is another

[16] *OC*, p. 526.

striking case of creative 'fever' requiring auscultation. This is the case of Dandy Red Scharlach, the evil genius of 'La muerte y la brújula', who leads the impeccably rational detective Erik Lönnrot into a trap and kills him. The Dandy's name is a give-away: *Scharlach* is the German word for 'scarlet fever'. Before he puts paid to his adversary, Scharlach explains to him how he came to hatch the marvellously ingenious plan by which he has trapped the artful reasoner:

Three years ago, in a gaming-house in the Rue de Toulon, you arrested my brother and sent him to prison. My men got me away from the shoot-out in a cab, with a police bullet in my belly. For nine days and nights I lay agonizing in this desolate symmetrical villa; fever had laid me low, the odious two-faced Janus who looks to both the sunset and the sunrise lent horror to my sleeping and my waking . . . In those nights I swore by the god who sees with two faces and by all the gods of fever and mirrors, to weave a labyrinth around the man who had imprisoned my brother.[17]

Scharlach's fever, like Dahlmann's, is a terrible effort at duplication, in which the solitary creator must pass from unity to duplicity, the origins of fiction lying in a dialectic. Scharlach 'agonizes' not because he is dying—he does not die—but because the making of a fiction involves an *agon*, or contest, like the contest between Scharlach and Lönnrot of which the fiction of 'La muerte y la brújula' consists. Janus, the god of duplicity or duplication, is 'odious' partly because such duplicity is taxing for the imagination, and partly for a reason I will discuss more fully in another chapter: because 'hatred' is the emotion appropriate to a dialectic, which can only originate in a conflict of desires or opinions. Janus, with his two faces, one looking to the sunset and the other to the sunrise, also presides over the synchronization, in a fiction, of phenomena whose coincidence is impossible in reality. The plot of the story depends absolutely on the conflation of these two incompatible times of day by the overlaying of one system of measuring time, the Christian, with a different system, the Hebrew. Borges's story almost achieves the impossible feat of making one man's sunset into another man's sunrise (but again, more of this later).

Fever, and the other congenerous states of mind which Borges sometimes invokes, such as nightmare or delirium, is a deceptive

17 *OC*, pp. 505–6.

Muse inasmuch as it seems to equate fiction with frenzy. The temptation is to say that Borges is having one of his jokes, that his fever cases are themselves urbane figments and a literary man's acknowledgment of Classical influences. But that would be going too far. Borges is serious, I believe, in that 'fever' symbolizes the unnatural state of mind the author has to cultivate if he is to make satisfactory, rigorous fictions. Isolation from reality is not enough, he also needs an abnormal concentration of the mind which might well be experienced as a kind of excitement. Where Borges is most truly misleading is in employing a symbol for literary inspiration which makes that peculiar state of mind seem so undesirable, an imposition on the mind by a disordered body. Borges makes fictions, as anyone makes fictions, because the pleasure of making them outweighs whatever strain is entailed; he does not write them because he cannot help himself. Borges's 'fever' is far from being a pathological condition, as one sees the minute one turns from its aetiology to its effects. These effects, in their supreme lucidity, are not merely discrepant from their advertised cause, they are contradictory of it.

CHAPTER 3

IDEALIZATION

THERE is more to Ts'ui Pên's Pavilion than the Solitude it procures him; it is a place also of limpidity. But limpidity is the last
effect we anticipate on the mind from an onset of fever: clearly,
the hallucinations to which the maker of fictions is professionally
liable are not of the usual random and disorganized kind. They
are, as Borges puts it in his piece on Shakespeare in *El Hacedor*
(*The Maker*), 'controlled hallucinations'. That definition, and the
other, synonymous definition which Borges also uses of the
'controlled dream' or *sueño dirigido*, probably qualifies as oxymoron. Oxymoron appeals to Borges because it is a combinatory
figure which brings into conjunction two terms we would normally
think of as contradictory of each other; it thus flaunts the freedom
which a speaker or writer enjoys of forming verbal combinations
for which there is no logical justification and no referent in the
real world. And so with the 'controlled hallucination', a perfectly
comprehensible idea but one which makes apparent a dominant
factor of mimesis: real hallucinations are not controlled but foisted
on us by the malfunctioning of our bodies or minds; 'controlled'
hallucinations can therefore only be the deliberate imitation of such
involuntary states.

They are also a verbal imitation of wholly or predominantly
wordless states. Hallucinations, possibly, and dreams, certainly,
may contain verbal elements but they are not, when they occur,
verbal experiences. They become verbal only once they are transmitted to someone else. The mimesis of dreams in literature is not
the mimesis of dreams themselves (which is possibly only for the
cinema) but of the accounts given of dreams by dreamers. Those
accounts, so Freud suggests in *The Interpretation of Dreams*, are
themselves a first attempt to 'control' the dream because the censor-
ship which the dream-work itself may have circumvented is now
reimposed and reworks the dream-work to make it less objection-
able to the dreamer; this reworking Freud, as an analyst, is entitled
to see as a crucial part of the dream which has been presented to
him by his patient.

But no dreamer, however inhibited, could ever control his dreams with the skill and objectivity of Borges. Borges's fictions do not at all resemble the dreams of our own experience, nor the more impressive, more grandly mythopoeic dreams reported in the oneirological literature. Nor, more importantly, do they resemble a third kind of dream, those invented by novelists on behalf of their characters and intended to stand in the same relationship to the waking events of the story as dreams in real life stand to waking events. The dreams one gets in Dostoevsky— especially Dostoevsky—are in their turbulence and opacity genu- inely mimetic of our own dreams. Similarly, James Joyce defended *Finnegans Wake*, the most exhaustive mimesis in all literature not of hallucination but of delirium, by saying that 'The action of my new work takes place at night. It's natural things should not be so clear at night, isn't it now?'[1] This is a statement of the purest, Aristotelian realism if ever there was one. The action of Borges's stories is very often set at night, but that, and his surreptitious dislocations of their logic, is about as far as his mimesis goes. He is much less interested in dreams than in control.

Literature is the dreams of authors not of men, and the author, as we saw in the quotation from Poe, is 'the literary *histrio*'. The equation of writing with acting is made by Borges himself in his piece on Shakespeare. The title of the piece is in English: 'Every- thing and Nothing.' Borges makes much of the continuity of Shakespeare's career: he was first an actor, then a dramatist, and acting is the profession 'to which he was predestined' (by that bigger dramatist still, God). The actor is someone who 'on a stage, plays at being someone else, before an assembly of people who play at taking him for someone else'.[2] Thus for actor and audience alike, or author and reader, the play, or story, is reality, and the other reality is temporarily in eclipse. By lending his body to the prepared text, the actor realizes the unreal. When he reverts to being a man, in Borges's alarmingly symmetrical scheme, the effect is to *un*realize the real; when he gives up acting, the Shakes- peare of 'Everything and Nothing', who is most emphatically not to be mistaken for the historical dramatist, is overcome by 'the hated savour of unreality'. In order to re-enter reality he becomes

[1] In a letter to Ezra Pound, quoted by Wayne Booth in *The Rhetoric of Fiction*, Chicago, 1961, p. 21.

[2] *OC*, p. 803.

instead a playwright, and persists for twenty years in 'that controlled hallucination'. Thus Shakespeare, first actor then author, is granted no reality at all as a man. Behind the dreamer, at most, there is 'nothing more than a little coldness, a dream not dreamt by anyone'.

Once one has begun to see the somewhat deviant sense of the word 'dream' Borges is using, talk of 'controlled' dreams looks a good deal less like oxymoron and a good deal more like tautology. To Idealists, or to those who, like Borges, have hoisted philosophical Idealism as their flag of convenience, dreaming is the very specification of mental activity; all our thoughts are fictions, only a great many of them also correspond with particular states of affairs in the outside world. Authentic fictions are those thoughts and sequences of thoughts which do not so correspond.

To 'dream', then, is to idealize, and we idealize simply by turning the world into words. Borges's world is the sum of what can be said, not the sum of what there is, so that to equate thinking with dreaming, and thus abolish the distinction between the real and the hallucinatory, is to inflate the world quite monstrously. But this inflation is temporary because it is fictive. A fiction may imagine that it is permanent but never make it so. At the end of the story of 'El Zahir'. ('The Zahir'), a literally unforgettable coin acquired banally enough in a Buenos Aires suburb, the narrator speculates about his ultimate fate, when the *zahir* is the only thing he can think of and he has become correspondingly incapable of the most mechanical human acts, such as feeding or dressing himself:

I shall not perceive the universe, I shall perceive the Zahir. According to the doctrine of idealism, the verbs *to live* and *to dream* are rigorously synonymous; from thousands of appearances I shall pass to a single one; from a very complex dream to a very simple dream. Others will dream that I am mad and I of the Zahir. Once everyone on earth is thinking, day and night, of the Zahir, which will be a dream and which reality, the earth or the Zahir?[3]

The Zahir differs not in kind but in number from the 'universe'; both are fantasmal. The universe is very many words, the Zahir only one. It might best be understood as the single word which subtends all the others: as the word 'word'. Borges makes the

[3] *OC*, p. 595.

Zahir a coin because a coin can be exchanged for a countless variety of things, just as the generic term 'word' can in a sense be exchanged for any item in the lexicon of a given language. The prospect the narrator holds out, of every mind on earth converging on the one figment, is the prospect of a perpetual fiction, like the infinitely recursive story adumbrated in *The Thousand and One Nights*.

The committed Idealist believes that we already have such a fiction: the world we live in. For Bishop Berkeley reality is not reality at all, so to speak, but the sign-system employed by God, and each individual human life is a representation scripted on high. In such a system God is the dreamer and the universe his dream. In the words long familiar in Spanish from the title of Calderón's play, *la vida es sueño*, life's a dream. But it is not living which is a dream for Borges, only writing, and it is perhaps dangerous to maintain, as Ronald Christ does, that *la vida es sueño* is 'the radical theme in Borges's writing'.[4] Calderón is proposing a complete transvaluation of reality, to be endured henceforth as the fantasmal prelude to something better and more real, cognizable only after death. Borges proposes no transvaluation of reality at all, and certainly no awakening to higher realities when we are dead. The dream, for him, is a passing distraction from reality; once the dream is over the dreamer must go back to living and to being the victim instead of the master of time. Borges's precedent is not Calderón so much as Prospero who, at the conclusion of the masque which he puts on for the young lovers, uses the transience of his own magical projections as a reminder that 'our little life is rounded with a sleep'.

Borges's 'controlled dreams', unlike life itself, are combinations of words or, as he likes to say, 'symbols'.[5] They are combinations, therefore, of general terms. Idealization, or generalization, is the founding principle of Borges's fiction, as it is the founding prin-

---

[4] Christ, *The Narrow Act*, p. 112.

[5] Whether he ought to call words 'symbols' is a moot point. Semiotics holds that words are not symbols but 'signs', the difference being that signs stand in a purely conventional relation to whatever it is they are signs of, while symbols enjoy a 'natural' relation: that is, there is some logical as opposed to arbitrary connection between signifier and signified in the case of a symbol. So-called road-signs, where they try and represent the hazard that lies ahead, are really road-symbols. What could be said for, if not by, Borges is that fiction uses words symbolically because it does not use them to refer to actual things; the language of fiction is thus symbolic of everyday language.

ciple of natural language. To put a name to something is to identify it with all the other actual and possible instances of that name, to identify the particular with the universal. This process can be mitigated, but never reversed. It can be mitigated by predicating attributes of the thing named which distinguish this instance of it from at least some other instances; or it can be mitigated by using language ostensively, like Wittgenstein's celebrated builder and his apprentice, whose language has simply four terms to refer to the four different building materials which the builder calls for and the apprentice brings.[6] But as soon as we pass beyond such primal scenes of nomenclature, and the building-materials to which the words refer no longer lie to hand, we come up against not the application of words but their applicability. The 'semantic space' they take up in our minds is then much enlarged and may not match at all closely the 'semantic space' they take up in the minds of the person we hear them from.

Borges keeps the necessary abstractness of language very much in view in his fictions; he is constantly challenging the realist illusion that general terms can be a full substitute for particular things. Even Aristotle, the arch-empiricist, was enough of a Platonist to declare that 'poetry is more philosophic and of greater significance than history, for its statements are of the nature rather of universals, whereas those of history are particulars'.[7] Borges, like Schopenhauer, has very little time for history or, to be more precise, historiography, which is in so many ways a fraud, a hopelessly insufficient and therefore misleading verbal representation of the past.

The history which Borges prefers, and which he has dabbled in himself, is more abstract, more in tune with the nature of language. It is not the history of life itself but of what has been thought or written about life: the history of ideas. Nowadays this is a subject much in vogue, and rightly so—a sign perhaps that historians themselves have become more sceptical of the adequacy of language to restore what has gone. Forty years ago Borges published first his *Historia universal de la infamia* and then the *Historia de la eternidad*, and established himself as someone concerned to supersede the pretentions of traditional historiography. He was taking

[6] L. Wittgenstein, *Philosophical Investigations*, Oxford, 1968, p. 3e.

[7] *Poetics*, trans. Warrington, London, 1963, p. 17.

advantage of the ambiguity in the word *historia*, which is both 'history' and a 'story', to show that the only past we have is the one variously idealized by historians. The *Historia de la eternidad* is a subversive title for a book; it makes eternity out to be a 'story', not a fact, and then saddles it with a 'history', which is the evolution through time of the supposedly unchanging idea of timelessness.

The ideal historian, in Borges, is someone who has no need to travel, or to study things as they really are. He appears as the narrator—the historian as story-teller—of one of the most involved and meaningful of the later stories, 'Guayaquil'. This narrator holds a chair of American History in Buenos Aires and is involved in a battle of wills with another historian, a Jewish immigrant to South America from Nazi Germany called Eduardo Zimmermann, who teaches in the University of the South. The two historians are rivals: both wish to travel to the Estado Occidental, or Western State, to examine and transcribe a historical document, a letter written by the Great Liberator, Simón Bolívar, in which he gives details of his famous meeting in 1822 at Guayaquil, in Ecuador, with the other great liberator of South America, José de San Martín. That meeting is held, at any rate in Borges's story, to be the sufficient cause of San Martín's withdrawal from the field in favour of his rival. The result of the corresponding meeting, almost a century and a half later, between the two historians, is the withdrawal of the narrator of the story in favour of his rival, who has in fact foreseen his success and bought himself an air-line ticket for the city where the letter is held.

The duel between the two historians is nothing so crude as a duel between the Ideal and the Real; it is a duel between different degrees of abstraction. The narrator of the story is a purist, if a reluctant purist: he is the perfectly sedentary man who will never leave the 'private office' (*escritorio particular*) in which he welcomes his more forceful opponent. He is in full occupation of the world of fiction; when Zimmermann rings his bell he opens the door to him 'with Republican simplicity', an odd phrase which is not Borges telling us what admirably democratic manners his narrator has but a small indication that the Professor of American History is the complete man of letters. For it is the famous republic of letters he belongs to and not the Argentinian Republic, and his simplicity is not a moral quality but a linguistic one: he is simple because he is a citizen of an ideal, abstract world where there are only words and no things.

Zimmermann is not yet fitted for such simplicity. The narrator's description of his rival makes it very clear he is not abstract enough:

> I can still see those garments of a loud (*fuerte*) blue, and with an excess of buttons and pockets. His tie, I observed, was one of those illusionist's knots adjusted by two elastic clips. He carried a leather briefcase which I presumed was full of documents. He had a sober (*mesurado*) moustache military in style; in the course of our colloquy he lit a cigar and I felt then that there were too many things in that face. *Trop meublé*, I said to myself.[8]

Trop meublé is more the sort of criticism one expects to be levelled at the descriptions of a Balzac, at the Pension Vauquer for instance, than at a man's face, and Zimmermann is indeed being snubbed for having not yet fought clear of the snares of realism. The documents in his briefcase, his military moustache—which associates him more immediately with the active, martial virtues than do the relics from the battles fought in by his own ancestors that hang on the narrator's walls—and, most subtly, his 'illusionist's' tie, which suggests that Zimmermann is a man insufficiently alert to the need for artifice to be *seen* to be artifice (the tying of knots, or literary plots, needing to be seen as performed by hand); all these are signs that his literary apprenticeship is incomplete.

Zimmermann is a man from the East; when the narrator corrects him, after he has made a small mistake in a historical name (he is not quite the complete Nominalist, one might say), he spreads his arms 'with an oriental gesture'. But he is on his way to the West, to the Estado Occidental where Bolívar's letter awaits him. This trajectory from East to West is also figured in the history of the people in whom he has specialized, 'the semitic republic' of Carthage—and the Bolívar letter he is after was itself written at Cartagena (in Colombia), a Western version of Cartagena in Spain, which was supposedly founded by the Carthaginians. Zimmermann's 'semitic' republic lacks the one cardinal point which will make it the equal of the narrator's more extensive, more purely ideal republic. This is a lack which he uses to establish, as he thinks, his superiority over his rival, as the man who must travel bodily to the documents: 'You, like the day, contain both

Occident and Orient, whereas I am reduced to my Carthaginian corner, which I shall now complement with a crumb of American history.'[9]

The narrator, meanwhile, must stay where he is; the ambition to leave his study was inappropriate. His role, Zimmermann tells him, will start once the famous letter has been published. The narrator, like all true authors in Borges, operates that is to say from the public sources, and is invited by his rival in this case, if need be, to refute them. The publication of the letter is the moment when the dialectic may begin. Zimmermann, like Bolívar before him, has imposed himself 'through his superior will, not through dialectic games'. History being the record of particular events, he is the sounder historian of the two, being as yet imperfectly abstract; but it is the narrator who triumphs by telling the story of his own defeat. That story is the dialectical game he has been playing right from the start. '*Votre siège est fait*', Zimmermann tells him at one point, 'your mind is made up', in a French phrase which brings out beautifully the full sedentariness of making up the mind. 'I have a feeling I shall write no more', the story concludes, '*mon siège est fait*'. There is indeed no more to be written; his mind is made up and it is the making up of that mind that we have been given to read.

If, as I believe, the story of 'Guayaquil' is one of a literary initiation, it is tempting to find Eduardo Zimmermann's function in the story, as the author who is not yet the finished Idealist, reflected in his name. Zimmermann's Z-ness is striking, and so is the fact that the word *Zimmer* in German means room, an indication perhaps of his authorial potential. It is profitable to compare Zimmermann with another of Borges's characters of the same initials, Emma Zunz, whose story is told in *El Aleph*. Emma Zunz is a girl who avenges the death of her father (which is in fact suicide) by murdering her employer. Her father had gone into exile in the East, in Brazil, after being falsely accused of peculation; the real culprit was the man for whom Emma Zunz now works, whose factory happens to be in the West of the city in which she lives.

Like Zimmermann, Emma Zunz is an initiate into the rules of fiction with something yet to learn about them. She carries out her murder but the sequence of events of which it is the inevitable

[9] *OC*, p. 1067.

conclusion is different, once it is complete, from the sequence of events she has foreseen when planning it. Before she murders the man, Aaron Loewenthal (another Jew), she gives herself physically to an anonymous sailor—a sailor, it so happens, from a Northern ship, the North being, as we know, that quarter from which fiction must depart: the quarter, in this case, of a humiliation calling for some fictive counterweight. Emma's plan is to blame Loewenthal for the violation to which she has voluntarily submitted. She will be killing him in truth because he had framed her father, that is her secret justification; she will be killing him apparently because he has raped her, and that is to be her public justification. She, in fact, will frame Loewenthal just as he framed her father. 'Once face to face with her victim, however, more than the urgency of avenging her father, Emma felt that of punishing the outrage she had suffered for it. She could not not kill him, after that meticulous (*minuciosa*) dishonour.'[10]

Emma's dishonour replicates the dishonour that has come, through no fault of his own, on her father; and it is dishonour which has to be avenged. The replication elevates Emma above a world of particular events into the fictional world of archetypal ones, where it is not this or that dishonour that must be avenged but dishonour itself, the word rather than the thing. Her vengeance achieved, she takes up the telephone and tells her prepared story:

The story was incredible, in effect, yet it imposed itself on everyone, because substantially it was true. Emma Zunz's tone of voice was genuine, her modesty was genuine, her hatred was genuine. Also genuine was the outrage she had suffered; all that was false were the circumstances, the time and one or two proper names.[11]

Nothing could be further from history, therefore, than Emma's justification of her crime; the real outrage of 'Emma Zunz' is perpetrated, on the strength of this casual conclusion, against that unadventurous empiricism whose criterion of the truth is a correspondence with the circumstantial evidence. Borges's Idealism recognizes no such criterion. The 'substantial' truth of Emma's account is that she has been violated, and that she has shot Loewenthal dead. She has, by arranging these two episodes into a fiction and making the second follow *from* as well as *on* the first, put a name as it were to the anonymous man who in fact violated her: a false name, but the only name he will ever get.

[10] *OC*, p. 567.   [11] *OC*, p. 568.

Here again there is a symmetry with what has happened to her father, Emanuel Zunz, who had changed his name after his disgrace to Manuel Maier. And when Emma goes with a friend to a club, she has to repeat and spell out the two parts of her name, and then smile at 'the vulgar jokes commenting on its revision'. These 'vulgar jokes' seem to be directed against what is, for Borges, the specific process of fiction, which imposes its own names as it proceeds.

What we imagine is altogether simpler than what, ontologically speaking, there is. Pictorial images, such as occur in dreams, are already a massive simplification of real perceptions, and that process becomes more drastic still when we pass from iconic to verbal representations. It is this simplification which seems to have some connection in Borges's stories with the letter Z. The most Z's of all come in the title-story of *El Aleph*, in which we get the landlords of the house where the wonderful microcosm is to be found, Zunino and Zungri, as well as the lawyer, Zunni, whom their tenant, the proprietor of the Aleph, plans to call in to stop them demolishing the house and depriving him of his source of inspiration; three Z's in a story named after the initial letter of the Hebrew and Phoenician alphabets presumably have something to do with the capaciousness of literature. However, rather than flounder about in the deep waters of 'El Aleph', I would rather turn to the story of 'El Zahir', with which it makes a kind of pair. The narrator of that story, like the narrator of 'El Aleph', has a Muse, a girl who acts, however indirectly, as an inspiration. Her name is Teodelina Villar and the early part of the story is taken up with the account of her life and somewhat premature death. Her life has been marked by her fanatical devotion to fashion, which she has followed with a rigour (always a promising word in Borges) exceeding that of the Hebrews and Chinese, who 'codified every human circumstance'. This, again, looks very like a first step on the creative ascent from the particular to the universal, and Teodelina is likened, sardonically, to a novelist, Flaubert, her fellow seeker after the Absolute. Her mistake is to have sought the Absolute in the 'momentary', in the fatally circumstantial shifts of sartorial fashion. Not until she is dead can she be released from her servitude to time.

At her wake, the narrator of the story, long her admirer, sees her not as she has become but as she was: 'At some stage of the confused night of the sixth, Teodelina Villar was magically what she had been twenty years before . . .'[12] Such, perversely, are the effects on her corpse of 'corruption'; the passage of time is inverted and her face returns stage by stage to what it had looked like at the period of her famous beauty, when her picture filled the magazines. Those were the days, naturally, when the narrator had been in love with her. The affair was platonic and, this being a Borges story, far more literally platonic than other platonic love affairs. What he has been in love with is the image of Teodelina Villar, and it is this image which he is able to recapture at the wake. She has been set free from circumstantiality and has entered on eternity. She is 'herself' because she can change no more, her self in the sense of the word famously laid down in Mallarmé's line from 'Le tombeau d'Edgar Poe' ('Tel qu'en lui-même enfin l'éternité le change'). Through the process of corruption Teodelina has 'put on incorruption', as advised by St. Paul; she has become the idea of herself. To the narrator this is an inspiration, because his image of Teodelina and the sight of her have fused. When he leaves the wake and emerges into the streets of the city at two o'clock in the morning, it is into a world where idealization has set in: 'Outside, the anticipated rows of low, one-storey houses had taken on that abstract look they are wont to take on at night, when the shadows and the silence simplify them. Drunk with an almost impersonal piety, I made my way through the streets.'[13] Anticipation, abstraction, and simplification are alternative descriptions of the one process, the exchange of the thing for the idea; and the narrator's intoxication prefigures the 'fever' which comes on him a few lines later after he has gone into a café, drunk some orange juice, and been given, in his change, the Zahir, the unforgettable coin. In the café, or *almacén*, 'as my ill luck would have it, three men were playing *truco*'. This episode which, were the story of 'El Zahir' by anyone but Borges, it would be tempting to say starts the story proper, is likened by the narrator to a figure of speech, to an oxymoron, because of the contrast it makes with the immediately previous episode of Teodelina Villar's wake. The contrast strikes the reader too, not in the almost ethical terms in which it strikes the narrator, but in terms of the story's logic. It is far from obvious in what sense Teodelina Villar is the logical prelude to the story of the Zahir. But her role as 'model' (which is

---

[12] *OC*, p. 590.   [13] *OC*, p. 590.

also the role she has had in the media of the day) for the narrator
seems to be confirmed by his reaction when he first receives the
Zahir: 'I reflected that there is no coin which is not the symbol of
the coins that glitter endlessly in history and fable.'[14] This coin,
in fact, is all coins, just as the word 'coin' is all coins, historical or
fabulous, until we add other words to it which will differentiate it.
We are in an ideal, verbal world where the real and the fictive
meet on equal terms and where time is no longer the enemy; the
glitter of these archetypal coins is 'endless'.

Borges, in his fictions, conducts a platonic affair with language.
It is an important part of his purpose to *show* that, in fiction, the
old philosophical modalities of *de dicto* and *de re* are one, that the
name of a thing is the essence of that thing. Just as one coin in 'El
Zahir' is all coins, so, in one of Borges's most explicit stories, 'El
Sur', one cat is all cats and one gaucho all gauchos. Juan Dahlmann, the protagonist of the story, comes across both cat and
gaucho in the selfsame locale as that in which the narrator of 'El
Zahir' is given the coin: in an *almacén*, an ideal place to seek that
distraction from routine and reality which fiction represents.[15]
After he leaves the sanatorium, to travel to the South and his
derelict *estancia*, Dahlmann finds he has thirty minutes to spare
before catching his train. This gap in his time-table is a reprieve,
like the ten days which are to elapse before Jaromir Hladík's
execution in 'El milagro secreto'; it is what one might call the
'story-space', thirty minutes of time which he can organize to his
own satisfaction before he must submit himself to the harsh and
impersonal chronology of the railway train. Dahlmann decides to
go and visit the cat in its café, an enormous cat 'which allowed
people to stroke it, like a disdainful divinity'. Disdain is a sentiment the cat shares with that other divinity, Teodelina Villar; in
her case it has been made 'perfect' by death. In the café Dahlmann
enjoys a cup of coffee, a pleasure which has been denied to him
during his spell in the sanatorium, and communes with the resident, oversized divinity: 'he thought, as he smoothed down the
black fur, that this contact was illusory and that they were separated as if by a glass, for man lives in time, in successiveness, and

---

[14] *OC*, pp. 590–1.

[15] Some French novelists associated or associable with the *nouveau roman*
have used cafés as settings in their books for the same reasons as Borges uses
them in his stories. One thinks particularly of Robbe-Grillet and the wittily
ingenious Raymond Queneau.

the magic animal in actuality, in the eternity of the instant.'[16] The café cat, like Keats's immortal nightingale, is perfectly quintessential because of the common assumption that animals, being without memory or foresight, dwell in a perpetual present. Like fictions, they escape not from time but from the conscious measurement of time. The encounter between Dahlmann and the cat is an encounter between the temporal and intemporal. It might seem that, being himself the creature of a fiction, Dahlmann should enjoy the same degree of eternity as the cat; but Dahlmann is only on the way to sharing the cat's eternity. Eternity awaits him at the end of the story, when he leaves a second *almacén*, this time in the South, to cross knives with the *cuchillero* who will no doubt kill him. The story of 'El Sur' is the story of Dahlmann's accession to his own essence, to his name. Shortly before the end of the story he is addressed by name by the proprietor of the café, even though the proprietor cannot possibly know who he is. This magical invocation, as Dahlmann understands, seals his fate.

It is in this second, symmetrical *almacén* that the equally quintessential gaucho appears:

On the floor, propped against the counter, sat huddled, unmoving as a thing, a very old man. Many years had reduced and polished him as the waters do a stone or the generations of men a sentence. He was dark, small, and desiccated, and as if outside time, in an eternity. Dahlmann remarked with satisfaction his kerchief, his flannel poncho, his long *chiripá*, and his horse-hide boots, and said to himself, remembering useless (*inútiles*) arguments with the men from northern parts or with *entrerrianos*, that no gauchos of this sort were left except in the South.[17]

This remarkable figure is the transformation of the cat in the first *almacén*, a second inhabitant of eternity. He is the archetype not of real gauchos, but of literary ones. He is the distillation of all the gauchos who have appeared in the prose and poetry of Argentina, the idealization of a book-reader. He is outside time now because time has done its work; his existence has consisted of the successive appearances made by gauchos in the work of Argentinian

---

[16] *OC*, p. 527.

[17] *OC*, p. 528. The *chiripá* is a long cloth worn round the lower part of the body and indigenous to Chile and the River Plate district. The *entrerrianos* are natives of the province of Entre Rios, the most easterly of Argentinian provinces, bordering Uruguay. Men from the North and the East are, we have already seen, strangers to fiction, or not properly acquainted with its rules.

authors, his essence is the semantic space occupied by the word 'gaucho' in the mind of another Argentinian author, Borges, or in the mind of any of Borges's readers. His status as a literary, and not a real, gaucho accounts for his assimilation to a form of words, to a 'sentence' polished over the generations.

A little later on in the story the old gaucho is described as 'ecstatic', as having the power, that is, of being bodily in one place and mentally in another (or of being in two places at once). For Juan Dahlmann he is a *cifra* of the South, and it is the gaucho who, when Dahlmann has been insulted and challenged to a knife-fight, provides him with a weapon: his one action in the whole episode: 'It was as if the South had resolved that Dahlmann should accept the duel.' The South has indeed so resolved, because Dahlmann's end has been predetermined and that end requires that he be killed in a duel. It is a literary end, predetermined by all the literary or more generally legendary precedents of a brave death in a *duelo a cuchillo*. Once the story is complete Dahlmann can take his own place in the literature alongside the rest of them, having been shown the way by, among other influences, a cat and a peasant who have acceded to eternity before him.

It is not so clear why the café cat in 'El Sur' should be of unusual size. Perhaps Borges is hinting at its identity with that most imposing of all his archetypes, the tiger, the 'big cat' which he says has meant so much to him. The tiger, above all, is the creature from which he, like Dahlmann, has felt cut off; the dividing glass stands not between him and flesh-and-blood tigers exactly, but between fictive tigers and flesh-and-blood ones. In a short piece in *El Hacedor* called—the title is in English—'Dreamtigers', Borges claims that 'In infancy I practised with fervour the adoration of the tiger'; even if, later on, 'tigers and the passion for them fell into disuse, but they are still in my dreams'.[18] Borges goes on, in 'Dreamtigers' and in a poem which overlaps with it, 'El otro tigre' ('The Other Tiger'), to enrich the archetype by making it ambivalent. The tiger of his dreams is desirable but not sufficient: it is not the real animal which stalks the living jungle. He knows he will never make the two coincide, and trap reality in his writing, but he will go on trying, he will keep after the other tiger, 'the one which is not in the line of poetry'.

The insufficiency of fictive tigers thus becomes Borges's

[18] *OC*, p. 783.

explanation of his will to go on writing—and creating more and more insufficient tigers. The pattern, apparently one of some primal loss, and obsessive, vain efforts at its recovery, is one that zealously psychoanalytical interpreters of Borges will jump at. But how autobiographical is he really being? The pattern, as always, is suspiciously neat. The tigers in Borges's life have been dream tigers from the start, and he was launched on their pursuit by his precocious adoration of them. There is no real tiger standing at the head of this long, fantasmal line. The young Borges stood and admired the caged tigers in the Zoological Gardens, but these are every bit as much a symptom of his fascination, not its source. The tigers which dominated his imagination are the 'striped, asiatic, royal (*real*) tigers, which only men of war could confront, on a castle above an elephant'.[19] These royal, or 'real' tigers, and the men of war who fought them, represent that side of Borges's, and his archetypal author's, ancestry which flows together with and is domesticated by the other, more peaceable, sedentary side. Borges's tigers are the equivalent of the 'ancient African appetites' of Ebenezer Bogle, or of the virile, martial strain in other of his fictional lineages. They symbolize whatever energy it is that keeps Borges writing, that obscure inspiration but for which he would never be able to practise his civilized skills in the making of rigorous, unemotional fictions. We do not believe, any more than he does, that his real inspiration is the superstitious belief that ultimately words will become the things themselves. The satisfactions of writing are the exact opposite: of making words suffice for the things themselves.

The dream tigers symbolize, therefore, obsession. In 'El Zahir' Borges includes an anecdote which he attributes, falsely everyone will presume, to Meadows Taylor, the nineteenth-century author of *The Confessions of a Thug*. It is of a 'cell' in India

on whose floor, on whose walls, and on whose ceiling a Muslim fakir had drawn (in barbarous colours which time, before expunging them, had refined) a sort of infinite tiger. This tiger was made, in some vertiginous way, from many tigers; tigers traversed it, it was striped with tigers, it included seas and Himalayas and armies which looked like other tigers. The painter had died many years before, in this selfsame cell; he had come from Sind or perhaps from Gujarat and his original purpose had been to trace a map of the world.[20]

[19] 'Dreamtigers', *OC*, p. 783.   [20] *OC*, p. 593.

The unfortunate fakir (who is also, for Anglophone readers, a faker) has 'looked on the tiger', just as the narrator of 'El Zahir' (who calls himself Borges) has looked on the too memorable coin.[21] The phrase, given in English, 'Verily he has looked on the Tiger', is one taken by Meadows Taylor in India to signify 'madness or sanctity'. But the fakir, in his captivity and his obsession, is also a maker of fictions. The lesson seems to be that to make fictions one needs to be a madman or a saint.

[21] In *Facundo*, interestingly enough, Sarmiento quotes the phrase *nunca ha parado un tigre* ('he's never stopped a tiger') as a typical gaucho insult about an effete townsman. I imagine that Borges's choice of the tiger as his heraldic beast may have something to do with this traditional use of it as the animal which sorts out the heroes from the milksops.

PART III

'To plan an assembly which would represent all men . . .'

CHAPTER 1

CONCEPTS AND CIRCUMSTANCES

FICTIONS which, like Borges's, avow themselves openly to be the systematic deployment of symbols, do not come easily under the heading of Realism—literary Realism, that is, and no longer philosophical Realism. It is the condition of art, Borges believes, that it should be seen to be art; instead of *ars est celare artem*, his motto might be *ars est divulgare artem*. His stories divulge not only the conventions and procedures of his own art but of the art of narrative in general, and to that extent they rank among the criticism of literature at the same time as extending the possibilities of creative writing.

Realism, as a literary mode, is something we recognize more easily than we define it, so proving the good sense of Wittgenstein's axiom that the definitions of a word are its uses, that the best we can hope for is to spot the resemblances between one use and another. As it is generally used in the discussion of fiction, Realism applies to that mode of writing in which the claims of reality are manifestly promoted at the expense of the writer's own claims. The Realist is the writer who has made the greatest possible sacrifice—or appears to have made the greatest possible sacrifice—of his own preferences and obsessions, the more dispassionately to register things as they really are. The fictions of Realism are recognizable by their concealment of artifice, by the normality or unobtrusiveness of their viewpoint on the world, by their constant particularization of place and person: in general, by the fidelity with which they seem to be transcribing a world and not making one up. And the world which is transcribed is one that exists independently of the writer; it was there before he came along and all he needs to do is express it, it is not a world which comes into existence only as he writes. The Realist, again, is someone who we believe is telling us what he has seen with his own eyes, and experienced in his own self, as a participant in the real world, not what he has read in the books of others, or got only by hearsay. He is a writer for whom the conventionalities of the genre are kept as far out of sight as possible so that they do not intrude and reveal the essential mediacy of language, or of literary protocol. The ideal Realist, perhaps, would be someone who wrote a novel about the society he lived in without ever having read a novel in his life, but who was yet so overflowing with the novelty of his social and psychological observations that he could not resist dramatizing them.

None of this is for Borges. Not for him the disavowal of artifice, the submission to the accidents of everyday life, the accumulation of circumstantial evidence of human behaviour. Nor, above all, the immediate observations of reality which seem to be constituents of all Realism. He is fitted for those neither by his temperament nor by his eyesight: he is bookish and has suffered most of his life from poor sight. Borges has written about his slow passage into blindness not, as I have said, because it is a personal catastrophe but because sightlessness symbolizes very well the condition of a writer of fiction, who needs to be able to think, not to see (it would be a better symbol still were the writer of fiction not also faced by the business of writing his fictions down; the dictation of them to someone else is a different process from their composition on paper, and the fact that the stories which Borges has written in old age, and has presumably had to dictate to others, are so much less intricate and rigorous than the earlier stories, surely has much to do with his inability to see them). The loss of his sight was no terrible disruption in the life of Borges the author. He was not, by his own account, a very assiduous or concerned observer of life even in the days when he could see quite well; he has always lived in what he has since called 'this abstract world in which I am'.[1] If blindness has affected Borges it will be as a reader rather than as a writer. It is thinking about what he has read that has provided Borges with the abstractions in which he deals.

Books stand between him and reality, like so many conceptual tigers between him and the real tigers of the forests. Borges may pretend that his deepest aspiration is for an immediate contact with reality, but to so aspire in a *medium*, like language, is self-defeating; Borges is exemplifying the real power, not the false promises, of words. For him, as a writer, words and books are reality, as they are for any writer. His acknowledgement that he

[1] A remark made to Victoria Ocampo in her *Diálogo con Borges*, Buenos Aires, 1969, p. 46.

will never, however many and various the tigers he imagines, accede to the real animal, is an acknowledgement that cuts deep into the pretentions of Realism, for which the mediacy we are talking of is supposed not to exist. Our idea of what Realism is may change quite radically if, for example, we discover that what we believed to be observation is in fact quotation, that this or that item which the Realist novelist has introduced to authenticate his fiction as observed fact turns out to derive not from his first-hand experience of the world but from his second-hand experience of it through the literature of his day. Much of what we credulously suppose to be Realist observation can be ascribed to prevalent convention; and anyone who doubts this should read Roland Barthes's brilliantly unfair but incisive study of Balzac, *S/Z*, where he demonstrates that arch-Realist's unsuspected dependence on the cultural stock of his time rather than on any immediate confrontation with real people and places. We should have realized before that Balzac, who wrote so much and so obsessively, had little time left for observing.

Realism, the mode of the documentary, is illusionism, the apparent mechanization of what is in fact hand-made—as we saw with Eduardo Zimmermann's bow-tie. Fiction-writers who are illusionists—the great majority—will not show their workings. Borges, like a few other equally playful and fastidious writers of the present time, chooses on the contrary to make those workings the subject of his fictions. He makes small dramas out of what has traditionally, in fiction, remained unseen in the wings.

Those simple souls who are taken in by illusionism emerge, in Borges, as a very low kind of philistine. The mark of civilization and intelligence is to be able to put a name to artifice when it is present. In the title story of *El informe de Brodie* (*Brodie's Report*), the narrator is an Aberdonian missionary who has rather thanklessly been taking the Word to central Africa and Brazil. He is the stern Presbyterian, one of the 'Protestant pastors' to whom Borges lays claim in his own family tree, engaged in dialectic with such 'ancient African appetites' as were admixed with Calvinism in the make-up of Ebenezer Bogle; he is the intellectual element in literary composition. The good doctor's report records his encounter not with some real population of heathens but with a literary population, of Yahoos. This uninviting tribe shows certain vestiges of culture, including one which is, in the context of a Borges story, of great significance: a language of disjoined mono-syllables each corresponding to a general idea. The Yahoos are therefore not without a capacity for abstraction. Brodie concludes from this evidence that they are not aboriginal but degenerate, and goes on to assimilate them to 'the tribes that roam the vicinity of Buenos-Ayres'. Many of the customs the Yahoos follow are suitably sordid if hard to interpret, but one is bound, after the mention of Buenos Aires, to try and read them in terms of the cultural life of Argentina, of whose degeneracy, as we saw in the first chapter, Borges is convinced.

One of the Yahoos' most striking failures is to conceive of artifice. Ornaments, for them, are natural objects, because they themselves are incapable of fabricating even the simplest thing. When Brodie, who, as the author of a report, presumably requires seclusion, builds himself a cabin up on the *meseta* or table-land, the Yahoos watch him build it and even help him build it, but once it is complete they continue to conceive of it as a tree. This looks like the most benighted Realism. The generic language of the Yahoos has here betrayed them, if the noun for 'tree' can be mindlessly extended to those artefacts fashioned from the wood of trees. But our own generic language may also betray us in exactly the same way, since we have only one set of terms in which to discuss what happens in real life and what happens in fiction. Consider the verb 'happens' in the last sentence; things really do happen in real life, but things really do not happen in stories: the one word assimilates the fictive to the real. The failure of the Yahoos is a failure to observe the conventions, and to understand that the works of men are not the works of nature. They are not only Realists but also Romantics, as may be seen from their treatment of their native 'poets', those members of the tribe who have the idea of 'arranging' a few 'generally enigmatic' words and shouting them in public because 'they can-not contain themselves'. The witch-doctors and the 'plebs' gather round:

If the poem does not excite, nothing happens; if the words of the poet take them by surprise, they all withdraw from him, in silence, under the mandate of a sacred horror (*under a holy dread*). They sense that the spirit has touched him; no one will speak to him, nor look at him, not even his mother. He is no longer a man but a god and anyone may kill him. The poet, if he is able, seeks refuge in the sand-dunes of the North.[2]

It seems that the Yahoos, both witch-doctors and plebs alike, are no more tolerant of the divine frenzy of poets than Plato was. Both as Realists in the matter of fabrication and as Romantics in the matter of inspiration, they fail to take account of the intellectual work in which art, for Borges, consists. They require, if any people ever did, the ministrations of the good Doctor Brodie; but he departs from them finally without having made a single convert. But the 'essential horror' of his time amongst them still haunts him now that he is back in Glasgow: 'In the street I believe they are surrounding me still.' 'El informe de Brodie' is a pessimistic story if one reads it in part as an allegory of the reception of Borges's own artefacts among a people unfitted to be offered them.

It is also the story which Borges singles out in his preface as being the only one in *El informe de Brodie* which is not 'realist'. The claim to be writing Realism is meant naturally to provoke, when Borges has all his writing life been classified as a fantasist, practising a mode of writing highly esteemed in England and in North America but not in South America. This distinction between Anglo-American and Latin American culture Borges puts down, typically, to the fact that Anglo-Americans appreciate fantasy in literature because they are such inveterate empiricists in life, while with Latin Americans it is the other way round. However, the preface in question should be quoted:

Apart from the text which gives this book its name [Brodie's Report] and which manifestly proceeds from the last voyage undertaken by Lemuel Gulliver, my tales are realist, to use the nomenclature in vogue at present. They observe, I believe, all the conventions of the genre, which is no less conventional than the others and of which we shall either soon tire or are tired already. They abound in the requisite invention of circumstantial actions, of which there are splendid examples in the Anglo-Saxon ballad of Maldon, which dates from the tenth century, and in the later Icelandic sagas.[3]

Now it is a fact that some of the stories in *El informe de Brodie* are less patently fantastic than Borges's earlier stories, and fall well

---

[2] *OC*, p. 1077. The italicized English phrase is given by Borges in the original Spanish version of the story, to lend a spurious authenticity to his reference.

[3] *OC*, pp. 1021–2.

short of the level of contrivance and methodical construction of the canonical *Ficciones*. Someone coming to Borges for the first time through them might take his claim to be writing Realism at face value; if they did, they would misread the more intricate stories, like 'Guayaquil', completely. *El informe de Brodie* does not break with the past, it simply fails to measure up to it; most of the stories differ in degree of artifice, they do not differ in the kind of artifice. If Borges claims to be a realist in 1970 then he might just as well have claimed to be one also in 1940.

That claim is unorthodox but not absurd. It is unorthodox because one needs to read only a few paragraphs of a Borges story to know that he does not belong to the school of Realism. The will to verisimilitude is decidedly weak in him; the story is self-confessedly a story. But this self-consciousness raises a fresh question: as to what exactly is the 'veri-' of which the Realist is hoping to create a similitude? Is the truth-to-life of fiction truth to life as we immediately experience it, or truth to 'life' as we have experienced it mediately in other fictions? The question is a large, obscure one I do not feel competent to pursue; the short answer must be that it is a bit of both: truth both to life and to 'life'. Realism should be both Realist, that is to say falling recognizably within a certain historical literary tradition, and realistic, that is, fit to be compared with what occurs outside books. Realism is thus doubly mimetic: of literary convention in the first place and of life in the second; and Realism evolves when some writer or group of writers believes that the mimesis of convention has gone too far, that it is time fiction tried harder to imitate life. This, however, it can only do by renovating its conventions, so that the process is perhaps interminable.

Borges, a writer for whom reality lies, by definition, outside literature—lies, indeed, outside language—is unconcerned with the mimesis of real life. He is concerned with the mimesis of convention. To the fundamental question of how one can reconcile the incompatible, the word with the thing, abstraction with reality, mind with matter, he gives a simple answer: one cannot, one backs out of that age-old illusionist game altogether and uses abstractions *as* the reality proper to literature. Borges is thus a realist of the absolute kind, in that the reality which he transcribes is the reality of his own mind. The verisimilitude of his fictions is unassailable, given that the private mental world of Borges is the only world to which they might legitimately be referred, and all we know of that world is what Borges has chosen to make public of it, in the composition of a particular story.

Borges puts us in the same position as he himself pretends to be in at the end of the story of 'La busca de Averroes' ('The Search for Averroes', or alternatively, 'The Search of Averroes': both translations are equally apt and the ambiguity in the original is obviously deliberate), when he draws an analogy between Averroes as author, commenting on Aristotle with a seemingly quite inadequate experience of Aristotle's world, and Borges as author, with an equally inadequate experience of Averroes's world:

I felt that Averroes, trying to imagine what a drama is without having suspected what a theatre is, was no more absurd than I, trying to imagine Averroes, with no raw materials but a few scraps of Renan, Lane, and Asín Palacios. I felt, on the last page, that my narrative was a symbol of the man I was while I was writing and that, in order to write that narrative, I had to be that man, and that, in order to be that man, I had to write that narrative, and so on *ad infinitum*.[4]

The coalescence of man and narrative defeats any attempt we might want to make to reach outside them, on one side to the real Averroes and on the other to the real Borges. This particular story is a conclusive lesson in how to make do with the second-hand, or mediate, given that the first-hand, or immediate, is inaccessible. As a writer Averroes practises what he preaches as a philosopher (just like Borges): he deals in 'the general laws of the universe', not in its specific, variable instances.

His problem, in Borges's narrative, is to determine what the terms 'tragedy, and 'comedy' might mean, as they occur in Aristotle, even though he has had no direct experience in his life of the theatre. He solves it, finally, by equating tragedy with panegyric and comedy with 'satire and anathemas'. This double definition tallies very impressively with what Aristotle indeed has to say early in the *Poetics* about the original divergence of the two major dramatic modes, tragedy having derived from those poets who chose to represent 'noble' actions and characters, comedy from those who preferred the meaner and ignoble. So Averroes reaches a conclusion which is essentially—or better, conceptually —correct despite the very different circumstances of his own life

[4] *OC*, p. 588.

and experience from those of Aristotle. Yet he has still not had any direct experience of the theatre, which had somehow seemed the prerequisite to a correct definition of the two terms. The experiences he does have in the course of Borges's story appear to have nothing to do with the quest which preoccupies him; in fact, though, they determine its successful outcome. Averroes's definitions are founded on all that has intervened between the beginning and the end of the narrative; they are the justification of what at first sight might be mistaken for a string of accidents—a few ragged children playing at being *muezzins*, a traveller's tale of an evening in Canton, where people enact stories instead of telling them, and so on.

Averroes uses what is to hand, and so does Borges; but what is to hand is never the real thing. In the final paragraph of the story its narrator tells us that his first intention had been to 'narrate the progress (*proceso*) of a defeat', but that the story turned out otherwise. The failure of an attempt to record a failure is a peculiarly Borgesian idea. Averroes is not defeated by his lack of direct acquaintance with Ancient Greece, nor is Borges defeated by his lack of direct acquaintance with Averroes's Spain; Averroes, who cannot read Greek, thrives on reading the translation of a translation of Aristotle, Borges, who can not read Arabic, thrives on reading translations of *The Arabian Nights*. The absence of all immediate contact between authors and their subjects is not 'absurd' at all, but the condition of authorship. Immediate contact would bring authors face to face with a limitless number of particulars which would prejudice their vocation as custodians of the universal. The responsibility of the author is with the concept and not with the circumstances, and the conceptual is the truly inherent aspect of things which we assume survives in transmission. What remains of Aristotle, in the translation of a translation which Averroes is forced to consult, is the essential Aristotle; the variations between the texts being only circumstantial ones.

'La busca de Averroes' ends with this statement of what looks like an unwelcome solipsism. The narrator of the story, like the Muslim fakir in his Indian prison-cell, has set out to represent the world but has ended up representing his own intimate obsessions. If this were really the case, then we might have to put him down as a frustrated realist, anxious but unable to transcend the reality of his own mind. But he is nothing of the sort; the story he has written is his own 'justification' because it is the material evidence of his authorship. We derive him from his narrative because that is all we know of him, our only first-hand evidence. His reality is circumscribed by what he has written.

If we are to admit Borges as a Realist, then, we need first to accept that fictions are inescapably solipsist. Instead of classifying writers of fiction as Realists and others, we must classify them all, in the first instance, as the transcribers of mental realities. They all deal in concepts, never in percepts. Having agreed this, we may next follow Borges's own lead and classify them according to whether they write more or less conceptually. Where conceptuality is concerned, more, for Borges, means better, because it is those writers who recognize the conceptual to be superior to the circumstantial who understand better the nature of literature.

In an essay written in 1931, called 'La postulación de la realidad' ('The Postulation of Reality'), Borges divides writers into two familiar classes, Classics and Romantics. The terms are not used historically, to designate individual writers, schools of writers, or literary epochs. They are used generically, as the names for two permanent and contrary attitudes towards the postulation of reality in literature. The Classic is strongly on the side of conceptualism; the Romantic strongly on the other side, of circumstantiality.

Borges wastes little time on the Romantics. He himself flirted with literary procedures in the 1920s which might well be called Romantic; once he abandoned them he was very sure of their weaknesses. The whole essay is meant as an antithesis to Croce's highly Romantic identification of the aesthetic with the expressive, and it is the strenuous 'expressiveness' of Romanticism, its cult of originality, its will to particularize, its boastful subjectivism, that Borges finds wholly distasteful. The sin of which Romanticism is guilty is parochialism: it is infatuated with the unique and the local.

What Borges prefers, and what he chiefly analyses in his essay, is the Classical postulation of reality, which, by comparison, seems casual and austere. To display the Classical style at its most accomplished, he quotes a lengthy paragraph from Gibbon's *Decline and Fall of the Roman Empire*. It would almost have sufficed, as Borges admits, to quote the very first clause of that paragraph, which reads: 'After the departure of the Goths.' This, says Borges, shows 'the mediate character of this way of writing, which is abstract and generalizing to the point of invisibility'.[5] Such a style of writing is a direct snub to our Realist expectations. The ambition of Realism is ultimately to make us *see* the reality it postulates; the triumph of Gibbon, as Borges would have it, is to ensure that we cannot see it. Realism would work to realize such a picturesque event as the departure of the Goths in as much detail and colour as it had time for; Classicism forecloses brutally on the whole procedure and reduces it to the one abstract, neutral term: 'departure', to which few of us, however incorrigibly Romantic our temperament, could easily put a clear image. Classicism insists on the communication of ideas; it does not pretend that the reality it conveys is the raw, unprocessed reality of immediate perception.

Classicism and Romanticism can no doubt be associated with different psychologies: those who admire the first above the second are temperamentally distinct from those who admire the second above the first. But rather than psychologize them, which would be an especially disloyal move in any study of Borges, it is more profitable to consider them principally as techniques of writing. They are techniques between which writers must oscillate, with a general, obvious tendency to favour one mode rather than the other. There are passages in Gibbon which are decidedly Romantic or Realist, in their will to recreate the circumstances of some event, even if Gibbon is, quite clearly, a Classical writer. Similarly, the great Romantics, Victor Hugo, say, or Dickens, pass frequently enough from the particular to the abstract, and from the mind's eye to the mind *tout court*. This, indeed, is one of the fundamental choices of writing, between what has sometimes been called the instant and the deferred nomination of an event. Gibbon was free to have itemized the departure of the Goths, which is a very complex event, analysing it into any number of scenes or episodes. He chose not to; perhaps there were no documents to inspire him, perhaps an innate Classicism forbade it. A complex event is thus reduced to a single noun, and its nomination made instant. The alternative is to tantalize, to keep us waiting for the Goths to strike camp, to withhold the word 'departure'. It is this technique of delay which, if Roland Barthes is right—and Barthes himself is an oddity, a Romantic with a profound, vastly intelligent bias against Realism—provides us, as readers, with some of our deepest gratifications.

[5] *OC*, p. 217.

All writing generalizes, therefore, and Classical writing generalizes absolutely. By so doing it proves itself the truly generic mode of writing. Romanticism, by particularizing, strives to contradict the founding principle of language itself. Borges considers three ways of postulating reality in his essay, and the third, which he calls 'the most difficult and efficient of all', is the invention of circumstances, that requirement which, as we have seen, he claims to have met in the stories of *El informe de Brodie*. Such is the technique of Romanticism, which is no doubt why Borges invokes its difficulty. Far from being difficult the invention of circumstances is the simplest of matters: the Romantic writer may circumstantialize to his heart's content because he is spared the rigours of a conceptual structure *à la* Borges. Most writers of fiction would find it far harder *not* to invent circumstances, than to invent them; circumstances are their stock-in-trade and they invent them in order to ingratiate themselves with an inexhaustibly circumstantial universe. Borges is disguising his scorn for a facile technique as an incapacity to practise it.

In the preface to *El informe de Brodie* he singles out two eccentric models of Realism: the ballad of Maldon and the later Icelandic sagas. The notion of an Icelandic saga being a work of Realism is a challenging one to say the least. But Borges allows that not all Icelandic sagas are works of Realism: it is the *later* ones to which he looks for signs of the invention of circumstances. He is in fact comparing these sagas with the earlier ones and finding a difference in the technique of their composition. If this comparison were impossible, there would be no way of telling that the later sagas incorporated 'invented' circumstances, because those circumstances might be perfectly traditional elements of all sagas. Realism is thus purely antithetical, a departure from the conceptualism of an earlier period.

In old age Borges's liking for Norse and Old English writings has grown remarkably strong but he first wrote about them early in the 1930s, in a celebrated essay on 'Las Kenningar' ('The Kennings'). Kennings were the periphrastic formulas on which Old Norse poets drew when they required a metaphor. Because they came from stock these figures were not 'expressive' in the way the figures of modern poetry are. The poet who employed them could not claim them as the expression of some sentiment peculiar to himself. Instead of inventing fresh, personal metaphors his task was to combine traditional ones, statutory syntagma which were a distinctive element in the literary language of the time. At the time of the kennings Classicism was institutionalized in Norse literature, which has the supreme virtue for Borges of being an anonymous, corporate enterprise whose code of conduct severely restricts the power of any individual to innovate or distinguish himself. The invention of circumstances which Borges claims to detect in the ballad of Maldon and the later sagas is nothing more than a modest shift in literary conventions.

It is also, as I have said, dialectical, because it opposes the Classical impulse towards abstraction and generalization. Circumstances, once satisfactorily invented, recall the mind of a reader from all things bearing the same name to that smaller class of things which bear not only the same name but also share this or that particular attribute. They recall the mind from the general to the particular and, illusorily, from the word to the thing. The process is one in which, as readers of fiction, we are anxious to connive; our tendency is to carry the process on well beyond the point where the author necessarily has to stop it, and to believe that we have been recalled from the ideal to the real. Borges, however, operates his own check on such a deceptive process by writing always of the *invention* of circumstances: the prime stand-bys of Realism are just as much figments as the abstractions of the Classical writer, they can recall us only from one mode of ideality to another. It is only once a fiction ends, and we close the book, that we are recalled from fiction to fact.

The maker of fictions is free to postulate a reality which observes the natural laws of the world we live in or one which infringes them. Borges, for whom reality is the reality of the mind—an ideality— infringes them so as to exploit fiction's independence. To the Realist, these infringements mark the intrusion of an unreality, a discrepancy between the way things proceed in stories and the way they proceed in the natural world. To the Idealist, the discrepancies remain but he disregards them. Idealism may well be more interested in the effects of referring the natural world to the mental world, and in the opportunities which this provides for finding ideality more real than reality. When we look around us and find that what we see coincides absolutely with what we expected to see, we are momentarily elevated on to the plane of what for Borges is eternity. At the end of his essay on 'La historia de la eternidad' he describes an actual experience of this kind (I think we can take it that this really was an actual experience, not an invented one). He was walking at night, and at random, in Buenos Aires, but was drawn by 'a sort of familiar gravitation' towards a quarter of the city 'whose name I want always to remember'. It was a thoroughly idealized part of the city, 'a confine which I have possessed totally in words, but little in reality, simultaneously neighbourly and mythological'.[6] The sensation it gave him seems to have been the sensation the narrator of the story of 'El Zahir' receives at the wake for his dead goddess: of a perception coinciding with an image. The scene around him is 'made unreal by its very typicalness', it is as simplified as the streets into which the narrator of 'El Zahir' emerges after the wake. In this reduced form Borges was able to identify the setting in which he found himself with the same setting thirty years before. He had 'a genuine moment of ecstasy and the possible insinuation of eternity'.

The experience is Platonic more than it is Proustian. Borges identified the streets of Buenos Aires now with the streets of Buenos Aires in the years before he was born; memory is not involved in the way it is with Proust. Borges, the Nominalist, has had an intuition of Realism. He could not have had it, one must suppose, in the daylight, when simplifications of our environment such as the one of which he writes are impossible. In the daylight the weight of circumstance is too great and we are led to remark what is distinctive about our experiences rather than what is essentially the same.

The circumstantial detail which is introduced in order to distinguish an experience that would otherwise be too abstract can thus become the element which exposes the unreality or untruthfulness to life of an ideal reality. Something of this sort occurs in the story of 'El otro' on which I have already touched. In this story the old Borges, sitting on a seat beside the Charles River in Cambridge (Mass.) in 1969, encounters the young Borges sitting on a seat beside the River Rhône in Geneva in 1918. The archetypal seat is the point where time is exchanged for the eternity of a fiction. Towards the end of the discussion between the two Borgeses the old one offers the young one an American banknote bearing the date 1964, to prove to the other that their encounter is real and not a dream. The young Borges reads the

[6] *OC*, p. 366.

date on the dollar-bill and recognizes that there has been a 'miracle'. The dated note is the circumstantial evidence of the reality of the experience. Unfortunately, as Borges casually lets on in a parenthesis, 'Months afterwards someone told me that banknotes do not carry a date'. From having been the evidence of a reality the note is suddenly transformed into the evidence of an unreality: the 'miracle' was impossible all along, contradicted by the actual practices of the United States Treasury.

The old Borges offers a final explanation of his experience:

I have pondered long on this encounter, which I have told to no one. I believe I have discovered the key. The encounter was real, but the other conversed with me in a dream and thus it was that he was able to forget me; I conversed with him while awake and the memory still torments me.

The other dreamt me, but he did not dream me rigorously. I understand it now, he dreamt the impossible date on the dollar.[7]

A story which had seemed relatively straightforward all but dissolves under the shock of this final rationale. Who now is dreaming whom? The old Borges is dreaming the young Borges dreaming the old Borges; which is the same as saying that the real Borges is dreaming two other Borgeses, himself at age 70 and himself at age 19. Those two selves have been set free from the constraints of time and meet as it were on equal terms; they are even described as being 'caricatures' of one another. This fiction is betrayed by the invention of a single impossible circumstance: eternity is destroyed by a date. The dollar-bill, a forgery if ever there was one, has been introduced into the game in order to put an end to it, to show that timelessness must have a stop. There could, in the fictive world of Borges, be no more deadly or intrusive circumstance than an impossible date.

The dollar-bill of 'El otro' is a lesson in the dangers that fiction runs when it purports to be imitating reality. Imitation invites comparison; if we believe that fictions are copying things as they are—and some degree of this belief is surely inherent in our response to Realism—we may decide to test it, and to see how well the copy measures up to the original. This is a naïve thing to do, but it is often done, and not surprisingly fictions are invariably found to fail the test; they turn out to be not such good copies of

[7] *El libro de arena*, p. 21.

reality after all. But such comparisons do not have to be so sterile; where we have extra-textual evidence of a particular state of affairs which we can compare with the representation of that state of affairs in a fiction, then we have a valuable insight into the ideology and methods of the fiction in question.

But the wise maker of fictions, suggests Borges, will deliberately *not* try to compete with reality. One of the earliest and still one of the wisest of his own representative makers of fictions, Ebenezer Bogle, understands this very well. Bogle's fiction is a man, the 'improbable impostor' Tom Castro. Castro's improbability is absolute. The man whose place and fortune he claims, Roger Tichborne, is slim, elegant, lively, and speaks with 'uncomfortable precision'; Castro is the opposite, fat, uncouth, somnolent, and with 'a conversation either non-existent or dim'. The two men are compared point for point and match nowhere. They are not merely dissimilar, they are systematically dissimilar, and this, perversely, appeals to the artful Bogle and to his 'insensate ingenuity'. Castro, the impostor, will be Bogle's *impos*ition. He is a reality which Bogle will impose on the Tichborne family and on the world at large; but Castro is not an original, he is a copy or translation of the original (just as Borges's version of the Tichborne story is). Castro's most marked characteristic is his lack of characteristics. He is excessively compliant and his features have 'an infinite vagueness'; he is an actor waiting to be endowed with a role. His failure to correspond bodily in any way whatsoever to the original of which he is to act as copy is, in Bogle's eyes, a virtue. Bogle's conclusive argument is that a resemblance between Castro and Tichborne would invite detailed comparisons; if Castro were to remind Lady Tichborne too much of her vanished son she might remark the exceedingly obvious discrepancies and suspect the imposture. But no one will suspect an imposture when the impostor is so unlike the original. As a deception, Bogle's scheme is 'insensate' because it is so patently a deception; small wonder that when he eventually shows off his creature, Castro, for the first time at the Tichborne home it is an unusually sunny day, and when he throws the windows open 'The light made a mask; the mother recognized the prodigal son and bestowed her embrace on him.'[8] The excess of light is the excess of Bogle's artifice; he is an illusionist who has succeeded by dazzling his audience instead of turning down the lights.

[8] *OC*, p. 303.

It is doubtful whether Borges's own illusionism works so well, or is intended to work so well, in the story of 'El impostor inverosímil': his Tichborne claimant will not be mistaken for the 'real' one. Bogle enjoys the additional licence of being himself a fiction, and enjoys also the pathetic credulity of his victim, the grief-stricken Lady Tichborne, her eyes veiled with tears when re-united as she believes with her son after a separation of fourteen years. If Bogle is a caricature of the maker of fictions, a forger so clumsy no one can believe he is a forger, Lady Tichborne is a caricature of the consumer of fictions, the reader who brings to his reading an indomitable will to believe.

As readers of Borges's story we might, if we were so minded, compare his Tichborne claimant with the original, because he has given us the literary source from which his version is derived—Philip Gosse's *History of Piracy*. By comparison with Gosse, Borges's story is the most blatant of fictions and all the more interesting for being so. He no more wants to imitate Gosse than Bogle wants to imitate Roger Tichborne. On the other hand, it is Gosse's story that we have to see as the 'reality' from which Borges's translation departs, and there are certain data common to both versions which constitute the fixed, essential core of the Tichborne story. The two versions vary in their circumstances, Borges having invented, for his purposes, quite different circum-stances from those invented, or selected, by Philip Gosse.

Ultimately, the logic of Borges's provocative interpretation of Realism leads to a pleasantly fantastic result. If Realism entails a correspondence with reality and if reality happens to be, as in the case of 'El impostor inverosímil', an existing literary text, then it follows that the truest Realist of all would be an author whose narrative matched, circumstance for circumstance, the 'reality' which first provoked it. This remarkable hypothesis, of a total correspondence between model and representation is one, natur-ally, which Borges was quick to realize: in the story of 'Pierre Menard, autor del Quijote', Menard, in his twentieth-century reproduction of a Spanish Golden Age text, repostulates a small part at least of a reality already postulated by Cervantes. The reality which Cervantes postulates tends very strongly towards the Classical, and is short on local colour; the same reality, repostulated by Pierre Menard three centuries later, is more Classical still, since it is no longer to be confused, even by the gullible, with the contemporary state of Spain. By interposing a text between an author and reality Borges cuts the last links with conventional notions of Realism; in his own dispensation everything which appears in a work of literature—every last circumstance—is displayed for what it is: a concept.

CHAPTER 2

REPLICAS AND REDUCTIONS

I HAVE looked at two of the three ways in which reality may be postulated, the Classical way of abstraction and the Romantic way of particularization. The last of the three techniques which Borges identifies in 'La postulación de la realidad' is subtler and more unexpected. It 'consists in imagining a reality more complex than the one declared to the reader and relating its derivations and effects'.[1] This method Borges finds to be the most literary of the three because of its dependence on language and on the manipulation of syntax. There are syntactical devices which can make us assume a premiss by presenting us with a conclusion; they involve us in what logic and semantics have now begun to study as 'presupposition'. Presuppositions are tacit; they are potential statements we are committed to accepting if we accept the statement which presupposes them. 'All Borges's books are written in Spanish' presupposes, trivially enough, that Borges has written some books. We presup-posit all the time when we speak, or write; presupposition makes for a crucial economy in words.

All forms of verbal economy appeal to Borges. 'I disbelieve in the methods of realism', declares the narrator of the majestic story of 'El Congreso' ('The Congress'), 'an artificial genre if ever there was one; I prefer to reveal straight out what I understood gradually'.[2] Like Gibbon with his Goths, this narrator will foreclose on a protracted process as quickly as language allows him to. Hence the attractions of the second, incidental method of postulating reality, which leaves certain things unsaid. The best example Borges gives of this method in use comes from Tennyson's *Morte d'Arthur*, and the description of Arthur's final battle with Mordred. After a panoramic (i.e. Classical) account of the fatal day and the destruction of the Round Table, there occur the words: 'then, because his wound was deep, fearless Sir Bedivere raised him up ...' This is the first news we have had that the King is wounded, and we learn it incidentally, in one of its immediate effects. (Borges no doubt picked on the *Morte d'Arthur* for his

[1] *OC*, p. 219.   [2] *El libro de arena*, p. 42.

examples because the 'reality' which Tennyson's work postulates is not a historical one: it is the reality of his literary source, Malory.) The method turns on the word 'because', which is here a sort of anachronism, having been placed in front of its logical antecedent. Such preposition is common and to most readers of prose imperceptible; Borges, who first isolates and then analyses it, is, among other things, an acute grammarian.

This whole technique, of which he gives other telling examples, is especially useful where a writer wishes to impose a self-evident fiction on his readers, to palm off known impossibilities as if they were possible. Borges considers this application of it in another essay: 'El arte narrativo y la magia' ('Narrative Art and Magic'), as used by William Morris in his *Life and Death of Jason* (and who but Borges would look to Morris and Tennyson as exemplars of narrative skill?). The impossibility in question is the centaur, and Borges praises the manner in which Morris, whose intention is assumed to have been the lifelike narration of Jason's fabulous adventures, first posits the centaur incidentally, by its effects, in the line: 'Where bears and wolves the centaur's arrows find.'[3] The centaur's arrows presuppose a centaur, and since there is nothing implausible about arrows as such, nor about the arrows' targets, bears and wolves, the centaur itself is as it were contaminated by plausibility. Morris is following the secular precept of Aristotle, that the correct way for the poet to argue is from a false premiss to a true conclusion.

Borges is not making the naïve claim that Morris convinces us that centaurs are possible; he is demonstrating that centaurs may be successfully postulated as elements of a fictional reality, as words among other words: he is demonstrating the autonomy of language. All Morris needs, says Borges, is 'our continued faith in his words, as in the real world'. Which may mean that we should trust what Morris tells us as we trust the world around us, or that we should trust Morris's narrative as we trust the narratives of our friends and acquaintances. The second meaning is more interesting than the first; the authority and licence which are conceded to those individuals who, in oral cultures, tell stories, are something which our own culture has lost sight of.

In Borges's own stories the incidental postulation of reality, which implies a reality more complex than the text has the time

[3] *OC*, p. 226.

or inclination to describe, is used more deviously and more ambitiously than ever William Morris used it. It is used to smuggle in impossibilities: Borges's stories are full of 'centaurs' or incongruities, often so slyly introduced that their presence goes unnoticed. It is also used to exemplify the gross discrepancy in scale between the postulated and the postulatable, between the reality which a given fiction represents and the reality it might in principle represent: the universe. Reality, even the most thoroughgoing Romantic would agree, is always more complex than any possible representation of it, so that the Classical writer, conscious that language can do no more than hint at the complexity of things, is again the one whose method more clearly embodies the actual conditions of all writing.

One of Borges's most engaging and persistent fantasies is of a total representation of Everything, of the world turned into words. This beautiful fancy is especially well suited to a writer of such extreme concision, a man too fastidious ever to have written a novel and who has suggested that the novels of other writers are too long and too random to be read with pleasure. It is right that an author who has stuck all his life to the shortest forms of prose writing, the story and the essay, should entertain the largest notions of literary possibilities. This is to turn the discrepancy of scale between life and literature into a joke.

But it is quite a serious joke. Borges may be pessimistic about the handicaps under which human systems of representation must labour but he does not deride them. He asks only that we should, like himself, be lucid and, it must be said, realistic, about them, not that we should be defeatist. In the Middle Ages, perhaps, it seemed quite a reasonable ambition to make microcosms, for the macrocosm was so much tamer and more manageable than it has become since; now it is an unreasonable, indeed an impossible, ambition, which is why Borges sees it as one of fiction's responsibilities to play with it. For the microcosm, that ideal epitome of Everything, can be idealized further: instead of concerning ourselves with the thing, with the making of a microcosm, we can concern ourselves with the idea of the microcosm.

The problems of representation are ones of scale. Is there perhaps a point where the process of abstraction becomes, as it has become in painting, non-representational, leaving us with a fiction that is merely abstract? Or is there a continuum between, at one extreme, a complete representation of reality, and, at the other, a complete abstraction? In terms of language, the first extreme would be the unimaginable sum of whatever might be said, the second the equally unimaginable reduction of that sum to a single word. It is to these unimaginable extremes that Borges, as is his way, steers our imaginations.

The representation which is coextensive with the reality it represents was an early invention of his. It is included as a last, short bibliographical spoof in the *Historia universal de la infamia*, and is so admirably succinct that it can be quoted in full: it is called 'Del rigor en la ciencia' ('Of Rigour in Science'):

> In that Empire, the Art of Cartography reached such perfection that the Map of a single Province occupied a whole city, and the Map of the Empire a whole Province. In time, these Disproportionate Maps failed to satisfy and the Colleges of Cartographers erected a Map of the Empire, which had the Dimensions of the Empire and coincided with it point for point. Less Addicted to the Study of Cartography, the Succeeding Generations understood that this protracted (*dilatado*) map was Useless (*inútil*) and not without Impiety consigned it to the Inclemencies of the Sun and of the Winters. In the deserts of the West there survive dilapidated relics of the Map, inhabited by Animals and by Beggars; in all the Country nothing else remains of the Geographical Disciplines.[4]

This wonderful representation of the Empire outdoes other maps by being three-dimensional, since its ruins can provide shelter for the underprivileged classes of animals and beggars. Its size on the other hand contradicted its function: a map that was coextensive with the area it mapped would require another, smaller map if we were to find our way about it. There is something self-defeating about this monument of Realism. Its most dramatic failing is that it takes up too much room. Representations of reality are themselves a part of reality, they are material objects for which room must be found. As things stand this is not a very serious problem; but a total representation of reality, 'Del rigor en la ciencia' points out, would take up as much room as the real thing—it would replace the real thing. It is merciful, therefore, that in Borges's Empire reality should have reasserted itself and cut the map down to size. Its vestiges serve as the reminder of what Cartography is capable.

---

[4] *OC*, p. 847. 'Del rigor en la ciencia' was reprinted by Borges in *El Hacedor* and it is as part of that later book that it appears in the *Obras completas*.

As it happens, the Imperial Map of 'Del rigor en la ciencia' is as much architecture as cartography. It is a collaborative work and it is 'erected', and since there is little point in consulting it it might just as well be lived in. It is one of the many edifices in Borges which symbolize the work of culture in general and the work of literature in particular.[5] The most intriguing and, I would say, the most misunderstood of these edifices is the fearsome 'Biblioteca de Babel' ('The Library of Babel'), which contains all the verbal representations of reality possible to a given alphabet.

The story dramatizes an idea mooted elsewhere by Borges in his 'Note sobre (hacia) Bernard Shaw '('A Note on (towards) Bernard Shaw'), where it is attributed to a hypothetical scholar by the name of Kurd Lasswitz (taking *lass* to suggest *lass*itude, or the French *las*, and *-witz* to suggest *wits*, we end up with the perfectly appropriate meaning for this name of 'Weary-wits'). Lasswitz, who flourished in the late nineteenth century, like so many of the real and counterfeit authorities in Borges, 'played with the overwhelming fantasy of a universal library, that would register all the variations of the twenty odd orthographical symbols, that is, everything it is possible to express, in every language'.[6] It is this wit-wearying fantasy which is realized in 'La biblioteca de Babel'. The architecture of the library is dire: it is built of an indefinite ('perhaps infinite') number of hexagonal galleries, with so many loaded bookshelves to a gallery. The galleries are linked by narrow vestibules each with two small 'cabinets', one of which is a latrine while the other is a horribly spartan bedroom large enough only to allow the librarians 'to sleep standing up' or, in the Spanish, *dormir de pie*—a phrase that the polyglot Borges has surely translated from the French *dormir debout*, as in 'c'est un conte à dormir debout', meaning 'a completely improbable story'.[7] In each vestibule, as in so many of the buildings that Borges has erected, there is a mirror: 'Men are wont to infer from this mirror

---

[5] They symbolize also the urban basis of culture and Borges's rejection of the false agrarianism of Argentinian culture. The process of civilization for Borges is the process of building permanent buildings and founding cities. When he symbolizes the making of fictions by the construction of buildings he is showing both activities to be the extension of culture into the territory of nature.

[6] *OC*, p. 747.

[7] If this interpretation is right, the library's sleeping quarters are a prime example of an architectural feature or reality more dictated by words than postulated by them, since their smallness has been determined by the phrase Borges wanted to introduce.

that the Library is not infinite (if it were really so, why this illusory duplication?) . . .'[8] The many mirrors which appear in Borges's stories, or, to be more exact and loyal to his own beliefs, the one mirror which appears in them many times, are there as symbols of representation itself; they are real objects but they do not really duplicate the reality reflected in them.

The library is not infinite, it merely exceeds our capacity to compute its size. Those of us who are innumerate cannot even understand how to begin to compute it. It is the *ars combinatoria* carried to extreme and almost repellent lengths. All the books in the library are different by at least one symbol from all the others, and all are possible combinations of twenty-five symbols: twenty-two letters of the alphabet, plus the full stop, the comma, and the space (that necessary void between words in the written language for which there is scant precedent in the 'reality' which written language represents: spoken language). Each book has 410 pages, each page forty lines, and each line eighty characters—values which, so far as one can see, have been fixed arbitrarily by Borges since they are bound to be insignificant. The division of the library's stock into volumes is wholly conventional; it could equally well have been contained, as a footnote to the story concedes, in a single 'perhaps infinite' volume.

The creation of literature by the mechanical combination of its graphic constituents is not a new idea. We have lived for years with the speculation that, given time, so many monkeys sitting at so many typewriter keyboards and hammering blindly away, *must* end by reproducing, Pierre Menard-like, *Paradise Lost*. (That speculation is now rather dated, in that it envisages the industry of monkeys being applied to the replication of a human artefact; nowadays we should be more inclined to examine their productions for evidence of some specifically simian creativity.) Borges does not believe for a moment, of course, that a work mechanically produced in this way would be the equal of a work produced consciously and intentionally; the most binding of all clauses in the contract which unites the author of a fiction with his readers is that the work is as he willed it, it is not random. It is noticeable that none of those who have searched the Library of Babel have yet found much sense in any of its volumes: the meaningful combinations of printed characters are vastly outnumbered by

[8] *OC*, p. 465.

the meaningless ones. Borges is not in favour of the combinatorial creation of literary works, but he is interested in it as a hypothesis, to see how it might change our notions of what literature is.

'La biblioteca de Babel' is a very subversive story. It is subversive in the first place of the common, and Romantic, view that authors, when they write, make language do exactly as they order it to; which is to give the author the entire credit for what he writes and his native tongue no credit at all. Borges's story calls our attention to the claims of language as an agency in literary creation. There *is* an element of combination in writing, as there is in any use of language. Once we have committed ourselves to one word, at the start of a sentence, we have partially determined our choice of a succeeding word. If we put down the personal pronoun 'he' we have committed ourselves to following it with a verb, and as the sentence grows so the choices before us diminish.[9] This element may not be strong in writing, but neither is it negligible.

Borges's story is subversive, secondly, of the idea that there are psychological, physiological, moral, or any other limits on what, as language-users, we can say. Those limits, according to 'La biblioteca de Babel', are in fact verbal: we can say anything that our language allows us to say. The combinations which the library contains are conspicuous by their total irresponsibility; they recognize no distinction between truth and falsehood, good and evil, sense and nonsense. The lesson is that anything, in theory and given sufficient time, may be said, however false, wicked, or nonsensical. Again, Borges is not saying that real authors are such paragons of irresponsibility, he is saying that we are too deterministic in thinking that they can but write what they do write, being the sort of people they are: a matter I shall come back to.

As a library, the Library of Babel is a failure then. So excessively wasteful is it that the most any librarian has ever found by way of

---

[9] This is what is known, by grammarians, as a 'finite-state' model of syntax, whereby the verbal chain becomes a sequence of ever more strictly governed choices of grammatical and lexical items. Chomsky has demonstrated the inapplicability to English of this model because it cannot account for the potential 'recursiveness' of sentences, meaning a language-user's ability to embed more and more clauses in them before completing them. 'Recursiveness' is a very Borgesian phenomenon, since it is, in principle, infinite; some Chomskyan Scheherazade might go on embedding clauses for a thousand and one nights without ever completing her original sentence at all.

sense in any of its volumes is the phrase 'oh time your pyramids'.[10] And 'pyramid', we learn later, is a possible meaning, in another language, of the orthographical symbols which, in Spanish, mean 'library', a sadistic complication this, which multiplies the virtualities of the library many times over, by forbidding us to limit it to a single language: its limits are alphabetical.

What the library needs is to be reduced. But because its holdings are total, it ought to include, somewhere within it, a catalogue. This ultimate reduction of chaos to order is, in more traditionally mystical terms, the Book of Books, 'a book which is the cipher and perfect compendium *of all the others*'[11] (Borges's italics). This magical compendium is the ideal towards which all representation, for Borges, points. It is not—and here is where the story of 'La biblioteca de Babel' is so often misread—a representation of the world outside the library (the world that has been displaced by the library, which no longer requires any such outside stimulation), but a representation of all these other representations. It is not a Book of Life but a Book of Books. The Library of Babel is not the real universe but the artificial universe of literature, the dystopia of a literary man envisaging the totality of literature, the moment when it has all been said. Borges's story becomes more alarming still when one realizes that the library is, like all representations, a huge simplification of the actual universe.

Two reductions are involved: a first reduction of reality to its representation, and a second reduction, of the representation. With Borges, as we have seen again and again, it is the representation which serves as his reality. Both reductions are movements from the Many towards the One. The unity of the Book of Books is as impossible as the multiplicity of the library, but the urge to reduce the second to the first is a real one, and a specifically literary one. In *El libro de arena* there is a story called, in English, 'There are more things', where the narrator is finally confronted

---

[10] It is not so much time that is pyramidal for Borges as causality. It is legitimate to look on the present moment as the point of time where the apexes of two pyramids meet; one pyramid stretches back into the past, containing the incalculable sum of moments or causes which have led to the present moment, the other pyramid, by analogy, stretches forward into the future, being the sum of all the moments or effects that will result from the present moment. As an alternative to the pyramid, in the story of 'Tlön, Uqbar, Orbis Tertius', Borges introduces a cone, which is one of the two ideal objects imposed on the real world by the ideal world of Tlön.

[11] *OC*, p. 469.

by objects in a house which he cannot describe because he does not understand their function. His powers of symbolization are defeated by this inexplicable 'furniture': the house, like the face of Eduardo Zimmermann in 'Guayaquil', is *trop meublé*. As he leaves the house, the narrator hears 'something', presumably its correspondingly monstrous inhabitant, coming up the stairs, 'oppressive, slow, and plural'.[12] The monster does not appear in the fiction because it is, by definition, what cannot be realized, its plurality disqualifies it.

The owner of the house in which the plural monster lives in 'There are more things' is, like Zimmermann, Jewish; Jewishness, in Borges's fictions, goes regularly with Romanticism, Realism, and multiplicity—his Jews are simply insufficiently abstract. The most Jewish of all of them is the poet David Jerusalem in the story 'Deutsches Requiem'. This story, involving as it does the death of a Jew in a Nazi concentration camp, is usually taken to be an uncharacteristically sombre and portentous one, and Borges himself, in an epilogue to the volume in which it appears, *El Aleph*, makes things worse by claiming it as an attempt to 'understand' the destiny of Germany. I do not believe that it is at all the serious, historical inquiry that claim might suggest. The 'destiny' Borges is concerned with is that supranational tendency of the human mind towards abstraction; the Germans he has long taken as models of that tendency. They symbolize, when they appear in his stories, the Classical urge to idealization.

'Deutsches Requiem' is pure artifice; it should not be read as some kind of commentary on the rise and fall of Nazi Germany. It opens in a quite jocular way, with a survey of the ancestry of its German narrator, Otto Dietrich zur Linde, which is the usual mixture of the martial and the theological. In one particular it is actually more bifid than usual, since the family name on his mother's side is *Fork*el. Nor are the more active exploits of his forebears very glorious: his maternal great-grandfather has been killed by French snipers in 1870, in the forest of 'Marchenoir', which looks suspiciously like *marché noir* or 'black market', while his father has distinguished himself, like Tristram Shandy's Uncle Toby before him, in the Siege of Namur, said to have taken place in 1914. No altogether serious story is going to start with games like these.

[12] *El libro de arena*, p. 69.

Zur Linde's passion is philosophical not political. It is for abstraction. As a young man it is music and metaphysics that have enabled him to 'face many unhappy (*infaustos*) years with valour and even with happiness'. He joins the 'Party' in 1929, out of admiration for 'the radically German spirit of Spengler'; but he has also differed from Spengler (i.e. he has entered the literary world by conducting a dialectic with one of its members), in an article, claiming that the 'most unequivocal monument of the features which the author [Spengler] calls Faustian' is not Goethe's 'miscellaneous drama' but the *De rerum natura* of Lucretius. The Faustian (*fáustico*) can be set against the *infausto*, as the source of happiness and satisfaction. Music and metaphysics, those most abstract of disciplines, are also Faustian. And so is the *De rerum natura*, the ideally compendious Latin poem which attempts to represent the universe known to Lucretius. The Faustianism in which zur Linde believes and which he also practises, is clearly not restricted to Germany. The 'Germany' of 'Deutsches Requiem' is a Germany of the mind, the fatherland of those whose will to abstraction is strong, like William Shakespeare, whose 'vast Germanic name' zur Linde invokes.

When the war comes zur Linde is not able to fight; he has been shot in the leg in a skirmish 'in the street behind the synagogue' in Tilsit and the leg has been amputated. On the day the German army enters Bohemia he is lying in 'the sedentary hospital' reading (who else?) Schopenhauer. Moreover, his hospital room contains, like Juan Dahlmann's café, its resident divinity: 'As a symbol of my vain destiny, there slept on the window-ledge an enormous, spongy cat.'[13] Zur Linde absorbs Schopenhauer's fundamental teaching that whatever happens to us happens because we have willed it so; the next thing that happens to him is that he is appointed 'sub-director' of a concentration camp.

Now concentration camps are meant for concentration, for the bringing-together in one place of all the representatives of a given class of person: in this case, Jews. A concentration camp is thus remarkably like a word, which also contains within it all the representatives of the class of things to which that word may be applied. It is the place where zur Linde's initiation into the power of language and of fiction will be completed. His chosen victim among the inmates of the camp is the poet David Jerusalem, an

[13] *OC*, p. 578.

unrepentant particularist who 'rejoices in each thing, with meticulous (*minuciosa*) love'. There is nothing so crude or historical as a gas-chamber in the camp where zur Linde is sub-director; he destroys Jerusalem by driving him mad or, we must be careful, by making him lose his reason. He does it by the well-tried method of 'El Zahir', by reducing the universalist poet to a single representation, of the map of Hungary. How he manages this we are not, understandably, told, but four years to the day after zur Linde had been wounded behind the synagogue the Jewish poet succeeds in committing suicide. For zur Linde, he has been transformed 'into the symbol of a hated zone of my soul'. The great Idealist has extirpated from himself the contrary will to Realism which might have held him back.

'Deutsches Requiem' ends euphorically, with zur Linde enthroned in a universe wholly unified, where nothing can happen without justification. The defeat of Nazi Germany is justified as the sacrifice which was called for by the need to build 'the new order' and that new order is the complete idealization of the universe. Zur Linde has achieved an apotheosis as a maker of fictions. He has been condemned to die, but that sacrifice too has been justified. He can glory in his own defeat and the defeat of his country: 'Let others curse and others weep; I am delighted that our gift should be orbicular and perfect.'[14]

The 'perfect', 'orbicular' gift makes for a smooth transition to that ideal compendium which will do here as a final example of Borges's microcosmic speculations: the Aleph. The Aleph is a 'small, iridescent sphere of almost intolerable brilliance'[15] to be found in the cellar of the house of Carlos Argentino Daneri, a comically stilted and ambitious poet who is at work on the poem to end all poems, a total representation of the known world to be entitled *La tierra* (*The Earth*). The inspiration for this vast literary undertaking has been the discovery of the Aleph. Daneri does not need to leave the house in order to document himself on the world he wishes to represent because it is all in the Aleph. This wonderful object is the pictorial equivalent of the Library of Babel, it is the sum of all the possible visual representations of the universe: all the possible snapshots from all the possible cameras. Reality, as ever, is excluded; Daneri, the fanatical Realist, works from representations of reality.

[14] *OC*, p. 580.   [15] *OC*, p. 625.

Reality, one might say, is what dies at the outset of the story. 'El Aleph' is constructed like 'El Zahir', and opens with the death of the narrator's Muse. Her name is Beatriz Viterbo, a name to evoke both Dante and Italy, and it is after her death that the narrator, who had worshipped here in her lifetime, meets her relative, Carlos Argentino Daneri, another explicitly italianate figure. At Daneri's house he communes with Beatriz's image: in the large number of photographs of her on display there. On the first such communion he studies the 'circumstances' of these portraits and lists the different periods and settings in which they were taken. In a second, symmetrical communion there is only one portrait, 'more intemporal than anachronistic', in 'dull colours'. Beatriz, in fact, is significantly less real than she was, less numerous and less colourful. The narrator, Borges by name, makes a florid little speech to her surviving image: 'Beatriz, Beatriz Elena, Beatriz Elena Viterbo, dear Beatriz, Beatriz lost for ever, I am I, I am Borges.'[16] This odd invocation completes the process of idealization: Beatriz, first a girl, then the photographic image of a girl, is now only the name of a girl. Similarly, in 'El Aleph' reality as a whole is first itself, then a representation in the Aleph, and finally the very partial representation of that representation in Daneri's poetry. There is something elegiac about the story. Nor does the transformation of a person into a name quite end the process, because in time the name itself will be transformed: to start with it will be the name inseparable from that particular image, but once the image fades and vanishes it will be nothing more than a name. In the end is the Word.

[16] *OC*, p. 624.

CHAPTER 3

DISCONTINUITY AND DISORDER

THE postulation, as in 'El Aleph' or 'La biblioteca de Babel', of a reality which exhausts the powers of representation of the camera or the alphabet, is one of Borges's most instructive hypotheses. The fantastic complexity of such a reality can, needless to say, be indicated but never reproduced. On these occasions Borges faces, in an extreme form, the problem that faces all writers of fiction all of the time: how to postulate a reality richer and more extensive than they have power to tell. Ordinarily, the inadequacy of our representations of reality is disguised by the plenitude and continuity of the words we use to represent it. The Romantic writer especially, particularizing in order to counteract the tendency to abstraction of language, amasses his circumstantial evidence to the point where the reader supposes that what has been said about a given person, scene, or object is all that there is to be said.

That is one illusion. A second illusion is that a continuous narration means a continuous narrative. We are accustomed to certain conventional interruptions of a narrative because they are signalled by interruptions in the narration: the division of a text into chapters, for example, or a shift from one narrative persona to another. But prose which is continuous we take to be logically articulated and events which succeed one another in a story to be causally connected. The continuity of a written narrative, be it said in passing, is mimetic of the continuity of an oral one, where the narrating voice never ceases even if the articulation of the events it is narrating is broken and haphazard.

If there were no discontinuities in a narrative, events would take as long to tell as they did to happen, assuming for the sake of argument, as I hope we can, that an event and the verbal representation of that event can be synchronized. Under this dispensation a wholly authentic autobiography, say, would require a second lifetime, of the same length as the first, in order to be narrated. Such a work would be the equal of the Map of the Empire, realizable only if reality could be displaced altogether. We have no trouble recognizing that to narrate events we must reduce them, that there need be no harm, if we are historians, in fitting the Hundred Years War into a reading time of twenty minutes.

Without simplification there can be no representation. The writer, who writes, as we know, from memory, could never begin were he visited by the gift we hear so much of, of 'total recall'. 'Total recall', were it possible, would submerge the mind in circumstances and take up a great deal of time: the same amount of time precisely as the events we are totally recalling. This inaccurate phrase is used to characterize autobiographical narrative of an excessively Realist kind. It is a comparison of one degree of Realism with other, less circumstantial degrees of it. 'Total recall', that is to say, is a literary convention and not God's gift to the autobiographer.

Borges, inevitably, alert to the uses and abuses of every narrative convention, has a character for whom 'total recall' is a reality: Funes the Memorious in the story of that name. Funes has all the advantages a writer needs: he has had an accident with a horse and now lies paralysed in bed, his world reduced to a few perceptions and a great many memories. His immobility he considers a trivial price to pay for the gift his accident has magically provided: his few perceptions and many memories are quite simply 'infallible'. But it is this infallibility which will stop him ever becoming a writer: he is incapable of the reductions and idealizations that authorship demands. Fate has gone too far in his case. He thinks he is fortunate, we know better—his name Funes marks him as *funes(to)*, as someone sad and unfortunate.

Funes is also doomed by his origins. He is not, unlike the narrator of his story, an Argentinian—a 'simple' republican, like the narrator of 'Guayaquil'—but a Uruguayan, with, as the narrator remarks, 'certain incurable limitations'. The limitations are those which, as we have seen, Borges associates with the East. Funes belongs to the Banda Oriental, whose arms are emblazoned on his teapot; the world is too much with him because he is unable to pass even in the smallest degree from the particular to the general. It is not only his memory that is perfect but also his perceptions, this no doubt to remind us that the simplification of reality starts at the moment we perceive it, that if we saw things in all their glory our minds would be swamped.

But Funes is denied even this first, elementary power to shut out those aspects of reality for which he has no use; no scene is too

complex for him to register it in full. Not for him the simplifications and consequent fictions of an ordinary memory:

A circumference on a blackboard, a right-angled triangle, a rhombus,
are forms which we are able to intuit fully; the same went for Ireneo
[Funes] with the tempestuous mane of a colt, with a herd of cattle on a
knife, with the changing fire and the innumerable ash, with the many
faces of a corpse at a long wake.[1]

Geometry is the ultimate in abstraction. The forms in which geometry deals are the most Platonic of entities, and as such they are
a-temporal, they belong in eternity. Funes belongs all too fully in
time. Even before his accident he had been abnormally accurate
and particular when it came to telling the time: he was the 'chrono-
metric Funes'. And his pedantry in respect of chronometry is
equalled by his pedantry in respect of proper names, those
irredeemably singular terms which alone among the words we use
refer to individuals and not to classes.

Funes, unlike the narrator of the story of 'El Zahir', could learn
no lessons from the corpse of Teodelina Villar. The passage from
temporality to eternity, from existence to essence, is barred to him;
he registers the entire process of change in the corpse's face, not
that crucial moment when it coincides with a particular memory of
it. Nor, were he to register that coincidence, could he conclude
from it that time had been abolished, that the face was the *same* as
it had been once before, because he would be forced to hold the
two experiences of the face separately in his memory, as two
experiences of a similar but not identical perception.

It is the narrator of 'Funes el memorioso' who offers the paralysed victim a chance of escaping from his excessive temporality,
through literature. The narrator is on holiday in Fray Bentos,
where Funes lives, and a holiday, we can take it, is a reprieve from
work and from necessity, from the ordinary measurement of time.
His holiday, however, is threatened; he receives a telegram telling
him to return home 'immediately' because his father is 'not at all
well' (*nada bien*). He has lent Funes two of the 'anomalous' books
he has brought away with him on holiday and he goes to get them
back. He learns Funes's story in a conversation, or monologue,
lasting throughout the night. The ship on which the narrator sails
for home the following day is the Saturn, and Saturn is the Roman

[1] *OC*, pp. 488–9.

equivalent of the Greek Chronos; the end of his holiday will see him devoured again by time, but not before he has had his one night of grace.

Like Saturn himself, the 'anomalous' books are Roman, or at least Latin: Caesar's *Commentaries*, an 'odd volume' of Pliny's *Natural History*, and two Latin works by Frenchmen, Lhomond's *De viris illustribus* and Quicherat's *Thesaurus*, later referred to as the *Gradus ad Parnassum*. Funes has been lent Pliny and Quicherat, plus a dictionary, since he does not know Latin. He knows it by the time the narrator visits him, and recites in both Latin and Spanish the 'cases of prodigious memory' recorded in the *Natural History*. The enumeration of these cases, by someone of infallible memory, is just the sort of conceit one would hope for from a Borges story. But instead of reciting Pliny, Funes might have learnt from him, for what Pliny has done is to reduce the world to an encyclopedia, or to make of *natura* a *historia*. And what Quicherat offers him is the way up from the empiricist morass in which he is trapped to the purer, literary heights of Parnassus.

In the course of his life Funes has in fact made two attempts to rescue himself from his absolute Realism. The first followed a recognition that the 'oriental' system of numbering is wasteful, that the number thirty-three, for example, 'requires two signs and three words, instead of a single word and a single sign.'[2]

Basing himself on this unexpected insight, Funes sets out to revise the two systems of representing numbers in the interests of economy, replacing the orthodox forms with a random assortment of nouns and those old favourites of his, proper names. His final gesture of independence is to replace the word for five hundred, *quinientos*, with the admittedly shorter but unfortunately already numerical word *nueve*, or nine.

Funes's system of numbering is a poor substitute for the original. There is nothing to be done with it by way of mathematics since its terms defy analysis; he has assimilated numbers to words by making them wholly arbitrary. His system is, in the words of the narrator of the story, a 'rhapsody of disconnected terms'. It is a sequence when it ought to have been a series, and if

[2] *OC*, p. 489. *Treinta y tres*, or thirty-three, is also the name of the most easterly of Uruguay's provinces, and was so called after the thirty-three patriots who led the independence movement in the country in the 1820s. It is a number, too, with a religious symbolism because it is the age at which Jesus Christ is supposed to have been crucified.

the original values of Funes's terms were lost they might be arranged in any order at all, they are meaningful only for as long as they can be translated back again into the system they have replaced.

Funes's second effort at abstraction is more promising. He resolves to reduce each day of his past, which is available to him in its entirety, to some 70,000 memories, and to define these by 'ciphers'. This looks to be on the right lines. But if the result of such a reduction and codification of the past is wholly desirable, the process of achieving it is beyond him. In order to classify his memories, Funes will need to remember them and since he has forgotten nothing at all he will never have the time to finish the task. Any new memories he acquires during the classification of the old ones will themselves have to be classified at some later date, and so on *ad infinitum*. Funes abandons the project because it is interminable and because it is 'useless' (*inútil*). The first reason is a good one for giving up, the second is not: the 'useless' is also the good, with Borges, for whom the practice of literature is specifically 'useless'. There can be no holidays for Funes, unlike his Argentinian visitor, no final access to Parnassus. His memory is an absolute against which there is no appeal. He dies at the age of 21 of 'congestion of the lungs'.

The ultimate paradox of Funes, however, is that he is himself an abstraction: he is the archetype of Memory. He is incapable of imagination because he is incapable of forgetting (it is not quite clear from the story how Funes could ever manage to tell his story, as he does, to the narrator during the night they spend together; the narrator is careful to tell us that the story we are reading is his no doubt defective account of what he heard from Funes, but the fact that Funes was able to say anything at all about himself indicates an unsuspected gift for abstraction). He stems from the Platonic doctrine that imagination and oblivion are one, that what we think of as creation is really imperfect memory. In Plato's version this anamnesis is not of what we have experienced since birth, but of an ideal, total experience before birth; for Borges it is the anamnesis of a purely conscious experience. But in either case creation depends on omission and omission means discontinuity, a disruption of what would, ideally, be one and whole.

Discontinuity, once it is allowed to show, becomes a source of obscurity and often of irritation among readers. In the *Crónicas de Bustos Domecq*, where a great many of Borges's literary hypotheses are dramatized more summarily and more obviously flippantly than they are in his stories, there is a successful writer called Tulio Herrera whose fame is to have introduced an aesthetics of omission. He creates new literary works by leaving bits out of old ones. The procedure extends to the titles of his works even; his novel is called *Hágase hizo* or *Let there be there was*, derived by omission from the biblical phrase 'Let there be light, and there was light'. Herrera is a figure of fun who omits the essential and as a consequence produces gibberish. But the aesthetics of omission is by no means a ridiculous idea when without omission, as we have seen, there can be no representation, no creation, at all.

Parataxis, or its equivalent figure in traditional rhetoric, asyndeton, which suppresses conjunctions between successive clauses and sentences, has been a standby of serious poetry in Europe for fifty years or more, and the greatest single reason, at a guess, why much modern poetry has been found hard to understand. The effect of leaving out conjunctions is to rob the reader of certain logical guarantees, that the successive sentences he reads are semantically as well as syntactically adjacent to each other. The words that are left out are the words on which the manifest coherence of a passage of prose or a poem depend, words like 'then', 'therefore', 'so', 'but'. The effect superficially is of disintegration, and the reader can palliate it only by reconstructing the intellectual scheme of the work for himself, in terms of what I. A. Richards, writing long ago about *The Waste Land*, called a 'unified response.'

In his early days, as something of an *avant-garde* poet, Borges met with and adopted the modernist technique of abrupt juxtaposition, a technique that was meant to shock and frequently did shock. Borges soon abjured it, but he has never abjured a belief that the representation of reality, whether that reality be an existing narrative, a person, or a scene, should be *seen* to be less, and other, than its model, that the discontinuities on which representation depends should be blatant. This is not simply the capricious adaptation to prose of a technique he learnt as a poet, but a demonstration that the activity of the human mind, and the nature of human language, can never match the complexity or continuity of what they seek to represent.

In the foreword to the *Historia universal de la infamia* Borges

accuses himself of overdoing such devices as 'disparate enumerations, the abrupt dissolution of continuity, the reduction of a man's
life to two or three scenes'.[3] This small piece of self-criticism is
perhaps his way of drawing attention to a strategy of writing whose
importance to him might otherwise have been overlooked. The
devices he incriminates are the most distinctive and enjoyable of
all those he has employed in his postulation of a too complex reality.
All three of them work by compression, all three of them are
dramatic; all three of them are basic to another art in which
Borges was keenly interested, and on which he wrote very in-
cisively in the 1930s, the cinema. As a film critic Borges displays a
rare and invigorating understanding of what, in recent years and
especially in France, has come to be called the 'syntax' of films,
that is to say the way in which the successive shots are articulated.

Now a film is nothing if not discontinuous, even if the continuity
of its projection to some extent disguises the fact. The cinema is
the most illusory of all techniques of illusion in the sense that what
we unthinkingly perceive as a continuum is in fact interrupted
several times a second, and each interruption, each transition from
frame to frame, is an opportunity for the maker of the film to show
his authority and change the camera-angle or the scene as a whole.
These changes may be startlingly abrupt, or smoothly prepared, or
they may be so slight that the majority of cinema-goers never
notice them. In the cinema, narrative is based on the 'cut': on the
cuts the camera makes within scenes and between scenes, and also
on the cuts the editor of the film makes after it has been shot,
which introduce all manner of elisions into its syntax.

Film syntax, like the syntax of dreams (and films, even more
than prose narratives, are 'controlled dreams', or dreams requiring
a 'director'), is notably poor in conjunctions, it lacks the wide
range of explicit logical relations between successive actions which
written syntax enjoys. The dream-work has its own ways of
representing logical relations, whose demonstration makes, for any
student of narrative, one of the most lucid and magisterial chapters
of Freud's *Interpretation of Dreams*.[4] The cinema, to date, has been
less resourceful and its syntax is still on the elementary side. This
is not the place to begin cataloguing the different logical relations a
film is capable of representing (without, I hasten to insert, resorting

---

[3] *OC*, p. 289.

[4] S. Freud, *Interpretation of Dreams*, London, 1954, pp. 312 ff.

to that degrading, a-cinematic device of a 'voice over'), but simply to emphasize that those relations are established at the moments in the film where its artifice becomes apparent: when there is a manifest interruption of its sequence.

The cut is the convention by which the cinema abstracts from reality, which is why Romantic extremists such as Andy Warhol have envisaged films without cuts, as an ideal representation of the real (though the absence of cutting from the projected version of the film may itself be an illusion, if the film was not continuously shot). But Warhol's protracted, rather uneventful documentary of someone sleeping, a notorious but not widely admired breakthrough in *cinéma-vérité*, is still not a film free from conventions—how could it be? Even a protagonist who is fast asleep has to be shown from somewhere, and there can be no such thing as a non-conventional camera-angle. To look down on a sleeping body is not the same experience in the cinema as to look up at one; nor, in more general terms, does the *expectancy* with which a cinema audience will regard the representation of a sleeping body take its justification from the feelings we have towards sleeping bodies in real life.

The mature, Classical way to cope with narrative conventions is, rather, to enjoy them. And to enjoy them may now and again mean to display them, to show them up as conventions. Such is Borges's own practice in the *Historia universal de la infamia*: in the story of 'El asesino desinteresado Bill Harrigan' ('The Disinterested Killer Bill Harrigan'), for instance, he writes: 'History (which, like a certain film director, proceeds by discontinuous images now proposes that of a dangerous tavern . . .'[5] To be exact, it is not history which so proceeds but historiography, for it is the discrepancy between reality and the records we make of it which is the very point at issue. But Borges, we know, enjoys the ambiguity of the Spanish word *historia*, which is as well able to imply the invention as the registration of past events. The less than historical stories of the *Historia universal de la infamia* are very filmic in their brevity and discontinuities, and the 'certain film director' to whom Borges alludes can only be Josef von Sternberg, who was very much a hero for him in the days when he was reviewing films, because of the sureness and intelligence of his technique. From von Sternberg Borges got what one imagines to be the highest satisfaction open to

[5] *OC*, p. 317.

him: 'intellectual pleasure'.[6] All film directors, and all historians, have to proceed in the same discontinuous way because they could not otherwise make films or write history; but Borges singles out one film director because he did more than merely accept the conventions of his trade, he revelled in them; that, for Borges, is a mark of the artist.

The cinema's most distinctive method of representing multiplicity is the montage, that economical sequence of more or less disconnected images which postulates a reality far more extensive and intricate than the human power of representation. The montage, which takes the specifically cinematic convention of the cut and intensifies it to the maximum, is the equivalent in a film of Borges's 'disparate enumerations', which likewise make very manifest the necessary discontinuities and inadequacies of prose. The enumeration, traditionally, is an epic resource and one whose effect seems to be to exhaust reality. Reading the Homeric catalogue of ships we come to believe that they have all been included, that Homer has encompassed the reality fully. With Borges it is the reverse, his enumerations are self-defeating; far from exhausting reality they indicate the absurdity of even trying to enumerate it. The long list of particular scenes which the narrator of the story of 'El Aleph' witnesses, lying uncomfortably beneath the cellar-steps and fixing his gaze on the infinite peep-show, is splendidly various and comical; but it is also disastrously trivial and local, like those paltry scraps of the world's topography which the Aleph's owner, Daneri, has managed to versify in his All-embracing poem:

by 1941 he had already dispatched a few hectares of the State of Queensland, more than a kilometre of the course of the Ob, a gasometer to the north of Veracruz, the principal business houses in the parish of La Concepción, the country house of Mariana Cambaceres de Alvear in the Calle Once de Septiembre in Belgrano, and a turkish bath not far from the accredited aquarium in Brighton.[7]

For anyone less manically ambitious than Daneri this enumeration of his achievements would perhaps be quite impressive, but measured against what remains in the world for him to write about, it looks, to say the least, sketchy. It looks, moreover, disorderly: Borges has subverted the orthodox purpose of an enumeration

---

[6] See Edgardo Cozarinsky, *Borges y el ciné*, Buenos Aires, 1974, esp. p. 29.

[7] *OC*, p. 620.

even more seriously by the pointless variety of its constituents. The places Daneri has 'dispatched' are utterly random, of different kinds and in different countries.

The most rightly anthologized of all Borges's 'disparate enumertions' carries this subversiveness to the limit. This is his allusion in his essay on 'El idioma analítico de John Wilkins' ("The Analytical Language of John Wilkins') to 'a certain Chinese encyclopedia entitled *Celestial Emporium of Benevolent Knowledge*':

In its remote pages it is written that the animals are divided into (a) belonging to the Emperor, (b) embalmed, (c) trained, (d) sucking pigs, (e) sirens, (f) fabulous, (g) unleashed dogs, (h) included in this classification, (i) which jump about like lunatics, (j) innumerable, (k) drawn with a very fine camel-hair brush, (l) etcetera, (m) which have just broken the pitcher, (n) which look from a distance like flies.[8]

This captivating miscellany Borges immediately follows with a sardonic summary of a particular Dewey-eyed system of classifying books in libraries, a system which has 'parcelled out the universe into 1000 subdivisions' and has reserved subdivision No. 263 for God the Father.

Borges's excerpt from his fictive Chinese encyclopedia is an offence against the very intellectual system it is alleged to exemplify, the system of calling the world to order by the logical classification of its contents. Borges's own procedure is analogous to that of encyclopedias in general: he represents the encyclopedia by a quotation just as the encyclopedia represents the world. That representation he shows in both cases to be not simply inadequate but impossible. What he proves is that language has possibilities in respect of taxonomy which science, concerned to classify phenomena in categories that are at least mutually exclusive, has not.

Borges's brief and memorable text teaches an object lesson in the principles of classification by showing their conventionality. It is a lesson well taken by the French historian of ideas, Michel Foucault, whose remarkable historical study of taxonomy, *Les Mots et les choses*, originated, he says in a preface, in his reflections on Borges's Chinese encyclopedia. It is Borges's 'a-topianism' which Foucault above all appreciates:

The monstrosity which Borges causes to circulate in his enumeration consists on the contrary in the fact that its common meeting-ground is

[8] *OC*, p. 708.

itself destroyed. What is impossible is not the adjacency of the things but the very site where they might be adjacent ... Where could the animals ever meet except in the immaterial voice which pronounces their enumeration, except on the page which transcribes it? Where can they be juxtaposed except in the nowhere (*non-lieu*) of language?[9]

Borges shows classification to be an arbitrary representation of things by himself juxtaposing incompatible or overlapping systems of classification. Two of his categories, (h) 'included in this classification, and (i) 'etcetera', are null, but the other twelve might each, in isolation, make a legitimate if eccentric division of Chinese fauna into two classes—the embalmed and the unembalmed, for example, or the flylike from a distance and the unflylike from a distance. The encyclopedia entry proves, as the Aleph also proves, that there is no achieving the Absolute via the accumulation of particulars; to be precise, the Absolute could only be achieved by an accumulation of *all* the particulars. Borges's bogus Chinese encyclopedia is called the 'celestial emporium' for the good reason that it will never be realized on earth. What it aspires to is the ultimate idealization of Everything, the incorporation into one 'almost infinite', Babel-like volume of every conceivable perspective on things.

Encyclopedias being what they are, which is a corporate attempt at the full representation of reality, it is right that they should have their place in Borges's fictions. As aggregates of facts about the world they stand as models for literature as a whole, understood as the aggregate of actual and possible fictions. Encyclopedias form the armature of the very first story in *Ficciones*, 'Tlön, Uqbar, Orbis Tertius'. Three encyclopedias are involved and they can be arranged, like the three elements of the story's title, in a series of ascending unreality. The series starts with a real encyclopedia, the *Encyclopaedia Britannica*, which as it were anchors the story in reality. Its next term is a bogus encyclopedia, invented by Borges, *The Anglo-American Cyclopaedia*, supposedly published in New York in 1917, which is 'a literal and also belated reprint' of the *Britannica* of 1902. Like the stories of the *Historia universal de la infamia*, this is an act of piracy, the imposition of a fresh name on old goods. There are, it seems, two copies of *The Anglo-American Cyclopaedia*, one belonging to the narrator of the story, the other to his, and Borges's, friend, Bioy Casares. The two copies are not identical: they offer a bifurcation. Bioy Casares's copy contains

[9] M. Foucault, *Les Mots et les choses*, Paris, 1966, p. 9.

four extra pages at the end of Volume 26 which the narrator's copy does not have, and those four pages contain the entry for the land of Uqbar. That entry reveals that the literature of Uqbar is fantastic and refers not to the reality of Uqbar itself but to the 'two imaginary regions of Mlejnas and Tlön': this being a second bifurcation, of which, as befits visitors to a labyrinth, we follow only one path, that leading to Tlön. The third encyclopedia in the series is *A First Encyclopaedia of Tlön*, of which only Volume 11 is known to exist even though it is reportedly one of a set of forty volumes, provisionally entitled *Orbis Tertius*. Even this massive enterprise—'the most extensive work men have undertaken'—is to be exceeded eventually by a more massive or 'meticulous' (*minuciosa*) one still, written no longer in English but in one of the languages of Tlön. Volume 11 has, one is pleased but not surprised to note, 1001 pages. The model on which *Orbis Tertius* has been based, by its founder, is the *Encyclopaedia Britannica*, so that the encyclopedic series forms in the end a circle. And just as there are two, slightly different copies of Volume 26 of *The Anglo-American Cyclopaedia*, so there are two, slightly different copies of Volume 11 of *Orbis Tertius*.

This elaborate chain of duplications, symmetries, and small variations sets the mind ricocheting uncomfortably from one degree of fictiveness to the next. The one point of stability is the *Encyclopaedia Britannica*, an arbitrary and incomplete taxonomy of the universe no doubt, but a reality none the less. The *Britannica* is the point of departure for a fiction. The two reproductions of it are alike in having the same title, unlike in that only one contains the article on Uqbar; it is the reproduction containing *more* than the original which provides for the continuance of the story. This same duplication is repeated exactly with Volume 11 of *Orbis Tertius*, which is tertiary in so far as it is the projection of a projection, the imaginary realm of the imaginary realm of Uqbar: Tlön is to Uqbar as Uqbar is to Borges, or to the narrator of his story. One copy of Volume 11 has been discovered in the bar of a hotel, where it had been left by one Herbert Ashe, an English engineer with a taste for inventing original systems of numeration, and more successfully than poor Funes the Memorious; the second copy turns up later (in a postscript to the story) in a library in Memphis, Tennessee, where a complete set of *Orbis Tertius* has been 'exhumed'—bars and libraries belong, of course, in the same paradigm for Borges, as places of inspiration and recreation. Ashe's copy of Volume 11 contains, as Bioy's copy of the earlier *Cyclopaedia* contained, something extra. Tlön is a 'congenitally idealist' planet, constructed to the specifications of Bishop Berkeley; there is no space or time there only succession, and the language has no substantives in it because the locals recognize no perdurable matter independent of their perceptions.[10] The extra item in Ashe's copy concerns the peculiar influence which Idealism may have on reality in Tlön; it may duplicate lost objects:

Two people look for a pencil; the first one finds it and says nothing; the second one finds a pencil no less real, but better fitted to his expectation. These secondary objects are called *hrönir* and, though graceless in form, are a little longer (*más largos*). Until recently *hrönir* were the casual offspring of distraction and forgetfulness (*olvido*). It seems a falsehood that their methodical production is barely a hundred years old, but so Volume XI affirms.[11]

The description of the *hrönir* in Ashe's copy of the encyclopedia is thus itself a *hrön*, a secondary and more satisfactory object than the *hrönir*-less account of Tlön in the Memphis copy of the same work. And this *hrön* is itself a replica of an earlier one, the four supplementary pages in Bioy Casares's *Anglo-American Cyclopaedia*. So we have two *hrönir* which are literary texts, together with the story's own example of a *hrön*, a pencil, which is the instrument texts may be written with. The influence of Idealism on reality, in our own world as well as on the planet of Tlön, is to add small, fictional objects to it, such as stories.

The discovery of Uqbar, we learn in the opening sentence of the story of 'Tlön, Uqbar, Orbis Tertius', is owed to 'the conjunction of a mirror and an encyclopedia'. This conjunction is not as wayward and provocative as the famous conjunction of an umbrella with a sewing-machine recommended by Lautréamont, but it makes the point that without conjunctions there can be no stories. The art of narrative is an art of composition; the discontinuous

---

[10] *Orbis Tertius* is the brain-child of the 'ascetic millionaire' Ezra Buckley, of Memphis, whose name indicates him as a fit though possibly degenerate successor of Bishop Berkeley. Buckley, unlike Berkeley, is not a religious believer, and this transforms the Idealism of his fictive planet. In Berkeley's system it is the unsleeping mental activity of God which sustains the universe and prevents it from being constantly annihilated; in Tlön there is no such sustention. There the trees do *not* continue to be when there's no one about in the quad.

[11] *OC*, p. 439.

elements from which a narrative is made have to be conjoined in an effective order. Uqbar, that exemplary country whose literature is purely fantastic, is, we can assume, dedicated to conjunction for the elaboration of its fantasies. But Uqbar, like so many of Borges's imaginary civilizations, also has its heretics, who challenge the orthodoxy prevalent in its literary circles. Indeed, the first mention of Uqbar in 'Tlön, Uqbar, Orbis Tertius', and the reason why the narrator and Bioy Casares start searching their encyclopedias for the entry describing it, is Bioy's quotation of one of its heretics to the effect that 'copulation (*cópula*) and mirrors are abominable because they multiply the number of men.'[12] This, it turns out, is a misquotation. On referring to his *hrön*, that is to say his copy of *The Anglo-American Cyclopaedia*, Bioy finds that the actual wording, 'perhaps literarily inferior' to his version of it, goes: 'For one of these gnostics, the visible universe was an illusion or (more precisely) a sophism. Mirrors and fatherhood are hateful because they multiply and publish (*divulgan*) it.'[13]

This particular heresiarch seems to be a man biased against literature. His 'visible universe' is a form of words, a 'sophism'; it is the sum of existing verbal representations of things, not the sum of things themselves. He is opposed to any addition to this sum, to any more sophisms being uttered. Those new, additional sophisms are created, however, by exactly the kind of misquotation of the existing sophisms of which Bioy Casares has been guilty; by his faulty transmission of what he himself has read Bioy has re-established the orthodoxy of Uqbar: fantasy has a future, as we at once discover. The main error in his quotation of the heretic's dictum was to put 'copulation' for 'fatherhood'. In this context 'copulation' looks to be a worse abomination since, if one takes the word in its widest sense—it is always as well to do this where Borges is concerned—it means a joining-together. For copulation we can read conjunction, and conjunction is the art of lending a plausible continuity to the necessarily discontinuous.

In Tlön itself, however, where philosophical Idealism has come into its own, continuity is a heresy: on that planet a troublesome sect of materialists argue the continuing existence of objects independently of the moments in which they are perceived by someone—this is the old challenge of empiricism to Berkeleyan Idealism. But Borges, as an author, subscribes fully to the orthodoxy of

[12] *OC*, p. 431.   [13] *OC*, p. 432.

Tlön: in the world postulated by a fiction there are no real objects to subsist once the writer or the reader's attention is withdrawn from them. Borges is understandably fond of the discontinuities which flaunt the Idealism of a fiction, and makes extravagant use of them in this story when he gets on to the 'splendid story (*historia*)' of how the fictive planet of Tlön first came to be invented by a secret society early in the seventeenth century. The originators of the fiction came to see that it would require more than one generation to carry it through: 'They resolved that each of the masters who had integrated it should elect a disciple for the continuation of the work. This hereditary disposition prevailed; after a hiatus of two centuries the persecuted fraternity re-emerges in America.'[14]

No sooner is the programme for the secret work's 'continuation' settled, then, before its history lapses, and lapses on the grand scale; a hiatus of two centuries in a history as fragile as this one might be thought destructive. Moreover, when the society reappears after this prolonged eclipse, it turns out to have been 'persecuted', though no instances of persecution are given nor any reason why anyone should have wanted to persecute it. Borges exploits the gaps in his story unmercifully. He does so, surely, because it is in the nature of language to disjoin before it can again conjoin, to exist as a lexicon of independent, general terms which it is the author's pleasure to combine.

[14] *OC*, p. 440.

PART IV

'Reality proceeds by events...'

CHAPTER 1

THE OBLIGATION TO BE INTERESTING

STORIES are not given but made. This would not be worth saying were it not the case that there are readers of stories who, like Brodie's ignominious Yahoos, have difficulty in telling the natural from the artificial, a missionary's wooden refuge from the trees it has been made from. Such people, perversely, are more apt to recognize that books themselves are artefacts, being another derivative of the tree, than their contents. A story of the commonest and most rudimentary sort, a news-story let us say, is readily taken to be a natural product, the inevitable conjunction of events themselves, rather than the composition of a journalist. Stories are not what reality makes by itself, but what we, by observing certain narrative conventions, make of reality. There are true stories and untrue ones, but their truth-values have nothing to do with the way stories are made. The form a narrative takes will not necessarily reveal whether it is made up from events that have actually occurred or events that have been invented.

We judge whether stories are true or untrue according to where we read them. Stories in newspapers, even the most obviously conventional and therefore suspect ones, we take to correspond with certain facts; stories in novels may contain all manner of 'truths', sociological, psychological, and several other -ologicals, but they are not true stories, they are not the representation of an actual state of affairs. True stories might, in principle, be verified; there should be no disagreement about the authenticity of the facts from which they are made, even if the selection and arrangement of those facts be held to misrepresent reality. The author of a true story, therefore, is responsible for its composition not for its components. These are contingencies, events befalling people in the real world. But where the real world is excluded, as it is in the composition of a fiction, the responsibility of the author of a story widens enormously. There is no longer the same strong element of contingency in his work; he still has to select the events of his narrative but he can select them from the whole range of possible events, free from the severe constraint on his choice which a correspondence with the facts imposes. The true narrative is more dictated than planned, the fictional narrative more planned than dictated.

This is a rather rough distinction but it is an important one for its effects on the readers of the two kinds of narrative. The reader of a fiction ought to read it in the belief that every element of it has been planned. This may not be, from its author's point of view, quite the case: there may be a considerable number of involuntary elements in his story, introduced instinctively rather than rationally while he was actually writing. Few if any novels can be rationalized down to the last sentence, and few if any novelists perhaps would see any reason why they should be. But when we read a story we are entitled to our belief that everything we read has been at least approved by its author, that it is there because he wants it there. The undoubted fact that it was originally an involuntary contribution to the fiction does not prevent us from reading it as a voluntary one.

If we do not read fictions as if they were wholly intentional, then we should not be reading them at all. Fictions deny contingency and they can only deny it by eliminating it. It is Mallarmé above all, with his 'Un coup de dés jamais n'abolira le hasard', who has taught us that the makers of fictions are not the servants of necessity but its masters, and it is to Mallarmé, more than any other literary thinker, that we owe the extraordinarily rigorous, self-denying philosophy of fiction which works itself out in the stories of Borges. Nothing passes by chance into those stories, everything they contain is there for a reason and there, moreover, for a literary reason, as a necessary part of that particular narrative. Borges has no time for the instinctive, only for the considered; he is an adept of Mallarmé's second, and higher, state of language: 'A desire undeniable to my time is to separate as if with a view to different attributions the double state of the word (*la parole*), brute or immediate here, there essential.'[1]

It is poets rather than prose-writers whom we expect to find using language in its refined, 'essential' state, because poets write less than prose-writers and can more easily accept such extremes of self-discipline. The prose-writer whose method leads him to ponder his text word by word is depriving himself of prose's major

[1] Mallarmé, *Œuvres complètes*, Paris, 1945, p. 368.

consolation, its facility. Borges, the exemplary writer of prose, rejects that facility, and constructs his stories with the care and unremitting attention to form of a poet. So carefully made are his stories, indeed, that it would have been unthinkable for him ever to have contemplated making a novel on the same principles—any more than the wonderfully scrupulous Mallarmé could ever have written a verse epic.

There is no need to assume that Borges's stories are free from contingencies, we know they are. Such knowledge transforms the story from a casual sequence of events into a planned one. Each event within that sequence, together with its place in the sequence, has a rational explanation if only we can find it, and the sequence as a whole is transformed from mimesis into mystery. All stories, if we read them properly, are to some extent detective stories, with ourselves conducting the investigation. Every element in a story can be questioned as to what it is doing there, what its value is in the economy of the narrative as a whole. 'In all my experience along the dirtiest ways of this dirty little world, I have never met with such a thing as a trifle yet', is the rebuke crushingly administered to a less gifted policeman than himself by the great Sergeant Cuff in *The Moonstone*. He spoke for the entire race of fictional detectives and for the attentive readers of fiction. The effect of a detective story is to make significant, for a short interval of time, all kind of trivial objects and actions that in normal circumstances would be overlooked. The insignificant domestic utensil may be the instrument of a crime, and has to be studied and interrogated with an intensity we would rightly regard as psychotic had its everyday function not been so dramatically supplemented. Similarly, the most commonplace words and gestures—the more commonplace the better, many writers and readers of detective stories would say—can for once in their lives be made fateful, and redeemed from their normal humdrum instrumentality. The general effect of a detective story is to inflate whatever it contains with potential meaning, and to show how a plot can seize on anything it likes, however mean or ordinary, and integrate it within a single meaningful, literary structure.

The most compelling of Borges's own stories of detection is 'Death and the Compass', than which no story could be more richly, more minutely contrived. As in *The Moonstone*, there are two investigators in the story, a dull one like Wilkie Collins's

Superintendent Seegrave, and a clever one, like the archetypal Sergeant Cuff. And also like Sergeant Cuff, the clever one reproaches the dull one for his failure to grasp the conventions essential to detective fiction. A crime has been committed: the rabbi Marcelo Yarmolinsky has been found stabbed to death in his hotel room. The policeman in charge of the investigation, Treviranus, has his own explanation of the crime, which is that it was an accident, that the rabbi has been murdered in error, having been sleeping in the very next room to the Tetrarch of Galilee, the possessor of some very desirable sapphires. The private detective Erik Lönnrot is not at all taken with this flat-footed explanation: "'Possible, but not interesting"—replied Lönnrot. "You will answer that reality does not have the least obligation to be interesting. I shall reply that reality may dispense with that obligation, but not hypotheses."'[2]

It is unjust of Lönnrot not to allow that Treviranus's explanation of the murder, for all its drabness, is still a hypothesis. It is a hypothesis, however, which has to be excluded right from the outset, since if it were found to be true it would be the start of a different story, of the investigation of an attempted robbery instead of a deliberate, planned murder. The ultimate disappointment, which no detective-story writer, one might think, could ever bring himself to inflict on his readers, would be the investigation of a murder which turned out to be an accident. Which is exactly what we get in the story of 'La muerte y la brújula'. It emerges at the last that Treviranus was right and Lönnrot wrong, that the murder of the rabbi *was* an accident, that the would-be thief of the Tetrarch's jewels has made two mistakes: he has anticipated by twenty-four hours the time for which the theft had been planned and he has gone into the wrong room in the hotel. He has erred in terms of both time and place. But if this first crime was an accident, those which follow it are not. Treviranus is right the first time but he can have no adequate explanation for the succeeding felonies; it is the hugely ingenious hypothesis of Lönnrot which sustains the story as a whole.

Lönnrot, like Don Isidro Parodi, is the ideal literary sleuth, a pure reasoner, and the hypothesis he develops in order to account, first for the death of the rabbi and then for the crimes which follow, leaves no room whatsoever for accident or chance. The series has

²*OC*, p. 500.

been rigorously planned, and a series which has been rigorously planned requires a rigorous planner. Lönnrot is the 'reader' of the crimes and a reader implies an author for the crimes. The author here is Dandy Red Scharlach, the demonic *metteur-en-scène* who ultimately shoots Lönnrot when the detective catches up with him. Scharlach ties the knots, Lönnrot unties them, until the final dénouement leaves him without a function and ready to be disposed of. Master criminal and the detective who reasons his way after him are twin virtualities of a single sequence of events. They are only partially to be differentiated, as their names confirm. Both are *red* (and *red*, in Spanish, is the word for a 'reticule' or 'net'), but Scharlach is the redder, his surname meaning 'scarlet fever' in German. Lönn*rot* is red, likewise in German, only the once, though his Erik may also suggest redness, as being the name of the celebrated Erik the Red; the Lönn- is not obviously significant on its own, though its form, and especially its umlaut, gives it a distinct family resemblance to Tlön and its *hrönir*.

Scharlach, German by name and German by nature, is the great Idealist. He is a dandy because he must eliminate the merely fortuitous from his schemes, like the lamented Teodelina Villar, who would wear nothing that had not been decreed by the arbiters of fashion. Scharlach begins from a contingency because there has to be a first, arbitrary datum in any fiction; thereafter contingency is eliminated and the plot proceeds with mathematical rigour. The contingency is the mistake made by one of his gang, Daniel Azevedo. But that mistake, committed because Azevedo was drunk, is also an inspiration for Scharlach: the plan to rob the Tetrarch is exchanged for a plan to trap his old enemy Lönnrot. Azevedo's errors of time and place in fact inaugurate a period in which the imagination is free to impose its own chronology and geography.

The Hôtel du Nord, in which Rabbi Yarmolinsky is murdered, has, as we saw in an earlier chapter, 'the numbered divisibility' of a prison: it is, like a fiction itself, a space which may be divided and subdivided as many times and along as many different scales as its author wishes. And 'La muerte y la brújula' exemplifies this freedom of the author to transpose the mathematics of the real world to suit himself. Lönnrot, like the engineer Herbert Ashe, and like the ill-starred Funes, plays the numbers game. There are, in the story, two series of numbers: a series of three and certain multiples or applications of three, and a series of four. The three-series incorporates elements of the story which are not, in Lönnrot's strong sense of that word, 'interesting'—though if they are uninteresting they are at least 'interestingly' uninteresting, since they have a significant, characteristically dialectical part in Borges's scheme. The president of this series is *Tre*viranus, the spokesman for contingency and for the prerogatives of reality. The robbery of the Tetrarch's sapphires had been planned by Scharlach for the fourth day of the month, but because of Azevedo's mistake it takes place on the night of the third. The victim himself, the rabbi, is exceedingly tertiary: he arrives on the third day of the month to attend the Third Talmudic Congress, having learnt resignation from three years of fighting in the Carpathians and, as the representative of his unfortunate race, from three thousand years of persecution. Three crimes are committed in all, each on the third of the month, three men are involved in the third crime, we are referred at a significant moment in the story to the thirty-third chapter of something called the *Philologus Hebraeo-graecus*, three years have elapsed since Scharlach's brother was imprisoned through Lönnrot's efforts, and so on. The most charmingly off-hand member of this entire series is the opening remark made by its president, Treviranus, to Lönnrot on the occasion of the first crime, that 'no hay que buscarle tres pies al gato', meaning, literally, 'no need to look for three feet on the cat', i.e. some unreal hypothesis to account for the crime of the sort that Lönnrot will very soon be developing.

The four-series is more compact. It is initiated by the Tetrarch of Galilee, the ruler of a fourth part of that territory under the Roman jurisdiction, maintained by various references to rectangular and quadrangular shapes, fortified above all by the invocation of the Tetragrammaton or four-letter name of God, each letter of which is supposedly spelt out by the successive crimes planned and executed by Scharlach. This series belongs with the 'interesting' side of the story, on the fictional side of the frontier. It is the transposition of reality, a mathematical operation on the 'facts' common to both Scharlach and Lönnrot, but a delusion for such irredeemably prosaic spirits as Treviranus.

There is, at the outset of 'La muerte y la brújula', a duplication just like the one in 'Tlön, Uqbar, Orbis Tertius', where we had two dissimilar copies of *The Anglo-American Cyclopaedia*: this time the dissimilarity is between the two hypotheses put forward to account for the murder of the rabbi. One of these hypotheses, Lönnrot's, offers *more* than the other, like Bioy's encyclopedia. Lönnrot, who prefers to work out a 'rabbinical' explanation for the murder of the rabbi, turns threes into fours, and in so doing re-creates the work already done on reality by Scharlach. After he has trapped the detective, Scharlach explains his plot to him, including the deception of the third crime in the series, which was not a crime at all but only the simulacrum of a crime. On this occasion, Scharlach has arranged for the words 'The last letter of the Name has been articulated' to be written up on a pillar, as if the Name were of three letters only: 'This writing divulged that the series of crimes was threefold. That was how the public understood it; I, however, interpolated repeated indications so that you, the reasoner Erik Lönnrot, should understand that it was *quadruple*.'[3] (Borges's italics.)

In the belief that the series is quadruple, having penetrated Scharlach's intentions, Lönnrot has been able to predict the day and the place—which is also the quarter of the compass—of the fourth crime which will complete it. He has discovered, as part of the Jewish lore necessary to his 'rabbinical' hypothesis, that the Hebrew calendar measures time differently from a Christian one, that the Hebrew day runs not from midnight to midnight but from sunset to sunset. The crimes which 'poor Christians' like Treviran-us compute to have taken place on the third day of the month must be reckoned, by those in the know—the 'Jews'—to have taken place on the fourth. The fictive explanation of the crimes offered by Lönnrot quite simply removes them from an orthodox, public calendar to a private one. Having determined by his impeccable logic where he needs to go in order to trap the master criminal, and when he needs to go there, Lönnrot sets off—southwards, inevit-ably—for the villa of Triste-le-Roy where, finally, his own death completes the series of crimes. But he sets off twenty-four hours in advance of the day when, according to his predictions, the final crime is to be committed. He dies on the third of the month, instead of the fourth. Before he dies, moreover, he finds that there have, in fact, been two previous crimes, that the third one was, as the non-fictional Treviranus 'divined', bogus. Lönnrot's murder therefore completes a series of three.

[3] *OC* p. 507.

The finale of 'La muerte y la brújula' thus returns us to reality, to our ordinary measurement of time, by reducing fours to threes once again. Lönnrot's impulsiveness, in going to Triste-le-Roy one day early, is symmetrical with the impulsiveness, at the start of the story, of Daniel Azevedo (Azevedo is one of Borges's own family names), who has blundered by killing the rabbi and who himself becomes the second victim of Scharlach, punished for his gross incompetence. When Lönnrot gets off the train that has brought him to his meeting with Scharlach, in the south, we are told that "It was one of those empty (*desiertas*) evenings which seem like dawns". By the Hebrew calendar on which the fiction depends it is so to speak a dawn, because sunset is the moment at which the new day, the fourth of the month, is held to start. A fiction for Borges, as we have seen, is a private world which allows its author the freedom of the compass; it is also a world, 'La muerte y la brújula' makes clear, which allows him the freedom of the clock. This is a story built on anachronism, like the great 'anachronistic' cape Yarmolinsky is wearing when he is murdered; it is a story which shows a fiction to be a slight, systematic misreading of reality.

Its chief lesson, perhaps, is in showing that fiction is 'interesting' while brute facts are not. Fiction is 'interesting' because it is intentional, brute facts are uninteresting because they are contingent. Borges's rules are strict, and those who infringe them die. The impulsives, Azevedo and Lönnrot, become the second and third terms of a series of murders which begins with the murder of the rabbi. Such impulsiveness is a treachery to be punished in the only way open to a maker of fictions, which is to incorporate it in a plot. Scharlach is the supreme structuralist who presses every contingent datum into service and thereby makes it intelligible. He is ·hat highly contemporary hero, *homo significans*, the bringer of meaning to an otherwise random universe. Those who form part of his structure, or plot, owe their loyalty to it, not to an unregenerate reality, they should take their time from the Hebrew calendar and not the Christian one. Scharlach himself knows the value of such fidelity: in the midst of his 'fever', when he was hatching his scheme of revenge on Lönnrot, to punish him for imprisoning his brother, an Irishman has tried to convert him 'to the faith of Jesus', but without success. This failed missionary can only be the Irishman already introduced into the story, a saloon-keeper with the pleasantly literary name of Black Finnegan, 'a former Irish criminal, crushed and almost annulled by decency'. Between the Red (Scharlach) of feverish, criminal conspiracy and the Black (Finnegan) of decency there can only be one choice for Lönnrot, who has 'something of the adventurer and even of the gambler in him'.

There looks to be something contradictory about a reasoner who is also a gambler, but gamblers are people who try to profit from contingency: they do not simply submit to chance but try to make money from it. And gambling, or gaming, as we saw with the game of *truco*, involves a submission to the rules of a world separate and distinct from the everyday world. In 'La muerte y la brújula' the gambling theme is important. Scharlach's brother has been arrested and he himself shot at a gambling-den in the Rue de Toulon; it is at Liverpool House, a tavern in the same street ('that briny street where there cohabit the cosmorama and the dairy, the bordello and the sellers of bibles'), that the second, counterfeit crime is committed, under the eye of Black Finnegan, adding his *noir* to Scharlach's *rouge*; the constant play in the story between threes and fours is also a play between the *pair* and *impair*, or even numbers and odd numbers. These elements converge in Lönnrot's reading of Hebrew mysticism, from which he discovers

The thesis that God has a secret name, in which is condensed (as in the glass sphere which the Persians attribute to Alexander of Macedonia) his ninth attribute, eternity—that is, the immediate knowledge of all the things that will be, that are, and that have been in the universe. Tradition enumerates ninety-nine names of God; Hebraicists attribute this imperfect number to the magical fear of even figures (*cifras*); the Hasidim reason that this hiatus indicates a hundredth name, the Absolute Name.[4]

Whatever the authenticity of this erudition, it plays a determining role in the economy of the story. Fiction is where Borges expects us to look for 'secret' names, 'Absolute' names, eternity, and *cifras*, all of which can be realized in the a-temporal world of Ideas. The 'magical fear' of which Hebraicists talk is also the fear of magic, or the power the maker of fictions enjoys to impose his hallucinations on others. The quest for the Absolute Name is also the writer's imposition of the name of which I have spoken earlier. It is open only to those, like Lönnrot, who understand what the conditions of natural language are, and what the specific freedoms and

---

[4] *OC*, pp. 500–1.

constraints of authorship. At its end there beckons an alternative, fictive universe which is no longer a chaos but a cosmos, and no longer fact but fiction. In the 'eternity' attributed to God, or to his literary surrogate, the author, there is no longer any place for chance because every least occurrence is now seen, from this superior, privileged viewpoint outside of time, to have its place in the scheme of things. What to the merely human mind, confined in time and place, appears contingent, is shown in fact to be a necessary part of the divine plot.

The most comprehensive of fiction's virtues, as Borges sees it, is to save us from contingency. A fiction offers us a model, a puny one it may be, compared with the infinite randomness of the real world, of a world in which everything is significant, and significant as an element in a narrative, or plot. What Borges teaches is that there are no scenes in fiction, only scenarios; the reality we are offered is a dramatic one. This is a point made, albeit cumbersomely, before millions of cinema-goers who will few if any of them have re-marked it, by the film version of Agatha Christie's *Murder on the Orient Express*. That story too lays bare the transformation of reality which all fiction entails. The 'place apart' into which the action withdraws so that the distinction from reality can be made more obvious is that stock fictional prop, the railway train. The protracted sequence of seemingly unrehearsed events, which starts when the Express starts and ends with the murder of the victim, turns out, on investigation by the passionately rational Hercule Poirot, to have been not an unrehearsed sequence of events at all, but, very precisely, a rehearsed one. Every circumstance has been planned, or foreseen, and contingency has been excluded, because there are enough conspirators to ensure that all the roles necessit-ated by an adequate mimesis of reality will be taken by actors. In the Orient Express, on which the unwelcome intrusions of con-tingency are further insured against by a providential fall of snow which immobilizes the train, there is no need for improvisation. So far as one can tell the entire preparation and execution of the crime goes as planned; no 'outsiders' are involved, requiring adjustments to the plot.

Borges and Bioy Casares use a very similar scheme to Agatha Christie's in 'Las noches de Goliadkin' ('Goliadkin's Nights'), one of the *Seis problemas para don Isidro Parodi*. In this story a crime is likewise committed on a train journey which, up until the moment when the crime *is* committed, had seemed to those involved a normal, spontaneous train journey. Parodi, in his prison-cell, having listened to the account of the journey and of the crime, knows better. Invited to elucidate the mystery, he proves that what, to Gervasio Montenegro, his informant as well as the victim of the crime (a robbery), had seemed to be merely passengers, assembled on the train by chance, were in truth plotters, assembled there by design. Montenegro, unwittingly, has played the part written for him in a scenario—and this in itself is a good joke, because the vain and florid Montenegro is one of his country's leading actors.

Parodi is considerably more alert than Hercule Poirot when it comes to detecting a fiction. Listening to Montenegro's account of his journey, he is made suspicious by the remarkable degree of differentiation between the various passengers on the train. It cannot be by chance, he concludes, that people so glaringly dissimilar from one another should be found together; they are being deliberately different, they have turned themselves from men and women into 'characters'. If their victim, Montenegro, had been a better actor instead of a ham, he might have seen through them. But Montenegro is, in Borges's terms, a Yahoo, with a poorly developed sense of artifice (he takes time off to tell Parodi of his detestation of that 'undesirable artefact', the microphone). Such a man is the inevitable dupe of the conspirators who have despoiled him, those conspirators whom he deludedly and pompously naturalizes as 'the human fauna that populated the confined universe which is a moving train'.[5] Montenegro is a disgrace to his profession, blind as he is to the distinction between the real and the artificial. He would be well advised to read Diderot's definitive *Paradoxe sur le comédien* and learn how the actor is to be distinguished from his roles.

Where *Murder on the Orient Express* and 'Las noches de Goliadkin' sin by exaggeration is in implying that, once they are realized, fictions go absolutely according to plan: that they are all script and no improvisation. But no conspiracy can exclude contingencies altogether, even on a railway train, and no scrupulous literary plotter, like Borges, ought perhaps to give anyone the idea that a plot as eventually perfected is exactly the plot as originally foreseen, that its actual implementation has not meant changing it in any way at all. It is the plot as finally realized, and as given to us to

[5] *Seis problemas para don Isidro Parodi*, p. 33.

read, from which all contingency has been banished; contingency can still intervene during the realization itself, as an impromptu element which it is the plotter's task to rationalize. The plotter's motto, faced with the unforeseen, should be the 'This weaves itself perforce into my business' of the machiavellian Edmund in *King Lear*, when he learns that the Duke of Cornwall and Regan will be arriving unexpectedly at his father's castle.

A more balanced model of conspiratorial activity demands, therefore, that foresight be mixed with improvisation. Such is the mixture in Borges's wonderfully artful story 'Tema del traidor y del heroe' ('Theme of the Traitor and the Hero'). There are three conspiracies in this story: the first is the conspiracy of the patriotic nineteenth-century Irishman, Fergus Kilpatrick, against the hated yoke of England; the second is the conspiracy of one of Kilpatrick's associates, Nolan, to present Kilpatrick's death in a false but favourable light as a contingency instead of an act which has been planned; the third is the conspiracy of a twentieth-century bio-grapher of Kilpatrick, Ryan, who is the hero's great-grandson and faced with the literary task of rationalizing his life into a narrative. Kilpatrick, 'a secret and glorious captain of conspirators', was, history has always believed, murdered on the eve of the 'victorious rebellion he had premeditated and dreamt of'—and the news of a victorious rebellion against the English in Ireland in the 1820s is certainly a well-kept historical secret. Ryan, as he plans his bio-graphy, comes quickly to distrust the historical account of Kil-patrick's death; he finds it, just like Isidro Parodi with Monte-negro's train journey, too theatrical to ring quite true. He senses that the apparently accidental may, on investigation, prove to have been the carefully contrived. Kilpatrick was murdered in a theatre, so prefiguring the death of Abraham Lincoln; he had been warned, like Julius Caesar—not the historical Julius Caesar, be it noted, but Shakespeare's Julius Caesar—not to go to the theatre that evening for fear of treachery; there have been 'false and anonymous rum-ours' of a fallen tower, like the tower Shakespeare's Calpurnia dreams of; a beggar who spoke to Kilpatrick on the day of his assassination has used words likewise prefigured by Shakespeare in *Macbeth*. In short, the account of Kilpatrick's end, as it has been recorded, is over-full of quotations: it looks to Ryan like the work of a literary man rather than of nature, or of that random, anony-mous conjunction of circumstances we must call history.

Ryan discovers, like Hercule Poirot on the Orient Express, that the assassination of Kilpatrick was a put-up job; it was not the treacherous intervention in the conspirator's schemes of an outside chance but the desperate improvisation of the conspirators themselves. They have learnt that there is a traitor in their midst and Nolan, Kilpatrick's oldest companion, is appointed to uncover his identity—to name him, that specifically fictional task. Nolan, who thus becomes Ryan's predecessor in investigation, finds that the traitor is Kilpatrick himself. Kilpatrick, nothing if not a conspirator, agrees, once his treachery is known, to save the revolution by having his own death disguised as an accident. He signs his own death-warrant. But far from being an accident, his death is the climax of a gigantic drama mounted by Nolan, the translator, it so happens, of the works of Shakespeare into the vernacular of Ireland. Nolan is a student of a remarkable cultural phenomenon discovered by Borges in Switzerland, the *Festspiel*: 'Vast and errant theatrical representations, which require thousands of actors and which reiterate historical episodes in the very cities and mountains where they occurred.'[6] The *Festspiel* employs, on a majestic scale, the fundamental strategy we are concerned with: it repeats history as art, it is history as interpreted by Parodi or Poirot. Nolan's own conspiracy is not the reiteration of a historical episode, but because he does not have the time to invent it in every detail he borrows from history—literary history, as always—calling on 'the English enemy' William Shakespeare. His 'public and secret representation' lasts several days:

The condemned man entered Dublin, debated, effected, prayed, reproved, uttered moving words, and each one of these acts which would reflect his glory had been prearranged by Nolan. Hundreds of actors collaborated with the protagonist; the role of some was complex; that of others, momentary ... Kilpatrick, borne along by the meticulous (*minucioso*) destiny which had redeemed and destroyed him, more than once enriched his judge's text with acts and words that were improvised.[7]

The conspiracy of Nolan is thus that interval of grace allowed to the condemned man, between the sentence of death and its execution: it is the interval of fiction. Nolan's representation only truly becomes a *Festspiel* when it is discovered a century later by

[6] *OC*, p. 497.   [7] *OC*, p. 498.

Ryan. Ryan's work undoes Nolan's. Where Nolan had disguised intention as accident, Ryan converts accident back into intention. Kilpatrick himself is another of the 'impulsives', whose treachery is redeemed by being integrated within a plot. Traitors, in Borges's stories, are traitors *to* the story, they threaten the coherence of the narrative. The treachery of a conspirator is one contingency that cannot be provided for in advance, and is therefore the most severe challenge imaginable to the resourcefulness of the conspirators who remain.

The power of the plotter is displayed at its highest in 'Tema del traidor y del heroe'. Kilpatrick, the awful contingency who could wreck the 'revolution', is redeemed; from being a traitor he is made into a hero, from being an accident he is elevated into the protagonist of a story. The elevation is, where history is concerned, a secret one. For the world at large Kilpatrick has always been a hero; it is only Nolan, Ryan, and now ourselves who know he was a traitor first. Ryan's discovery complicates the historical record rather than invalidates it.

History is altogether pragmatic, it attends only to the public effects of conspiracies, not to their secret preparation. 'Tema del traidor y del heroe' is a lesson in how to make fictions, not how to make or rewrite history. As an analysis of the conspiratorial process it is, as one of Borges's most incisive and sympathetic French readers, the novelist Claude Ollier, says: 'an epitome of the mechanism—functional and constitutive—of any fiction. It offers besides a remarkable model of the technique of appropriating the "everyday": the ordering of its peripeteia in accordance with a preceding literary structure.'[8]

Borges's own story is a brilliantly successful conspiracy, a resounding snub to contingency. More than that, it is the successful conspiracy for which Kilpatrick has given his life. Kilpatrick has died not to drive the English from Ireland, but to drive the merely accidental from a narrative. If he is an Irish rather than any other race of hero, that is perhaps because Ireland was the home of the man whose Idealism informs this, and every other fiction, Bishop Berkeley of Cloyne.

[8] C. Ollier, 'Thème du texte et du complot', in *Navettes*, Paris, 1967, p. 158. This essay by Ollier, a fearsomely rigorous and systematic writer of fiction himself, is short but one of the most enlightening comments there is on Borges's methods.

CHAPTER 2

GAMES OF CONSEQUENCES

HISTORY, we have heard it said too often, is just one damned thing after another—which is no doubt true of history but not, let us hope, of historiography; narrative, under its aspect of plot, is just one damned thing causing another. The sentimental verdict on Fergus Kilpatrick would be that he died for the cause, a more philosophical verdict that his death was caused. He did not, above all, die of natural causes, because there can be no natural causes in a fictional plot. In fiction characters die because their authors have so determined, because the plot demands it; if their death is then put down to natural causes all well and good, but we should, as readers, have the sense to recognize those natural causes to be artificial ones. Natural causes as such are simply not 'interesting' enough, in the particular sense that word has by now I hope acquired.

A literary plot is very much a conspiracy against nature, a denial of contingency and a denial of chaos. The events of which it is composed form a temporal sequence but they are more than just successive; each new turn of the plot is justified by some other element of which it is either the cause or the consequence. Fiction enriches facts by making them interdependent, its sequences are chronological but they are also structural, and to that extent they are spatial as well as temporal. The full logic of a narrative is not to be grasped before the narrative is complete, when we are free to reverse its flow and justify what comes earlier by what we now know was planned to come later.

It is recapitulation that turns a story into a plot and rationalizes for its readers the author's process of composition. This is a rationalization the majority of plot-readers do without; they prefer stories to plots. Stories are for the simple-minded, for telling, in E. M. Forster's supercilious words, 'to a gaping audience of cave men or to a tyrannical sultan or to their modern descendant the movie-public . . .'[1] Plots, on the other hand, demand 'intelligence and memory also', intelligence to perceive the author's connections

[1] *Aspects of the Novel*, p. 117.

between causes and their effects and memory because in a narrative a cause may be separated from its effect by a great many pages and other peripeteia.

Forster's own example of the difference between a story and a plot is well known, and remains very serviceable: '"The king died and then the queen died" is a story. "The king died, and then the queen died of grief" is a plot.'[2] If there is a weakness in this example it lies in the formulation of Forster's 'story', not in that of his plot. For his very short story surely *is* a plot, of an admittedly subdued kind, since to co-ordinate the deaths of two people as closely related as a king and a queen is to hint a little too strongly at some causal link between them. The story could have been made marginally less conspiratorial by parataxis: 'The king died. The queen died', which is as far as one can go in the suppression of all connection between the two events without actually separating them by the insertion of other elements of narrative. But even this does not help much; we know that kings are married to queens and suspect that there must be more to the bizarre symmetry of their fate than mere accident. We are not surprised to be told that the second death was brought about by grief at the first. The queen's death at least is not a natural one, it is by the author's fiat that she has died of grief rather than of some other cause. The natural cause of her death is the one that appears on her death-certificate, and no death-certificate, I imagine, has ever allowed itself the sentimentality of ascribing death to a particular emotion. A death from grief is a fictive death because it informs us about the character of the queen; death from viral pneumonia informs us only that she was unlucky. An author, on the other hand, is absolutely entitled to introduce a 'natural' death into his fiction as an artifice indistinguishable from other artifices: contingency may be, and frequently is, represented in fiction.

Forster's distinction between plot and story is the ancient one between what occurs *post hoc* and what occurs *propter hoc*, what follows after and what follows from. This is a distinction more easily observed in life than in fictions. Life is random and diffuse, fiction intentional and concentrated; to read causal sequences everywhere into life may be the symptom of a psychosis, to fail to read them into fiction is certainly evidence of literary incompetence. In fiction *post hoc* asks constantly to be interpreted as *propter*

[2] Ibid., p. 116.

hoc. Where the logic of a narrative is not explicit its readers will contribute a logic of their own, making the connections which the author has deliberately left out or has neglected to make. A fiction is that privileged world within which everything makes sense. Everything that happens is in principle explicable by reference to other elements of the fiction. The queen's death from grief is the index of her character and that character will itself be constructed partially by the reader from the perceived consistency of her behaviour; her grief is thus both symptom and evidence. Her 'character' too will ultimately be justified by the place it occupies in relation to the other characters of the fiction, to the character of her heartless sister, let us say, who is incapable of grief, or to the character of her dead husband, a man not worth feeling grief for. Motivation—the author's motivation—is everywhere in a plot.

The only times when this motivation lapses, in part, are when particular sequences of causes and effects are determined by natural law. The author decides whether he needs to include such sequences or not, but once they have been introduced he will seldom feel free to infringe natural laws. Bodies heavier than air fall quite normally to the ground even in fictions, and there is nothing conspiratorial about the laws they observe by doing so. It is only when one of them strikes someone on the skull that we have the makings of a conspiracy; then the victim becomes the luckless intruder on a natural sequence of events. His intrusion becomes, in terms of plot, a contingency, to be justified. The plotter may choose to retrace the victim's movements, to determine why he happened to be passing that place at that moment. The falling object is given its place as the culmination of a narrative and its accidental fall is transformed into a destiny. The impact of object on skull may be shown to be the just conclusion of a conspicuously villainous career, or the unjust conclusion of a saintly one. In the second case, God, or nature, is inculpated for his heartlessness and failure to live up to our own ethical principles, in the first case we are reconciled with the management of the universe by finding that it thinks the way we do.

In life falling objects are acts of God (for insurance purposes if not for metaphysicians); in fiction, as I have suggested, they *represent* acts of God. There can be no true accidents in a fiction when such accidents as it contains have been put there on purpose.

Freud, notoriously, seems to have believed the same of real life, that accidents are caused by the subconscious desires of their victims to be the victims of an accident. Such, certainly, was the belief of Freud's favourite German Idealist, Schopenhauer, for whom the universe is compounded of Will and Presentment; since every Presentment is evidence of the activity of Will there can be no accidents at all. In Schopenhauer's scheme the Patient turns out, however obscurely, to be also the Agent. The successive Presentments of a fiction, too, are evidence of Will, of the author's Will, and our job as its readers is to try and explain to ourselves what that Will was about when it presented this particular fiction.

For the space, and time, of a fiction, its author thus plays God. It is he who determines the concatenation of events. The reality imposed by a fiction might have been other than it is and whenever its author has made a choice we could in theory ask ourselves why. Why has he caused the queen to die? Why to die of grief? And so on. It is the knowledge that fictions are so largely arbitrary in this way that has pained such fastidious souls as Paul Valéry, who said he could never bring himself to write the words 'The marquise went out at five o'clock', with all the questions that incipit would raise: Why a marquise? Why does she have to go out? Why at five o'clock? But most readers of fiction never stop to put such questions to the text, they acquiesce gladly in an author's decisions and in the apparent necessity of the narrative he has to tell. Valéry's extreme delicacy is an excellent reason for never writing a fiction, a less good reason for never reading one. It is not normal to read fictions in the *constant* awareness that they might have been other than they are.

A fiction is one possibility among many, an arbitrary composition of causes and effects presented as a necessary one. If the maker of fictions is to impersonate God successfully, a certain reticence is required of him; he must not do anything that would reveal the arbitrariness of his proceeding. He should not interrupt his plot either to comment on it and show it up for the conspiracy it is, or to address his readers in some other persona than as the narrator of his story. This is something for which Borges criticizes H. G. Wells:

While an author restricts himself to relating events or to tracing the tenuous deviations of a consciousness, we can suppose him to be omniscient, we can confuse him with the universe or with God; as soon as he stoops to arguing, we know he is fallible. Reality proceeds by events, not by arguments; we allow that God should affirm (Exodus 3: 14) I Am What I Am, not that he should state and analyse the *argumentum ontologicum*, like Hegel or Anselm.[3]

Borges here stands up for pure narrative. Wells's sermons are a derogation of authorship because they invite their readers to quarrel with him; they undermine that very postulation of reality in which narrative consists. There is a good deal more to the notion of authorial 'omniscience' as Borges understands it than there generally is when that term is invoked in the discussion of narrative. Over the past twenty years or so such omniscience has been largely involved with the question of narrative 'point of view', a topic that has a mysteriously powerful hold over many students of fiction. The 'omniscient' novelist, so called, is one who does not limit himself to a single point of view in his fiction, but moves uninhibitedly from place to place and character to character, viewing them at will from within and without. Rather than omniscience this is ubiquity and an exploitation by the author of his liberty to place himself where he likes; and to place oneself where one likes is, in a sense, to place oneself nowhere. 'Omniscience' has had something of a guilty conscience ever since Jean-Paul Sartre attacked it so furiously in François Mauriac, interpreting it as a serious case of *mauvaise foi* in a novelist who, as a Christian, should have known better than to show the fate of his characters to have been predetermined and the characters themselves to be fixed essences, denied the existential freedom to create themselves as they went, free from determination by their past. 'Well, no! It is time it was said, the novelist is not God' was Sartre's angry conclusion.[4]

Such solemn proscriptions cut no ice with Borges, for whom the whole issue of 'point of view' must look rather petty. His narratives do not jump from consciousness to consciousness because they are so determinedly behaviouristic, quite uninterested in the 'tenuous deviations' he talks of in the essay on Wells. But they are flagrantly, delightedly godlike; Borges, unlike Sartre, sees no reason for an author to pretend he is really only a man, with all the limitations on his perception of the world which that implies. The pleasure of authorship, on the contrary, is to be free, provisionally, of the

---

[3] *OC*, p. 698.

[4] J.-P. Sartre, 'M. François Mauriac et la liberté', in *Critique littéraire* (Situations 1), Paris, 1976, p. 55.

calendar and the map and to arrange things to satisfy oneself. For Borges the maker of a fiction stands in the same relation to his own small creation as God, seen as the author of the universe, stands to creation as a whole. God, we can take it, is outside time and place and needs to recognize no past, present, and future. His concatenations of cause and effect are instantaneous. His purview, moreover, is not limited to the actual but also takes in the potential. Each realization of his will leaves alternative realizations unrealized, unless we believe, as people have before now believed, that those alternatives which are unrealized in our universe are realized in another, and that every time the course of events bifurcates a new universe is created, *hrön*-like, not quite the same as the old. The monstrous proliferation of causes and effects entailed by speculation of this sort is exactly what Borges needs in order to dramatize to the full the process of cause and effect itself.

An aesthetics of omission is nowhere more effective than in the matter of causality. Such chains of cause and effect as we care to manufacture are barely commensurable with the chains of cause and effect that together constitute the past, present, and future of the universe. The reduction of one, or the idea of one, to the other, provides great opportunities for drama. Borges is a man to enjoy such speculations as that of Pascal about the effects in human history of the length of Cleopatra's nose. He enjoys, a little malignly, the discrepancy it is possible to establish between a single, trivial cause and its multiple, ponderable effects. The discrepancy is of course a fiction: it is created by the elimination of all the intervening causes and effects which could, potentially, lead us from the cause in question to its remote consequence. It may be striking, or strikingly comic, and the technique employed either to show, as many sceptics like to show, how the fate of empires may hinge on trifles, or, as by Borges, how indescribably complex the universe is when viewed in a consequential spirit.

There is no more choice enumeration of the heterogeneous effects of a single cause than the one which opens the story of 'El espantoso redentor Lazarus Morell' ('The Dreadful Redeemer Lazarus Morell') in the *Historia universal de la infamia*:

In 1517 Father Bartolomé de Las Casas took great pity on the Indians, wearing themselves out in the laborious infernos of the West Indian gold-mines, and proposed to the Emperor Charles V that they should import negroes, who might extenuate themselves in the laborious infernos of the West Indian gold-mines. To this curious variation in a philanthropist we owe infinite events: Handy's *blues*, the success ach- ieved in Paris by the oriental painter doctor D. Pedro Figari, the fine runaway prose of the also oriental D. Vicente Rossi, the mythological dimensions of Abraham Lincoln, the five hundred thousand dead of the American Civil War, the three thousand three hundred millions spent on army pensions, the statue of the imaginary Falucho, the admission of the verb *linchar* into the thirteenth edition of the Dictionary of the Academy, the impetuous film *Alleluya* . . .[5]

Of such catalogues of effects are the pyramids of time constructed, reaching out ever more widely and variously into the multiplicity of history from an arbitrarily isolated event. The final consequence in this particular catalogue is Borges's own story, 'the culpable and magnificent existence of the atrocious redeemer Lazarus Morell', who extorts money from slaves in the Southern United States by persuading them to flee from one plantation and be sold to another, Morell and the slaves to share, or so he promises, the purchase price. The consequences of Bartolomé de Las Casas's 'variation' (a word carefully placed by Borges, because it is always by 'varia- tion' from a given reality that he shows fiction to originate) thus encompass the real and the fictive, the great and the small, the direct and the indirect; in the catalogue, itself a literary fabrication, they meet as equals.

Enumerations of this kind symbolize, in their variety and dis- continuity, the laughable inadequacy of the human mind to measure the full consequences of a single event. As Borges chooses to look at it, the present moment—if we allow that to be a simple, determinate event—is subtended by the whole of the past. Starting from the here and now, *any* here and now, one might in principle work one's way through the whole of human history from cause to effect. A single 'variation' postulates the universe; or, as Henry James put it, 'really, universally, relations stop nowhere'.[6] Were the history of the universe to be written it would therefore be a narrative of infinite ramifications. These ramifications enter the merely human fictions of Borges in the form of another favourite symbol, the labyrinth, which reduces the potential ramifications of any given event to the more manageable power of two. The labyrinth faces those who would penetrate it with a series of

[5] *OC*, p. 295.

[6] H. James, *The Art of the Novel*, New York, 1947, p. 5.

alternatives, but never more than two at any one time. It is a pity, where Borges is concerned, that the labyrinth should so readily be taken as the symbol of a hopeless confusion, a place into which we enter only to blunder this way or that without a hope of reaching the centre. But labyrinths are man-made and even if we fail to 'read' them properly we know their code can be cracked.

A Borges story is not itself labyrinthine; it does not face us with alternative continuations.[7] It is the writer of a narrative, not its reader, who must tackle the labyrinth, because it is he who is confronted, at every turn of his story, by alternative ways of continuing it. By the time the reader follows him the alternatives which he has discarded have vanished. As readers, we understand that any narrative could have taken a different path from the one it does take, but that hardly makes its pursuance a passage through a labyrinth. If Borges suggests that there is something unpleasant about labyrinths, the unpleasantness is all for the maker of the fiction, who has constantly to choose and, much more important, to choose rationally. In stories as rigorously constructed as Borges's own, each moment of choice is obviously far more taxing than for less meticulous writers.

The labyrinth is born of duplication, of the postulation of an alternative to a given reality, and founded on duplication thereafter. Labyrinthine man is one who lives and works by twos. A prime example is Herbert Quain, of 'Examen de la obra de Herbert Quain' ('Examination of the Oeuvre of Herbert Quain'). Quain, another of Borges's Irishmen, is a writer for whom there is no discipline 'inferior to history', a discipline which, among other faults, has no room for the alternative sequences of events that are his own stock-in-trade. Even in his death Quain is dogged by the tendency that has marked his life: he gets two obituaries, one in the *Times Literary Supplement* which is itself equivocal, since each of its 'laudatory' epithets is 'amended' by an adverb, and another in

---

[7] It is hard to see how any sequential narrative could ever be truly labyrinthine, in the sense that it might make us retrace our steps and try some other path through the story every time we get to what is obviously a dead end (but what, in a narrative, *is* a dead end?). The nearest approaches to labyrinthine narratives are those in which, as in Robbe-Grillet's *Dans le labyrinthe*, the narrative regularly contradicts itself, or those 'programmed' as if for a computer, in which alternative developments are numbered and can be selected by the reader according to his own preferences of the moment.

the *Spectator*, which manages to compare him to two other writers, Agatha Christie and Gertrude Stein.

It is Quain's first novel that the *Spectator* likens to the work of Agatha Christie, a detective story called *The God of the Labyrinth*. It was not a success, and its failure is ascribed to the coincidence of its publication being followed only a few days later by the publication of *The Siamese Twin Mystery*, whose 'agreeable and arduous involutions' set the two cities of London and New York 'to work'. A coincidence indeed, when one detective story is instantly followed by a second (*The Siamese Twin Mystery* is a real title, written by Ellery Queen), whose title alludes to just such an instance of duplication: the mystery of two linked but not identical congeners. *The God of the Labyrinth*, it turns out, is a more than usually labyrinthine construction because it has two solutions, a first, explicit solution reached in the text, and a second, superior solution which the text indicates but does not divulge. This alternative solution has to be found by the reader, who is given the clue to its existence right at the end of the story and has then to go back and reread the earlier parts. The alternative hinges, predictably, on the reader understanding that an event in the narrative which had seemed to be a chance event—'the meeting of the two chess-players'—was not a chance event at all but a planned one. The rereading, which produces the 'right' solution to the mystery, thus depends on integrating this intrusive, anomalous event into the structure of the fiction. The two chess-players here are the author of the story and his reader.

Anyone who has tried to analyse one of Borges's own stories knows well the advantages of rereading. The first time round one gets only a dim idea of its structure, of the small symmetries which are the best clue to its logic. A second reading may still not be enough, but it is more intelligent than the first reading because it is teleological, it enables one to interpret the earlier parts of the story in terms of the later, or the whole narrative in terms of its known conclusion. Succession begins to turn into a logical sequence. Until we are made free of chronology in this way we cannot expect properly to appreciate the intricacy of any literary structure. It is only when we relate the parts of the structure to each other that we realize its necessity, that is, the elimination of contingencies. In his preface to a Spanish version of Valéry's 'Cimetière marin', Borges argues against the 'superstition' that a translation—which is, after all, a text as much reread as rewritten—is bound to be inferior to the original: 'There is no good text which does not declare itself sure and unconditional if we practise it a sufficient number of times. Hume, as we know, sought to identify the concept of causality with that of invariable succession. Thus a mediocre film is consolingly better the second time we see it because of the stern inevitability it has donned.'[8] To invoke Hume on induction in order to justify sitting twice through the same mediocre film is a witty example of Borges's own way with causality. Applied to the business of translation, his argument is somewhat specious, since the readers of books in translation are those people least likely to know the work in the original. But this does not at all affect the general point that a literary sequence which we re-cognize is more significant to us than one we merely cognize.

In *The God of the Labyrinth* the rereading is made necessary by a 'long and retrospective' paragraph at the end of the book; and from the rereader's point of view a second reading of the narrative is exactly that, 'long and retrospective'. What it retrospects is the first reading. In so far as it works backwards from the conclusion it reverses the direction of that original reading. In this it imitates the chronology of the investigation of a crime, which works simultaneously forwards and backwards: forwards through 'real' time and backwards through the recreated time-scale of the events which led up to the crime. It also imitates the chronology of the construction of a narrative, where the end of the narrative has been determined in advance and the various peripeteia inserted in order to justify it.

The rereader, who is, for Borges, the archetypal reader, is thus free in a sense to reverse the sequence of a narrative, to justify what comes before by what comes after, since it is not until he himself has reached and understood the consequence that he is able to identify the earlier cause. This notion of reversibility is introduced clandestinely into 'Examen de la obra de Herbert Quain'. The *Spectator* obituary of Quain, as I have said, compares *The God of the Labyrinth* to a book by Agatha Christie. A few lines later the narrator of the story introduces his short account of the novel with the words: 'I regret having lent the first one [book] he published, irreversibly, to a lady.' This irreversible decision can only be the one he himself has taken as the narrator, or maker, of the story; the

[8] *Prólogos*, p. 164.

lady is Agatha Christie, the author of the detective story of which Quain's has been seen as a derivation. There is no going back now on that decision, which has carried the story forward and represents a moment when one path through the labyrinth has been taken and an alternative one ignored—the 'lady' could, to offer a simple alternative, have been a 'gentleman', and it is noteworthy that the duplication which the story does allow itself at this point, the duplication of Agatha Christie by Gertrude Stein, is never pursued. So the allusion to Agatha Christie has become inevitable, with this allusion to the allusion; it was not, of course, inevitable when it was first made, as the story itself says quite directly: after the comparisons with Agatha Christie and Gertrude Stein have been made we are told that these are 'evocations which no one will judge to be inevitable and which would not have pleased the deceased.'[9]

They would not have pleased Herbert Quain because he is something of a specialist in inevitability. His second book, *April March*, is a 'regressive, ramified novel' which starts at the end, so to speak, with 'the ambiguous dialogue of some strangers on a railway platform', and then works backwards through three alternative and mutually exclusive 'evenings before', and then three more alternative and mutually exclusive 'evenings before' each of the 'evenings before.' *April March*, whose title is itself an advertisement for the freedom a narrative enjoys to reverse the calendar, is thus slightly more than labyrinthine because it proceeds by threes instead of twos. Quain himself comes to recognize that this structure is a little too ample. Once *April March* had been published he 'repented of the ternary order and predicted that the men who imitated him would opt for the binary . . . and demiurges and gods for the infinite: infinite stories (*historias*), infinitely ramified'.[10]

Not many men, so far, have imitated Herbert Quain, because makers of fictions see no virtue in robbing their readers of the single, uncontroverted sequence of events they are accustomed to. Writers of detective stories advance rival, mutually exclusive justifications of particular events, but only because their readers trust that in the end one justification will turn out to be true and the others false. It is worth noting that when contradictory hypotheses are introduced into the one narrative they do not cancel one another out, they coexist; the one which is subsequently falsified is as much a constituent of the narrative as the other. Generally, alternatives will only be invoked in a narrative in order to promote the claims of one of them to be the truth above the claims of the others. In Diderot's *Jacques le fataliste*, that early and spirited text-book in narrative strategy, alternative continuations of the story are more than once rejected as being too stereotyped and self-evidently fictional, the better to convince us that the continuation we are given is unprecedented and authentic.

It is our awareness, as readers, that the making of a narrative is a sequence of choices by the author, which can make innovators, or authors, of us all. Change one intermediate link in the narrative chain and the narrative changes; it is forced to take a different direction, though perhaps leading to the same conclusion. Herbert Quain's career after the publication of *April March* offers still more lessons in duplication. First he writes a play, a 'heroic comedy' (a new and rather oxymoronic genre, one would have thought) called *The Secret Mirror*. This play, like Jaromir Hladík's tragedy, has two acts. The first act dramatizes the veneration of a playwright, Wilfred Quarles, for one Ulrica Thrale, a Muse who never appears and whom 'we suspect is not wont to visit literature'. In the second act the events of the first are shown to be the projections of another playwright, John William Quigley, who collects society photographs of the 'real' Ulrica Thrale. Quarles and Quigley are duplicates, as projections of the playwright Herbert Quain, and the two acts of *The Secret Mirror* are rereadings of each other. Chronologically, Act Two precedes Act One, Act One being the glorification of the often disagreeable circumstances of Act Two. But all is not well in Act One, in which 'Almost wholly imperceptible, there is some curious contradiction, there are sordid details.'[11] Quarles, for instance, has a rival for the favours of Ulrica: the Duke of Rutland; the newspapers announce the Duke's engagement to her, the newspapers then deny his engagement to her. The procedure may be thought typical of a certain irresponsible kind of newspaper but this is not Borges satirizing the Press; it is Borges showing how contradiction works in the temporal world of the *periódicos*, where affirmations should be supported by facts. It is only when one makes up stories that one is free to decide for oneself whether the Duke of Rutland is engaged to Ulrica Thrale or not. There are

[11] *OC*, p. 464.

other signs of alternative developments in Act One of the play, or of duplicity, not least 'a secret duel on the terrace'. When *The Secret Mirror* is finally put on, the critics—and no one who has read Borges's story attentively will be surprised by this—are put in mind not of one name but of two: Freud and Julien Green. 'The mention of the first', declares the narrator, 'seems to me totally unjustified', and there is no worse solecism in a Borges story than a lack of justification. If the name of Freud is an intrusion that is because Borges recognizes only literary justifications of literary creation. Quain, like all his other authors, creates new works of literature by a conscious transformation of the old: Act One of *The Secret Mirror* is the transformation of Act Two, not the transformation of his own life. With literary artefacts as rigorous and rational as his, what sense can there be in invoking the name of the man for whom artistic effort is pure expressionism and psychic necessity?

The whole idea of bifurcation, or trifurcation in the case of *The God of the Labyrinth*, defeats the Freudian's ambition of explaining a fiction by reference to its author's personality. No psychic determinism is possible where an author makes such systematic use of his freedom, unless we are to deduce a different 'personality' for him from each sequence of events which he creates. The only psychic trait which a figure like Herbert Quain requires in order to explain him is the will to differentiate himself, to add to what there is by deviating from it at a given point. He is nothing more nor less than the principle of literary invention, that invention which he acknowledges to be the 'highest' of literature's pleasures. The last item in his own œuvre is, suitably, an attempt to pass on to his readers the pleasures he has had from invention himself. It is a set of eight stories, each one of which 'prefigures or promises a good argument, deliberately frustrated by the author. One of them—not the best—insinuates *two* arguments. The reader, distracted by vanity, believes he has invented them'.[12] The lesson is clear: as soon as there are two arguments in one story, as soon, that is to say, as the author of a story shows that the events of the narrative we are reading *could* have been different, the reader appreciates the principle on which narrative is founded and becomes, potentially, a writer, capable of departing from the model along bifurcations of his own. But he has also been warned against claiming too much credit for such inventiveness, which is the product of 'vanity';

[12] *OC*, p. 464.

Borges is insistent, as we shall see, that narratives do not belong to those who narrate them but to the common literary repertoire. As story-tellers we can borrow stories, adapt them, tell them, and in telling them return them to the pool from which we took them in the first place.

There is a last twist in the 'Examen de la obra de Herbert Quain' which is typical. The narrator's final admission is that he himself has extracted one of his own stories from a story in Quain's collection, *Statements*. The story is 'Las ruinas circulares' ('The Circular Ruins'), another parable of fictional creation, which is the third story in the collection *El jardín de senderos que se bifurcan*, the same collection as contains the story we have been reading. 'Las ruinas circulares', we are told, has been 'extracted' from the third story in *Statements*, which is called 'The Rose of Yesterday'. As to what exactly happens to a story when it is 'extracted' we are left pleasantly in doubt, though translation has been involved, since Quain's stories are in English and the narrator's in Spanish. *Statements*, one observes, contains eight stories, Borges's *El jardín de senderos que se bifurcan* only seven, unless, of course, we were to count Quain's collection as an eighth fiction to be added to Borges's own.

The bifurcations of which Quain is the master do not, one should be clear, dissolve the logic of a narrative; there can be a great many alternative justifications of the one event, all as logcially necessary as each other. Borges keeps his finger steadily on the old paradox of determinism which is that, once they are done, deeds can be seen to have been determined, even though we know, before they are done, that we are free not to do them. In the story of Fergus Kilpatrick, Ryan, the traitorous hero's descendant and subsequent biographer, not only penetrates Nolan's plot but believes that Nolan wanted someone, in the future, to penetrate it: '[Ryan] understands that he too forms part of Nolan's plot (*trama*) . . . After insistent hesitations, he resolves to suppress the discovery. He publishes a book dedicated to the glory of the hero; this too, perhaps, had been foreseen.'[13] Having come to a fork, Ryan chooses one continuation—the publication of a book in praise of Kilpatrick—rather than the other; with hindsight we can say that his choice was determined. What we cannot say, on pain of falsifying the whole process, is that it was inevitable while it was still

[13] *OC*, p. 498.

under way. It is inevitable only once it is complete. And while we are still talking of bifurcation, it is worth noting that the alternative which Ryan rejects, of betraying Kilpatrick the betrayer, is the alternative which Borges has realized, by telling the story of Nolan's plot. There is really no end to Borges's duplicity.

CHAPTER 3

POINTS OF DEPARTURE

A ROMANTIC primitivism continues to dog much discussion of
fiction, which believes that language alone mediates between an
author and reality. Given a respectable command of his native
tongue, an author is fully equipped for turning life into words, and
once the transcription is done it is his, an original document.
Romanticism refuses to allow that its authors are slaves of convention; the works they produce will be recognizably, all too
recognizably sometimes, of a particular genre when they are
completed, but the formal constraints which that genre imposes
are not seen as a serious impediment to the author's freedom. He
is inspired and directed by life itself, not by other books.

Classicism takes the other view: that literature as well as
language intervenes between reality and the author. Classicism is
conscious of convention in any literary genre and of the need for
anyone writing books to know how books are written. We could
none of us tell a story if no one had ever told us a story. The stories
we tell, supposing we graduate as narrators, will generally be
different stories from the ones we have been told; but not so very
different and not always intentionally different, since we may set
out to repeat a story and fail. On the other hand, the stories told to
us may have seemed to call for adjustment or improvement; they
may have been solemn when we would have wished them funny,
clean when we would have wished them dirty, and so on. There
are, in short, all kinds of ways in which we can appropriate narratives and put our own signature on them. In every case the tendency
will be, where the oral transmission of stories is concerned, to make
the narrative more and more patently fictive, more and more what
an anthropologist would perhaps recognize as a myth:

Imagine, for example, a historical narrative transmitted orally in a non-
literate society. Unless a concerted effort were made to preserve it in its
initial form, certain episodes would soon be forgotten, while others
would be magnified; the whole—here impoverished, there enriched—
would acquire a more regular structure, a greater symbolic import,
a memorableness that the original did not have; in short, it is transformed

into a culturally exemplary, psychologically salient object which, once adopted by a society, becomes—precisely—a myth.[1]

It is interesting that a Romantic view of literary creation, as taking place more or less *ex nihilo*, is not at all borne out by what we know of literary creation in supposedly unsophisticated societies. Originality, in the process Sperber imagines, consists in the quite modest departures made by different individuals for different reasons at different times from the model bequeathed to them. The result of such originality will be the existence of several versions of the 'same' myth, since a new version never annihilates the old ones but coexists with them.

This is exactly the view which the exemplary Classic, Borges, takes of narrative in a highly literate culture. He is a librarian by conviction, as well as by profession. Literature he sees as cumulative; an author, whatever his degree of acquaintance with what has already been written, brings something to the stock which it lacked. He does not add to it by accident, as it were, because he cannot help himself, but because he judges it to be incomplete, out of date, or unsatisfactory in some other way. An author competes not with reality but with the representations of reality already in existence when he originates his own. He must distinguish himself from them by whatever variations he sees fit to introduce.

This sensible doctrine is also that of Formalism, for which the history of literature is essentially dialectical, with new writers learning from and departing from the old. It is dialectical, moreover, whether one looks at it from the writer's or from the reader's point of view—and in Borges's case there is seldom need to distinguish those two points of view. The literary experience of the man who writes a book and the man who reads it will never be the same, but a new experience of writing will also be a new experience of reading. The writer departs from precedent, the reader, symmetrically, assimilates and comprehends that departure by relating it *to* precedent. New works which break too violently with precedent are those, notoriously, which resist comprehension the longest. We reach the position, quite legitimately, where, as Viktor Schklovsky has it: 'a work of art is perceived against the background of, and by

---

[1] Dan Sperber, *Rethinking Symbolism*, trans. Alice L. Morton, Cambridge, 1975, p. 79.

way of association with, other works of art . . . Creation as parallel with and contrast to some model is a description applicable not just to parody but to any work of art in general'.[2]

The considerable originality of Borges is to have dramatized so distinctively the conditions of originality itself. He began as he meant to go on. His first book of fictions, *Historia universal de la infamia*, is very much a set of parodies, in the broad sense of the word, as Schklovsky uses it. The apologia with which he prefaced it (though not until the reprint of 1954; the original 1935 edition of the book makes no such diffident noises) is well known: 'They are the irresponsible game of a timid man who did not have the courage to write tales (*cuentos*) but amused himself by falsifying and tergiversating (sometimes without aesthetic justification) the stories (*historias*) of others.'[3] The *historia*, clearly a less fictive thing than a *cuento*, is both a datum for Borges and an ambition, since his own inventions arise as modifications of the *historias* of others and are finally offered to us as a *Historia universal*. They thus become the data for another inventor. Borges has inserted his fictions into a chain of transmission. He has transmitted them both to ourselves, his readers, who might pass them on orally, modified not by artistry as strict as his own but by neglect; and also to another generation of writers of stories, who will inherit, because of his intervention, a different repertoire of narratives from the one he inherited. Actually, they will inherit a larger repertoire, since the versions on which he has based his own versions will remain alongside them.

There is a very strong element of pretence in all this; Borges's stories look, in fact, definitive or, better, a dead end. It is hard to imagine anyone refining or improving on them. The same pretence has had a renaissance in some of the stories he has written in old age, and is prominent especially in those of *El informe de Brodie*, where several of his narrators claim they are merely handing on the story we are about to read, that it has been told to them before being told by them, and that their one contribution has been to modify it slightly. Students of Borges know all too well that the chain of transmission is likely to end with Borges. To transmit one of his more complex narratives is an impossible task, it resists translation into fewer, or other words than his own.

[2] Quoted by B. Eichenbaum, in *Readings in Russian Poetics*, ed. Matejka and Pomorska, Cambridge, Mass., 1971, p. 17.
[3] *OC*, p. 291.

Nevertheless, even if his own narratives largely elude the process, the process is a real one. It is more obviously real in cultures where transmission is oral than in those where transmission occurs mostly in print. Borges likes to subscribe to it because he is the complete print-man in a culture far less bookish than himself. He pays lip-service to the survival of conventions we ourselves find very quaint partly in order to bring out the traditional, epic role of the story-teller, as the anonymous custodian of local myths. The dramatization of the act of narration as a part of the narrative makes possible the identification of narrator and hero, and shows how the first is aggrandized by recounting the feats of the second. The stories which pass from mouth to mouth are taller than those which pass from book to book, because tall stories are more easily imposed by the physical presence of the story-teller. Borges's own profoundly bookish inventions make a sardonic comment on all that the story-teller must give up by confining himself to his library, and to the printed word.

The effect of transmission on narrative above all is to reduce it to the essentials. If we want to determine what the plot of a particular work of fiction is, the only thing to do is to prepare that work for transmission: a plot might be loosely defined as the account of a narrative given by one person to another. Reduced to its essentials, a narrative is, in Borges's terms, archetypal; it becomes a literary Form. As such, its link with reality is weakened and its standing as a literary artefact improved. Whenever, within one of Borges's stories, a narrative is conspicuously well told, its authenticity as a record of the facts is put in doubt. In 'La otra muerte' ('The Other Death'), a story of the duplicate deaths of a gaucho, Pedro Damián, Colonel Dioniso Tabares recalls the far-off military campaign in which Damián dies for the first time: 'He spoke of Illescas, of Tupambaé, of Masoller. He did so with such faultless periods and in so vivid a manner that I realized he had related these same things many times, and I feared that behind his words there remained almost no memories.'[4] It is good to be reminded that a 'vivid' account of a war, contrary to the common belief of what vividness implies, may be quite unsupported by personal memories of that war; vividness is an effect of prose and more readily achieved by a competent author who has never been to war than by an incompetent one who has.

[4] *OC*, p. 572.

Freedom from the given, then, from the *historia*, grows with repetition and with the increasing idealization which narratives, just like any other phenomenon in the natural world, undergo. Borges attributes to his father the subtle observation that we in fact remember something only once, because the second time we remember not the thing itself but our first remembrance of it. This disturbingly cumulative view of memory is one which quickly widens the gap between mental images and the reality which first imprinted them. In 'La otra muerte' the narrator has seen the dead Damián once but cannot remember what he looked like. All he can remember is a photograph of him, but when this has been lost, and he tries to recall Damián's features, he finds he has been recalling a different image altogether, 'that of the celebrated tenor Tamberlick in the role of Othello'.

Damián, like so many of Borges's protagonists, is dead before the story starts; he is no longer there to be referred to. His face, and even the representation of his face, have gone. In its stead we have his story, which, metaphorically, we can read as if it were his true face, as in the lines of one of Borges's poems:

> the colours and lines of the past
> will define in the darkness a face,
> sleeping, unmoving, faithful, unalterable . . .[5]

This essential, eternal 'face', which might equally well be the essential, eternal 'name', is the brief form of words to which we might all, in principle, be brought, once we are dead but not quite forgotten. It is only by courtesy of a figure of speech that words can be said to provide an 'image' of an absent reality.

The removal of Damián, the referent, at the outset allows him an intermittent posthumous existence as a memory. Colonel Tabares remembers him as a coward, remembers him as a hero, and fails to remember him at all. The first two alternatives originate divergent narratives in which Damián is the protagonist, the third one naturally leads nowhere. The coexistence, within 'La otra muerte', of contradictory versions of Damián's fate follows the sensible advice of Herbert Quain, that bifurcation is for mortal authors, infinite ramification only for the gods. The narrator of the story finds an 'explanation' for this divergence in the work of an eleventh

---

[5] 'Del infierno y del cielo', *OC*, p. 866.

century Italian theologian, Piero Damiani, who in his *De Omni-potentia* apparently maintained that God is so all-powerful as to be able to 'effect that what once was has not been'. Whatever God's powers in this respect, our own are enormous: if the past be construed as whatever we remember of the past then all we need to do to abolish what once was is to forget it. The real past, however, is potentially recuperable; a fictive past is all that we are told it is and nothing more. There can be no reference to some actual state of affairs that would belie the account we are given. The god of the labyrinth can undo even a death and show that it was not 'really' a death. In 'La otra muerte' the narrator of the story, Colonel Tabares, and Damián himself, who dreams a heroic death in battle for himself to compensate for his cowardice many years before, have all learnt from the historical Damiani how history can be rewritten.

One would not be surprised to learn, in turn, that Borges has driven his point home by misquoting *De Omnipotentia*, since to misquote *is* to rewrite history (or the *historia* which Borges likes to posit as his source). He, indeed, can allow no useful distinction between quotation and misquotation: both entail a transformation of what someone else has said or written. For Borges all writing is really the rewriting of the already written, and is thus full of quotations. It is not full, on the other hand, of quotation marks, which are a Romantic contribution to typography if ever there was one. By singling out quotations in the way we habitually do we imply that whatever is not explicitly attributed is the author's own invention. Quotation marks are a convention imposed by the fetish of 'originality', and a convention, moreover, which has the backing of the law of the land, as Northrop Frye wittily observes: 'In our day the conventional element in literature is elaborately disguised by a law of copyright pretending that every work of art is an invention distinctive enough to be patented . . . Demonstrating the debt of A to B is merely scholarship if A is dead, but a proof of moral delinquency if A is alive.'[6] The effect of such fanatical individualism is to separate works of literature from one another to an unnatural degree, and the effect of that effect is to set a whole academic industry in motion, tracking down the hitherto unacknowledged 'influence' of one writer on another, with the unspoken corollary that where no influence is demonstrated there we have

[6] N. Frye, *Anatomy of Criticism*, Princeton, 1971, p. 96.

total originality. In the Classical view Literature is one, and the writer can move about in it at will, taking and using whatever he wants.

His justification, should he be asked for one, is that whatever he takes will be put to a new use. Here again the convention of isolating explicit quotations between distinctive marks (when we write, though not, interestingly, when we speak) easily blinds us to the fact that the words in question have literally been translated: they have been moved from one location to another. We have little trouble in understanding that the meanings of single words change with the context in which they are found; but show reluctance to grant that the same holds for whole sentences, paragraphs, or even chapters. Quotation can never be a simple affirmation of the original statement; it may be a reaffirmation or it may be the excuse for a refutation. A quotation is ambiguous; in the terms we have been using in this chapter it is a historical datum, and like all historical data it can be made the locus of a bifurcation.

Take Borges's story of 'Los teólogos' ('The Theologians'), a very intricate drama of quotation and misquotation.[7] This begins with the sacking of a monastic library by Huns, and the burning of its books. Book Twelve of Augustine's *Civitas Dei* alone survives 'almost intact'—the 'almost' being just the precaution the trained reader of Borges would expect and one whose import becomes rapidly clear. This book records Plato's teaching of the circularity of time and the return of all things. As the one relict of the vanished library this Platonic text is especially venerable 'and those who read and reread it in that remote province persistently forgot that the author only stated this doctrine the better to confute it'.[8] Here then we have a first example of how quotation can go wrong: Augustine is remembered as having endorsed Plato instead of refuting him, because the quotation has lost its context. It would have been better had a volume of Plato survived the Huns rather than a volume of Augustine.

---

[7] Theologians make, for Borges, ideal representatives of his own trade, dealing as they inescapably do in fictions; the statements of theology are distinctive for being incapable of verification. The history of theology, what is more, is unusually dialectical. New doctrine is born of old doctrine, new theologians establish themselves by disagreeing with old ones. Short of some divine intervention there seems no reason why this perfectly non-empirical process should ever stop.

[8] *OC*, p. 550.

A century (or what one might term a suitable hiatus) later, the Platonic doctrine confuted by Augustine is professed in the same remote province by a heretical sect called the *monótonos*, or else the *anulares*. It is confuted this time by the rival theologians—the alternative theologians—Aureliano and John of Pannonia. Aureliano's confutation is very long-winded, and depends on quotations from Plutarch, Origen, and Cicero. John's confutation is 'almost laughably brief' and quotes from the Epistle to the Hebrews, St. Matthew's Gospel, and Pliny. The short confutation is preferred to the long one, and the arch-*monótono*, Euforbo, goes to the stake.

Subsequently, a further, more resourceful heresy arises, that of the *histriones*, who seem to have several doctrines. Their sacred books have disappeared, and all that have come down to us are the 'insults' they gave rise to; a contemporary 'theologian' has suggested that these 'insults' *are* the lost gospels, an identification familiar to us from the earlier identification of Plato with his adversary Augustine. The heretics in Aureliano's diocese are an unusual sect who argue that 'time does not tolerate repetitions'. Aureliano prepares a report on them and their dangerous doctrine, but finds himself at a loss for words 'when he sought to write down the atrocious thesis that no two moments are equal'. Like the ingenious Nolan staging the assassination of Fergus Kilpatrick, he is saved by quotation. He remembers a particularly apt 'prayer of twenty words', which turns out to be not his own invention but that of his great rival, John of Pannonia, and to have occurred in John's successful confutation, years before, of the *monótonos*. The words used then to confute the believers in a doctrine of Eternal Return are now used a second time to confute the believers in an exactly contrary heresy. Their true authorship is revealed, and John of Pannonia, transformed by time into a heretic himself, is burnt at the stake. After his death, and the death, subsequently, of Aureliano, in a fire lit not by men but by lightning, the two theologians merge in their posthumous eternity.

'Los teólogos' travels, as the best of Borges's stories invariably do, in a circle. The twenty words of John of Pannonia's prayer against the *monótonos* are all that have survived of his writings, an 'almost laughably brief' corpus compared with the 'many volumes' of Aureliano which posterity enjoys. They survive as a quotation robbed of its context, just like the quotation of Plato by Augustine with which the story began. The burning of John of Pannonia, the burning of the heretic Euforbo, and the burning of the library by the Huns form a series of events, each of which has left behind a quotation: Augustine's quotation of Plato, Euforbo's dying re-statement of his doctrine of temporal circularity, John of Pannon-ia's confutation of that same doctrine. The relationship of the four authors involved here is simply organized: John is to Euforbo as Augustine is to Plato. John and Augustine argue the uniqueness of each moment, Euforbo and Plato its inevitable recurrence. Un-fortunately, however, the confutation of Euforbo by John is a recurrence of the confutation of Plato by Augustine, and if the Platonic doctrine has every right to self-fulfilment through such a recurrence, the alternative doctrine, that no two moments of time are alike, does not. John of Pannonia, contesting the belief in recurrence, is himself contested by the fact that he is re-enacting a scene enacted once before. In short, the recurrence makes of him an inhabitant not of time, but of eternity, not of history but of literature. In his concision, and universality, he is exemplary; his treatise against the heretics is both 'limpid' and 'universal': 'it did not seem to have been written by a concrete person, but by any man at all, or, better, by all men'.[9]

Quotation, with Borges, stands for that necessary plagiarism of other men's writings without which no writer can survive. Whether we agree with the thoughts we borrow or borrow them only in order to disagree with them, we cannot do without them. Quota-tion makes manifest the dialectical process of literary invention, and reminds us that language is more fruitfully employed in contradic-tion than in corroboration, which is why the alternative universe of Literature is so notably discordant. Borges's universal library is a library of Babel because every single proposition advanced in one of its volumes is confuted in another. He is not saying, surely, that Literature would be a Babel, were his fantastic project ever realized, but that it is a Babel now. He might even claim that it became a Babel the moment a second literary work was added to the first, since the second will have been composed as an answer to the first. Or, if it was not expressly composed to that end, it will have been read as if it were, since its readers could not avoid assimilating it to the only other literary work they knew of. (In official histories of literature books may be studied in the order in which they were written; but we each of us have a private history of

[9] *OC*, p. 552.

literature where chronology is not supreme and where the succession which matters is the order the books have been read in.)

The sharpest lessons of all about the function of reading, and the equation of invention with the modification of existing texts, occur in the story of 'Pierre Menard, autor del Quijote'. That story is itself inserted into the dialectical sequence of literary history by being offered as the critique of an earlier account of Menard's 'visible' work. That earlier account, described as a 'treacherous catalogue', has been prepared by Madame Henri Bachelier, and prepared, moreover, for a 'certain daily paper whose *protestant* tendency is no secret', so that the newspaper, like the story, is seen to be in the confutation business. 'Decidedly, a brief rectification is inevitable.' The story we read sets the record straight by examining the invisible work which Menard produced and which naturally has found no place in a catalogue prepared for a medium as hopelessly temporal as a daily paper.

The list of Menard's published works is extravagantly dialectical (the only omissions from the definitive version are 'a few vague *circumstantial* sonnets' (my italics)): he engages in controversy with other writers, notably Paul Valéry; he emends existing literary texts—his own; he debates philosophical issues; he speculates on the possibilities of 'enriching' the game of chess by abolishing one of the pieces in it; and in general shows an advanced understanding of what the Borgesian literary man should be expected to understand, that to criticize is also to create.

His secret ambition to reproduce *Don Quijote* seems, in this light, most heroic. It is closely prefigured in his scheme to improve the game of chess—and who but Borges would plan to 'enrich' a game by reducing its scope? This scheme Menard 'puts forward, debates, and ends by rejecting', which is secret work with a vengeance, a nugatory exercise in dialectic which leaves the rules of chess untouched. In Borges's terms, such work is exemplary, and thoroughly creditable. The man who advances hypotheses of his own and then rigorously rejects them is not a lesser man for doing so but a greater one, because he embodies both roles in the dialectical process instead of simply one; he is self-sufficient, as an author has to be.

So it proves when Menard moves on to *Don Quijote*. His wish is to redeem that well-known work from the spontaneity of its first production by Cervantes, and to endow it with the 'inevitability' of a poem. This wish has been prefigured in the story by the narrator's own wish to produce an 'inevitable' rectification of Madame Bachelier's catalogue, that lady being, on the evidence of her name, a 'novice' (and an echo of Cervantes's *bachiller?*) Nothing is to be left to chance in the reproduction of the great novel:

> I have contracted the mysterious duty of reconstructing his [Cervantes's] spontaneous work literally. My solitary game is governed by two polar rules. The first allows me to try out variants of a formal or psychological type; the second obliges me to sacrifice them to the 'original' text and to justify this annihilation in an irrefutable manner ...[10]

The text of *Don Quijote*, therefore, like the rules of chess, will not in the end be changed by Menard's activity. His 'solitary game' is very much a game of one-man chess, in which he first reasons out the moves he will make and then reasons out the counter-moves which invalidate them. And the 'polar rules' to which he adheres are an early indication by Borges of how, in his stories, he uses the opposed points of the compass, North and South, East and West, as the extremities between which a fiction can be shown to move. In 'polar' terms, Menard starts from the North, which is the reality of Cervantes's text, travels in imagination to the South, which is a possible variation of Cervantes's text, then back once again to the North, where he rejoins reality.

Menard has time before he dies to write only two chapters and a bit of *Don Quijote*, but these fragments are, the narrator of his story assures us, a great enrichment of the original. They are the work not of a Golden Age Spaniard but of a twentieth-century Frenchman, someone who is a stranger to the age, the locality, and even the language of Cervantes. One begins to see how very much more considerable an intellectual feat this is than that of the original author. A quotation from *Don Quijote* is used to demonstrate the greater significance of Menard's text over Cervantes's: 'truth, whose mother is history (*historia*), the emulator of time, depository of actions, witness to the past, example and warning to the present, admonition to the future'.[11] As written by Cervantes,

---

[10] *OC*, p. 448.

[11] *OC*, p. 449. The quotation is truncated, and comes from the ninth chapter of the first part of *Don Quijote*. This chapter is a very playful one in which Cervantes bridges the gap between the first and second parts of his narrative, claiming to have discovered the continuation of the knight's adventures in an Arab historian, Cide Hamete Benengeli. Arab historians, it seems, are not to be

this is 'a mere rhetorical eulogy of History'; as written by Menard, 'the contemporary of William James', it is an 'astonishing' piece of philosophical Pragmatism, whereby 'Historical truth is not what happens; it is what we adjudge to have happened'. The play on, and in, the word 'history' is thus exploited to distinguish the spontaneous Cervantes from the rigorous Menard. For Cervantes history is the extra-historiographical reality of the past, the Past-in-Itself, as it were; for Menard, the protégé of Berkeley as much as William James, it is whatever is recorded of the past. For Menard history includes the *historia* of *Don Quijote*, from which he will diverge the better subsequently to rejoin it.

What Menard ultimately produces is not an unusually short version of *Don Quijote* but an unusually long quotation from it. The words are the same but their sense has changed. Nowhere does Borges's thriftiness in respect of language appear more provocatively than here; given time, it would seem, a small number of different formulas might come to mean a great many different things. This is the gist of Borges's speculation elsewhere, that 'Perhaps the story of the universe is the story of the diverse intonation of a few metaphors'.[12] If that is so, one of those metaphors might have to be the word 'intonation', as Borges adapts it. In point of fact intonations are possible only for the spoken language, not for the written one. The written language's resources for reproducing such acoustic variations are feeble, though quotation marks can certainly be accounted one of them. Borges is again here doing honour, ironically I imagine, to the greater potency of an oral over a written narrative. The man who speaks can alter the sense of the words he quotes without resorting to any additional words; the man who writes must appear to concur in what he quotes unless he gives it a different context.

In literature the diversity of intonations will be considerable, so considerable that only readers as archetypally minded as Borges

[12] 'La esfera de Pascal' ('Pascal's Sphere'), *OC*, p. 636.

---

trusted to the degree Spanish historians might be, because they are members of a 'mendacious' race! Borges's story of Pierre Menard alludes in a number of ways, I suspect, to this particular chapter of *Don Quijote*, not least to the firm belief of the narrator of that novel that the knight cannot have lacked 'some wise man who should be responsible for writing of his unprecedented exploits (*nunca vistas hazañas*, i.e. exploits never seen)'. It is a short step from Don Quijote's 'never before seen' exploits to the invisible achievement of Pierre Menard.

will be competent to penetrate to the common meaning which underlies them. Those few common meanings are a kind of ultimate abstraction, Platonic entities informing the full variety of the universe of books. It is a dismaying scepticism which sees these matrices as themselves metaphorical: the foundations on which Borges's literary universe rests are perfectly insubstantial.

Pierre Menard is, in his way, the embodiment of Time: what he does to the text of *Don Quijote* is no more and no less than what Time has done, he changes the meanings of words without changing the words themselves. When we read *Don Quijote* ourselves we reproduce it just as Menard does, because we are people of the twentieth century; and if we have previously been readers of William James we are quite entitled, in the a-temporal universe of ideas, to find evidence of Pragmatism in the work of a seventeenth-century Spaniard.

ODIUM THEOLOGICUM

Not least among the admirable tortuosities of 'Pierre Menard, autor del Quijote' is that it culminates in the one truly abortive conclusion open to the maker of fictions: a coincidence between his own invention and the invention of someone else. Menard's ambition, like that of any true author, is antithetical, but it is also so perverted that the synthesis he eventually produces is identical with the thesis from which he first began. The dialectical process seems to be short-circuited. The identity, however, is purely textual; as soon as a reader is introduced into the scheme, that textual identity lapses. From the reader's point of view there can be no ideal coincidence between Menard's chapters of *Don Quijote* and the original. Indeed, from the reader's point of view there have never been two identical texts of any book because no book has ever been read with identical responses by two people, nor by the same person twice.

Before the great day comes when he accomplishes the coincidence he is seeking, Menard experiences a great many failures. He has to go through a lot of rewriting before he rewrites Cervantes. These failures are fictions—faulty translations of *Don Quijote*, it could be said—which we are not invited to read; in fact we have the story's word for it that Menard has destroyed them, that it was his custom to walk at dusk through the outskirts of Nîmes and 'to make a merry bonfire'. These evanescent works of literature have perished, like those tossed into the flames by the Hunnish cavalry. They are condemned by their author in conformity with his 'polar rules', whereby all unjustified innovations—and that, in this case, means *all* innovations—must be annihilated. By first inventing fictions and then abolishing them again, Menard is playing a double game; in the very appropriate jargon of espionage services, he is a double-agent. He is, as I have said, engaged on a game of chess against himself. The *Quijote*, as it happens, is not the first Spanish book he has 'translated', he has also published a French version of Ruy Lopez's *Book of Liberal Invention and Art of the Game of Chess*. The 'liberality' of that title prefigures the spontaneity which Menard is anxious to correct in the work of Cervantes. There is nothing at all 'liberal' about the inventions he approves of.

Unlike other of Borges's inventors, unlike Dandy Red Scharlach, say, Menard requires no adversary but himself. But in order to be an inventor he has got to find, within himself, a principle of division, a germ, as it were, of schizophrenia, since until a man be divided internally he is not able to launch himself on the creation of a fiction. That fiction is dialectical through and through: dialectical in respect of the fictions which already exist at the moment of its creation, dialectical in respect of its narrative form, which is a whole series of potential contradictions, dialectical in its 'characterization'. That word, in Borges's case, must go into quotation marks because it is used in an etiolated, formal sense. The characters in his stories are not psychological entities, merely proper names. They are, as all fictional characters are to a greater or lesser extent, functions of the plot, and Borges gives them names as a concession to the protocol of fiction; they could as well have been identified more symbolically, perhaps by an algebraic notation.

Characters, like any other element in a literary structure, derive their meaning in the first instance differentially: it is by comparing one character with another, and seeing what the differences are, that we get our first understanding of their presence in the fiction. The differences between them matter, and so, equally, do the similarities, for if there are no similarities between two characters then there is no incentive to measure the differences between them. So the first step towards classifying the characters in a narrative is to observe what is common to any two of them and what is unique.

With most fiction we should normally set about doing this in psychological terms, distinguishing one character from another by the way they behave and deducing that these are alternative psychological 'types'; in one situation we observe two different reactions. With Borges, however, that possibility is removed, since his characters have no psychology, no inner life worth speaking of. It is always *possible* to interpret any act psychologically and to take it as evidence of a distinctive personality, but it would be perfectly sterile to attempt that with the acts which Borges's characters perform. His characters are there to serve the plot, they are 'mere subjects of the action' as the preface to the printed version of two of Borges's and Bioy Casares's film scenarios puts it.[1] There are characters in any narrative because there can be no narrative without them; they may not be human characters but animals or even inanimate objects, but they are characters none the less, and the actions of the narrative will be distributed purposefully amongst them.

If there are no psychological characteristics to distinguish one character from another in a story, then we are thrown back on their names to do the job. Proper names matter far more in fiction than is sometimes allowed, and far more than in real life. They matter because they are distinctive. When people are present to us we do not distinguish them by their names but by their looks; when they are absent it is quicker and more effective to distinguish them by name, rather than by some brief résumé of their appearance. In a fiction, where there are no physical presences, we depend greatly on having the characters identified for us by their names, even if, as the fiction develops, we come to 'recognize' characters by their mannerisms and obsessions. (An extreme Formalist might argue, with reason, that those mannerisms and obsessions are themselves demanded by the conventions of narrative, that the content thus stems from the form.) There has been much resentment when novelists deliberately fail to name their characters, so that they become harder or impossible to keep apart. In some instances, as looks to be the case with Virginia Woolf, they may want us to identify them by their intimate foibles; in others, as is certainly the case with Nathalie Sarraute, they may not want us to identify them at all, when so much even of our secret, psychic life is quite lacking in 'authenticity' and therefore undeserving of attribution to one person rather than another. In general, though, characters *are* distinctive, and much more distinctive than real people. This extra distinctiveness we acknowledge almost every day when we encounter real people who, because of the extravagance of their behaviour, we call 'characters'.

It was the distinctiveness of 'characters' as opposed to the homogeneity of real people which, we saw, alerted the shrewd Isidro Parodi to the plot against Montenegro in 'Las noches de Goliadkin'. Alert spectators of *Murder on the Orient Express* might, though I doubt it, have likewise penetrated the plot on that train. But the diversity of Agatha Christie's characters on that

[1] *Los orilleros. El paraíso de los creyentes*, Buenos Aires, 1955, p. 7.

occasion is rich and overwhelming, and reinforced by the need to give a variety of important film actors their chance in a 'character' part. Borges could never be so florid in his exposure of convention.

It is a principle of linguistics that meaning may be instituted by very small differences between linguistic units, by the minor, acoustic variation, say, between the words *pull* and *bull*. The variations through which meaning may be instituted in a fiction will need to be more decisive than that, but not exaggeratedly so. In one of Borges's later stories, 'El encuentro' ('The Encounter'), there is an allusion to two old *cuchilleros* called Juan Almanza and Juan Almada. They bear each other a grudge for the apparently frivolous reason that 'people mixed them up'. The pair of them never in fact meet, even though both are recorded as having died, Almanza of a stray bullet, Almada of natural causes. The story into which this ill-differentiated pair is introduced is the story of two other men who *do* meet, in a knife-fight. Unlike Almanza and Almada these two, by name Uriarte and Duncan, are not knife-fighters. When they fight, however, they show an unexpected expertise and one kills the other. Their expertise is an attribute not of the men themselves but of their weapons, which have been taken from a show-case full of famous knives dating back to the legendary past of Buenos Aires's *cuchilleros*. 'El encuentro' is a story in which the encounter matters a great deal and the identity of the rivals little. They fight because an encounter, *any* encounter, requires two adversaries; they are functions of the plot, a necessary, formal duplication. The story is doubly archetypal: it is archetypal as an Argentinian story, approximating to the Platonic ideal of the story of a *duelo a cuchillo*; and archetypal for being founded on conflict, on the disjunction without which there could be no story.

It is this disjunction for which Almanza and Almada fail to qualify because their names are too alike and people confuse them. It is to them, however, that the weapons used in the fight by Duncan and Uriarte are eventually traced back: the encounter between the two bourgeois is the fulfilment of the rivalry between the two *cuchilleros*. The tone has been raised, and in the future it will be raised still further, because the witnesses to the duel agree amongst themselves that they will 'lie as little as possible and raise the duel with knives into a duel with swords'.[2] This, it seems, will keep the authorities quiet; the encounter is now in circulation as a

OC, p. 1042.

narrative and can progress towards the status of a myth. The names of the duellists, Uriarte and Duncan, are distinctive, as are their persons and the weapons they fight with, and the story, as Borges tells it, contains regular hints at the inevitability of its conclusion. The name of Duncan, who is eventually murdered by Uriarte's 'dagger', is presumably an echo of *Macbeth*, planted, as by Nolan in 'Tema del traidor y del heroe', so that we shall recognize the story's plot to be a conspiracy, part plagiarism and part improvisation.

I have said that the reason why Almanza and Almada hate one another is the 'apparently frivolous' one that people get them muddled up. It is only 'apparently frivolous' judged by the psychological criteria we normally bring to the discussion of motive in fiction. As a psychological explanation of a rivalry it looks most inadequate; but it is not a psychological explanation. It is a formal, literary explanation, in terms of narrative. Almanza and Almada have, in their names, everything it takes to be two characters in a fiction: they are similar but not identical. They invite comparison. The fact that they are, to judge by the story of 'El encuentro', a little too similar to be made into fully blown characters does not disqualify them. They can be listed among the embryonic, apprentice characters in Borges, like others we have considered. Their deaths are random, they have failed to take the chance their names offered them of a significant conjunction.

But they embody the principle of bifurcation, or division, and that is the reason they hate one another. Hatred is the emotion which divides, the emotion most obviously appropriate if we want to establish a motive for the dialectic principle itself. Where love brings together, hatred drives apart, and the various pairs of rivals in Borges's stories hate one another because they are rivals, they are not rivals because they hate one another. It is hatred which is justified by the disjunctions of the story and, very strikingly, by the disjunction within a single character whereby the story originates.

In the course of the highly creative fever which follows his operation in the sanatorium, Juan Dahlmann, the protagonist of 'El Sur', 'hated himself meticulously (*minuciosamente*); he hated his identity, his bodily necessities, his humiliation, the beard that dristled on his face'.[3] This is his cue to divide himself, like proto-plasm, into two, to inaugurate an alternative, fictive self which will

[3] *OC*, p. 526.

suppress his identity, or oneness, set him temporarily free from biological constraints, and compensate him for the shortcomings of reality (a theme in Borges I shall return to in the last part of this work). I have no good explanation for Dahlmann's animus against his beard, unless it represents the facial contingencies he will rise above on his subsequent expedition in search of his definitive, 'eternal' face. The important thing is that Dahlmann has now duplicated himself and will soon be on his way to his Romantic death in the South.[4] This duplication, into a sedentary and a heroic self, is one conditioned, as so often in Borges, by his ancestry, in which there are German pastors—the Protestant or dialectical element again—and Argentinian military heroes. Dahlmann himself is the secretary of a public library and feels 'deeply Argentinian'. He will die what is, in literary terms, a 'deeply Argentinian' death, in a knife-fight. Like Uriarte and Duncan in 'El encuentro' he does not know how to wield a knife, for if he did his fate would be evitable.

Dahlmann's self-hatred turns him literally from a patient (in a sanatorium) into an agent, or into an agent who is both agent and patient in one, true to the assertion of Schopenhauer, that 'I demonstrate the same being in the actor and the sufferer'.[5] But patients may well not enjoy their transformation into agents, since the process of bifurcation does not end there; indeed, it only *begins* there. The alternative self stands at the head of a sequence of narrative choices, the labyrinth through which he has to pick his way to his inevitable fate. He may feel, like another of Borges's fever patients, Dandy Red Scharlach, that all this duplication is too arduous. The presence which dominates Scharlach's inventive sickness is that of the 'hateful' two-headed Janus. His feelings towards his suffering body are like Dahlmann's but more negative: 'I came to abominate my body, I came to feel that two eyes, two hands, two lungs, are as monstrous as two faces.'[6] For Scharlach the human body itself has labyrinthine possibilities.

[4] It might be more accurate to say that Dahlmann is now three, not just two Dahlmanns: the 'original' Dahlmann plus the two alternative Dahlmanns. There are some memorably acute remarks about these duplications within a character in Borges's note on a film version of *Dr. Jekyll and Mr. Hyde* (*OC*, pp. 285-6), where the film-makers were confronted with the problem of a facial as well as a nominal duplication. Borges's suggested solution of this problem is far more intelligent than theirs.

[5] *Selected Essays of Schopenhauer*, London, 1914, p. 156.

[6] *OC*, pp. 505-6.

Hatred, whether of one person for himself or of one person for another person, results in fictions. Haters are no respecters of facts. In the story of 'La busca de Averroes' the philosopher dines in the house of Farach, the local theologian or 'Koranist'; among the other guests is the traveller Abulcásim Al-Asharí, whose memory, like that of any potential Borges hero, is 'a mirror of intimate cowardices':

> Abulcásim said he had reached the kingdoms of the empire of Sin (of China); his detractors, with that peculiar logic which comes from hatred, swore that he had never set foot in China and that in the temples of that country he had blasphemed against Allah.[7]

The 'peculiar logic' of hatred thus thrives on contradiction. The two charges made against the traveller—the teller of tales—by his adversaries are incompatible. Those adversaries want the best of both worlds, want Abulcásim both to have been in China and not to have been in China. They are dialecticians on principle, who disregard the incompatibility of the premises from which they are arguing. Their two fictions against Abulcásim can never be reconciled, so if they were ever to coexist in a narrative—apart from their coexistence in Borges's narrative, as a specimen paralogism— one must be annihilated. If hatred inspires disagreement with existing narratives, it has subsequently to be controlled by logic of an orthodox sort in order to ensure that such disagreements are not mutually exclusive. Logic works by excluding middles, or the coexistence of contradictories, and so, once it is finalized, does narrative, but, as Borges repeatedly demonstrates, a narrative still on its way to being finalized works by discarding alternatives which are incongruous.

Of the alternative charges laid against Abulcásim, that he was a liar or a blasphemer, there is more to be gained by studying the second. To blaspheme is a peculiarly literary act: it is to depart, verbally, from the prescribed formulas of devotion. Blasphemy is a minor, less elaborate branch of heresy, and there is, very logically, nothing that Borges likes better than a systematic heresiarch. The heretic is someone who distinguishes himself by his departure from orthodoxy; his motive is *odium theologicum*, supposedly the most visceral of all hatreds. Heresy, with Borges, is identical with authorship in general, both in its motives and its products: it reorganizes the old fictions which it hates into new ones.

[7] *OC*, p. 583.

The most persistent and outrageous of Borges's heretics is Nils Runeberg of Lund, protagonist of the 'Tres versiones de Judas' ('Three Versions of Judas'). Runeberg, dissatisfied by the Gospel story as given, invents three theological fictions of his own, which we are bound to see, from the narrative point of view, as improvements on the original. He is interested not in the story as a whole, but in its conclusion, with the betrayal of Jesus. He is interested in fact in the relationship of Jesus with Judas. Now these two names, in view of what we have just been saying, are something of an *hasard objectif* for Runeberg (or Borges), a coincidence in 'nature' which invites their incorporation into a story. The names are similar but not identical, like those of Almanza and Almada.

Runeberg's variations on the New Testament account of Jesus and Judas are exercises in what he calls 'the economy of redemption', but he does not use the word 'redemption' in quite its normal theological sense. He wants to redeem Judas Iscariot, and to do so by giving him a more and more decisive role in the narrative of Jesus's betrayal. The gravest sin which, as a maker of fictions, can beset him, is the sin of contingency, or the haphazard, and it is this sin he plans to redeem by integrating it within a story. Judas's betrayal of Jesus will be treated like the betrayal of Scharlach by his impulsive henchman, Azevedo, in 'La muerte y la brújula': it will be ransomed by being turned into a different, more satisfactory, and more 'interesting' narrative. As an act of redemption this is unorthodox but not wholly unorthodox, since the redemption of the human race through the sacrifice of Jesus also works by endowing our collective and individual histories with finality: it is a proof, if we accept it, that the world is not fact but fiction, a story willed by God.

Runeberg starts from what he sees as a crucial weakness in the Gospel account: the superfluity of Judas's treacherous kiss in the Garden of Gethsemane. This is superfluous, he argues, because everyone must have known what Jesus looked like already, so that there was no need for him to be identified in this way. Now a fiction, as we have several times remarked, has as one of its functions to establish the identity of its hero, to trace his essential features; if that identity is already established, further fictions are redundant. But such redundancy is a virtue, because it means that whatever further fictions are elaborated they cannot affect the 'historical' record: the history of Jesus remains unscathed by

Runeberg's speculations. A superfluous action in a narrative, however, is an offence for a mind as rigorous as his, and he will work to justify it: 'To suppose an error in the Scriptures is intolerable; it is no less intolerable to admit a casual fact into the most precious occurrence in the history of the world. *Ergo*, Judas's betrayal was not casual; it was a predetermined fact which has its mysterious place in the economy of redemption.'[8]

Runeberg's successive reinterpretations of Judas's value in this economy promote him rapidly and scandalously from the most ignominious of roles to the most glorious. His first version has Judas being sacrificed in order to mirror, on the merely human level, the sacrifice of God himself on the divine level. In the second version Judas is seen as a supreme ascetic, mortifying not his body but his soul for the greater glory of God, and becoming the equivalent in Hell of Jesus in Paradise. In the third and final version Judas, having first reflected and then equalled Jesus, supplants him; it is now he, and not Jesus, who is seen as the Son of God, God having decided to espouse humanity in its lowest form. Runeberg's Redeemer is thus to be found in Hell, which must rank as something of a last word in Christian heresy. But the last word in heresy is also a triumph of narrative logic, and Runeberg ranks high on the list of Borges's methodical makers of fiction. The weakness of the Gospel has been repaired. Judas, a traitor not to Jesus but to the rigorousness of the story, is redeemed.

Borges comes back to the story of Jesus and Judas in a later story, 'La secta de los treinta' ('The Sect of the Thirty'), in terms exactly similar to the story of Nolan's Festspiel in 'Tema del traidor y del heroe':

In the tragedy of the Cross . . . there were voluntary and involuntary actors, all of them indispensable, all of them inevitable . . . Only two were voluntary: the Redeemer and Judas. The latter threw away the thirty pieces of silver which were the price of the salvation of souls and immediately hanged himself. At that time he was 33 years old, like the Son of Man. The Sect venerates them as equals and absolves the others.[9]

The Sect are advanced students of fiction. They know that, in structural terms, there is equality between all the elements of a narrative,

---

[8] *OC*, p. 515.   [9] *El libro de arena*, p. 85.

and that they all contribute to the one end. Nothing could make the point more succinctly than the provocative reasoning whereby the money which Judas received for his treachery becomes 'the price of the salvation of souls'. This is teleology taken to its limits: the Sect, which has taken its name from these thirty ill-gotten shekels, argues that but for Judas's betrayal there could have been no Redemption, that whatever is part of the story leads to the culmination of the story. Jesus needs Judas just as much as Judas needs Jesus; but for the one's infamy the other could have not known glory.

Runeberg's three fictions have the effect, therefore, of transforming the lowest of the low into the highest of the high. Fiction, for Borges, glorifies. The protagonist of a story, after all, however villainous, is technically its hero. Many of Borges's protagonists are, by their own confession, cowards, or alternatively are shown to be cowardly and treacherous. In a fiction they can, like Judas Iscariot, change places with the loyal and brave. Like another of Borges's traitors, Zaid in the story of 'Abenjacán el Bojarí, muerto en su laberinto' ('Abenjacán the Bojarí, Dead in his Labyrinth'), they can become king for a day. This is another of the A to Z stories. Zaid is the cousin of an African king, Abenjacán el Bojarí, who is himself the architect, in exile, of an imposing labyrinth in the wilds of Cornwall. Abenjacán lives in his labyrinth guarded by a lion and a Negro slave and tells his story to the local rector (Rector Allaby, a character borrowed by Borges from Samuel Butler's *Way of All Flesh*, where Rector Allaby is the father-in-law of Theodore Pontifex). In alliance with his cousin, Zaid, Abenjacán has despoiled his people and then, when they rebelled, fled his kingdom with his cousin and the loot. Subsequently he has murdered Zaid and built his labyrinth as a refuge. But this account proves false; Abenjacán calls on the Rector again and tells him that Zaid is alive and pursuing him, indeed that he is already inside the labyrinth. His own body, together with that of his lion and his slave, are later found in the labyrinth, their faces carefully expunged.

The 'explanation' offered of these events is that the inhabitant of the Cornish labyrinth was not the brave Abenjacán at all but the treacherous Zaid, that the labyrinth has been built not as a refuge but as a lure, in the knowledge that when Abenjacán heard of it he would travel to Cornwall in pursuit of his cousin, who, in the flight together, has robbed him of his treasures. When Abenjacán finally arrives and penetrates into the labyrinth, Zaid murders him and flees back to Africa. This murder and ensuing flight are the realization of the fictive murder and ensuing flight in Zaid's story to the Rector. In that story he has impersonated his enemy and so turned himself into a hero. He has alienated his treachery from himself by projecting it on to the third-person Zaid of his narrative, and that Zaid is 'dead'. The story of 'Abenjacán el Bojarí, muerto en su laberinto' is one of the replacement of the King by his cousin, of the letter A by the letter Z. Hero and villain are interchangeable because it is only their names, and above all the initial letters of their names, which separate them; the face of the dead man in the labyrinth has been destroyed, so that they can no longer be identified by their bodies. 'He pretended to be Abenjacán, he killed Abenjacán and finally *he was Abenjacán*' (Borges's italics) is the story's dying verdict on Zaid.[10] The traitor has been transformed into a hero, except, of course, for us, before whom the actual deceitfulness of that transformation has been exposed.

The glory Zaid achieves, like the glory Runeberg procures for Judas, is a reflected glory. Both are usurpers of a dignity which, 'historically' speaking, belongs elsewhere; Zaid is not a 'real' king, any more than Judas is a 'real' redeemer. A reflected glory is one which comes from moving to the centre of a story. In Zaid's case it comes from telling one's own story as if one were its hero rather than its villain. As a story-teller Zaid subscribes to a fundamental principle of narration, which is that the stories we tell can make men of us; his story comes very much under the heading of what, in *Evaristo Carriego*, Borges calls 'the narratives of iron which shed their valour on whoever is recounting them'.[11]

It is this acquisition of a reflected glory which seems to be supported in Borges, albeit rather obscurely, by certain astronomical (or should it be astrological?) arrangements in the stories. In several of the stories play is made of the relationship between sun and moon. We have come across the moon at least once already, reflected in the rectangular *fuentes* of London when Ebenezer Bogle sets off through the streets in search of creative inspiration. Elsewhere, as in the story of 'El inmortal' ('The Immortal'), it is associated with the onset of 'fever', and we know by now what that means. The moon is the planet appropriate to Borges's fictions

[10] *OC*, p. 606.   [11] *OC*, p. 116.

because, as 'controlled dreams', they are pointedly nocturnal. But the moon is a source of illumination only by the grace of the sun; its glory is a reflected glory. It may replace the sun during the hours of darkness but it cannot shine without it. As a bringer of light, the moon is a fraud if not a fiction. There is evidence of a sun/moon relationship in the relationship between Abenjacán and Zaid. When the presumed Abenjacán first lands in Cornwall with his lion and his Negro slave, the lion, the King of Beasts we may assume, is described as having 'the colour of the sun', while the slave has 'the colour of the night'. Abenjacán himself, who is Zaid pretending to be Abenjacán, is, rather surprisingly for someone emerged from darkest Africa, 'a man of lemony (*cetrina*) skin'. He is, one might say, yellow: literally yellow in the colour of his skin and figuratively yellow, as it will turn out, in his cowardice. Thus in addition to the King of Beasts who is the colour of the sun, and the slave who is the colour of the night, we have an intermediate presence who is the colour of the moon. As the story develops, Zaid is a moon who substitutes himself for the sun, for the King, a substitution he achieves as both hero and narrator of a story, that is to say as the elucidator of a mystery.

This symbolism may seem alembicated and incredible. It is repeated, however, perhaps more clearly, in another story: 'La forma de la espada' ('The Form of the Sword'). This is also a story of treachery told by the traitor himself, and it is set in that privileged location, Ireland, much of it indeed in the country-house of a certain General Berkeley, conveniently removed for the duration to another of Borges's occasional campaign-grounds, India. Ireland is in a state of civil war, which we can take to be that very state of internal dissension we have seen to be the nursery of fictions. The story is told *to* the narrator in Uruguay, by an Englishman 'whose real name does not matter'; since his 'real' name is Moon, we may dispute that casual aside. It concerns a young recruit to the cause of Irish independence against the English, a twentieth-century Fergus Kilpatrick. His name is John Vincent Moon. Moon, propitiously for a Borges story, is a 'dialectical materialist' and also strongly deterministic, being convinced that 'the revolution was predestined to triumph'. And triumph it does, as with Kilpatrick; only it is not the conspiracy against the English which comes to fruition, it is the conspiracy against reality.

Moon, alas, is a coward. He betrays the fellow-conspirator who has, being a true hero, risked his life to save Moon from capture. It is this hero who, so it appears, is now telling the story of the treachery. After hearing Moon arranging, on the telephone, like some more technological Judas, to have him arrested as he crosses the garden, he pursues the 'informer' through the 'black corridors of nightmare and deep staircases of vertigo' of General Berkeley's labyrinthine house. Eventually he takes down a sword and marks his adversary for life: 'with that half-moon of steel I put my mark on his face, for ever, a half moon of blood'.[12] This tell-tale mark is one we have been introduced to already, as crossing the face of the nameless Englishman who is telling the story. John Vincent Moon, the Judas, has appropriated the glory of the nameless Irishman whom he has betrayed by the simple, grammatical expedient of turning himself into the third person 'he' and his saviour into the first person 'I'. The 'I', as the narrator of the story, is automatically its hero, the 'he', or its narratee, is the infamous traitor in need of redemption.

Moon, the provisional source of light, is ultimately exposed as a sham. He is also a man in a state of civil war, a man divided. He is both agent and patient. As agent he inflicts on his patient half the mark—a half-moon—which symbolizes his divided state. But that division lasts only as long as his narration lasts, it is a division forced on him by the necessary disjunction of narrative itself. Once the 'solitary game' is over, Moon can revert to being a full moon again, instead of two warring halves. The true hero of his story has been shot by the English, and it is, as ever, the death of that 'reality' which has opened the way for Moon's own fiction of self-aggrandizement. There is a last irony, however: by telling his own story to a stranger Moon negates the redemption that story was invented in order to achieve. Should we admire him or despise him all the more for the expertise of his deception?

[12] *OC*, pp. 494–5.

PART V

"the final discharge which would redeem him . . . from the vain
task of imagining"

CHAPTER 1

THE MEANS TO AN END

JOHN Vincent Moon, of 'La forma de la espada', is a conspirator who believes that his cause is predestined to succeed. His cause being the cause of fiction, he is correct to hold that belief. At the conclusion of his own narration he tells his listener that he has told the story in the way he has 'so that you would hear it to the end'. The trick he has pulled, of objectifying himself as the cowardly Irishman Moon, is the trick all authors pull, even when they appear more directly in their work as 'I', because that 'I' is still an object-ification.[1] The exposure of that trick is, in two senses, the end of his story: it is both a conclusion and a destination. It is, better, a predestination, the end to which his story is bound to bring him if it is to conform to the rules which Borges, at least, lays down for stories.

All stories, and not only stories as rigorous as Borges's, will appear, once we have read them, to have been purposeful, to have progressed towards an end appointed in advance. In a great many cases this end really has been appointed in advance; the author knew, from the outset, what the destination of his journey was to be, what he did not know was exactly how he would get there, nor how long it might take. Stories do not just stop. In English, to guard against the merely contingent connotation of the word 'end' we have the additional term 'end*ing*', which introduces a much stronger notion of agency and even of craftsmanship.[2] Endings we

---

[1] The author, any more than Berkeley's Will or Spirit, can never finally appear in his text as a subject. The representation of a subject is, inevitably, an object, requiring a further, invisible subject as its representer. Thus we set off along that infinite regression of authorial selves which Borges explores, with consummate brevity, in his 'Borges y yo' ('Borges and I') in *El Hacedor* (*OC*, p. 808).

[2] It is interesting that in France, where the one word *fin* is regularly and ambiguously used for both 'end' and 'ending', they should look to English for guidance. The English term they have their eye on, and which they need, is 'ending', the alternative to which for an English person tends to be the French word *dénouement*! Unfortunately, the word they end up by borrowing generally seems to be 'end', so that one is constantly coming across references, in French critical works, to a very awkward and unnecessary hybrid: the 'happy end'.

judge by their conclusiveness; the only endings that are unsatisfactory are those we find inconclusive, which leave, indeed, too many loose ends. And conclusiveness, in a narrative, is its own reward; from the technical point of view all endings are happy endings, whether they involve happiness ever after or an Elizabethan blood-bath.

Where the predestination of plot is concerned, the most purely exemplary writer of fiction ever was surely the rich and neurotic Raymond Roussel, for whom constructing a narrative was very like filling in an acrostic: he started from one set of words—a quotation, it might be, or a proverb—and ended with another very similar but not identical set. The narrative was a rational transition from one set to the other. Roussel created the second set by tampering phonetically with the first, so as to quite transform its meaning. All he then needed to do was to create a fiction which would justify the new state of affairs he had created. His tamperings were sometimes very slight, sometimes considerable, but their effect in general was to disarticulate the sentence he began with and to introduce more nouns into it. The sentence towards which he could then progress was more tempting the more static and heteroclite its contents. Roussel created several books out of these verbal experiments, which make strange and instructive reading.[3] In their bare, mathematical way they exemplify the movement which any fiction must follow, from a datum, or given state of things, to a destination, which is the same state of things transformed for the author's gratification. Between datum and destination there comes the choice of justifications. Roussel, like any other maker of fictions, had set himself something to justify, a predetermined end, but he was free to justify it in a number of different ways. It would not be hard to find alternative plots to those he actually uses in his books; there is no call to confuse this high degree of finalism with a complete determinism. Roussel himself seems to have wanted to get from start to finish of each individual narrative as economically as possible; another writer, adopting the same technique, might want

---

[3] No one would ever have known the method Roussel followed if he had not divulged it, posthumously, in a book called *Comment j'ai écrit certains de mes livres* (Paris, 1933 and 1963). Since this remarkable apologia was reprinted, in 1963, the interest and significance of Roussel's career have been widely appreciated in France. His books have not made much headway elsewhere, for the obvious reason that the extreme logic of their inspiration is utterly destroyed in translation.

to spend longer on the way, embroidering and amusing himself, before reaching the same conclusion. Roussel's narratives are an extreme reduction—a *reductio ad absurdum* some would no doubt maintain—of narrative in general. Like the narratives of Borges they are all plot and no psychology. What the two writers share is a fierce wish to remain *in*expressive, to let language and logic between them do the work. There is no evidence, and no likelihood, that Borges has ever read Roussel; and absolutely no need for him to have done so. They merely share a certain Classicism and a certain rationalism. Roussel, as a man, was not a success, and early on in his life was treated by one of the most celebrated of contemporary psychotherapists, Pierre Janet. He was desperate to recover what seems to have been a moment of mystical happiness and illumination in adolescence, an experience he himself spoke of as 'la gloire'; but since 'la gloire' is also, in French, the conventional term for the fame a great writer acquires, this justification of his literary career on psychological grounds looks rather suspect. It is as if Roussel had tried to organize the narrative of his life on the principles we have been discussing, by extending it between two meanings of the one word *gloire*. Again like Borges he is an author whose autobiography is all of a piece with his fictional creations. The two writers share a passion: which is for self-effacement; but we cannot argue from their common taste for literary austerity to a common temperament determining that taste.

The ends which Borges sets himself in his fictions are more ordinary than Roussel's, they are the predictable dénouements of quite familiar plots. The end is what is delayed: the archetypal end is the execution of the condemned Jaromir Hladík in 'El milagro secreto', which is bound to happen and eventually does happen, but not until we have been let into the secret of his miracle. The interval between now and then, between the beginning of a story and the inevitable end, is filled with imaginings, and imaginings, as we have seen, are an ordeal for the imaginer, setting him off on his journey through the labyrinth of choice. The appointment of an end is a responsibility which Borges's protagonists often long to be rid of. They long to pass from the complications of thinking to the simplicities of doing.

One of the keenest of Borges's anticipators is Emma Zunz, the girl who avenges her father's suicide by shooting her employer, the man who had once framed him. When she gets the letter telling her her father has died of an overdose of veronal

Her first impression was one of discomfort in her stomach and knees; then of blind guilt, of unreality, of cold, of fear; then she wanted it to be the next day. Immediately afterwards she realized that this wish was futile (*inútil*) because her father's death was the only thing which had happened in the world, and would go on happening without end.[4]

The report of her father's death has removed Emma from the real world into an unreal one. To date this unreal world contains only the one event, her father's death. That is the event which launches the fiction and which, to that extent, is irreversible; but if it cannot be expunged it can be justified by being built on. Emma looks ahead to the time when that justification is complete, to the end of the story. She has, in fact, all that she needs to start organizing the future: she has the inspiration of a dissymmetry, her father's death, which she will eventually balance out, and the *wish* to remove herself from the present, which is also the wish to find herself in a different, more comfortable situation. The *inútil* is, for Borges, another word, and by no means the pejorative word one might think, for the fictive; the death of Emma's father gives rise to a distraction from reality.

That first death is ultimately matched by a second: the murder of Aaron Loewenthal, whom Emma's father had sworn was actually guilty of the peculation for which he himself had been disgraced. Emma, her plan made, anticipates its realization: 'On Saturday, impatience awoke her. Impatience, not anxiety, and the singular relief of it being, finally, that day. She no longer needed now to plot (*tramar*) and imagine; in a few hours she would achieve the simplicity of acts.'[5] The joy of doing, as opposed to imagining, is that it is 'simple', that is to say it is *single*; to act is to make a choice between alternatives and so escape from the bifurcations of the labyrinth. No wonder that the relief which Emma feels should be 'singular'. The death of Loewenthal will mean her release from the responsibility of invention. Before she shoots Loewenthal, however, she learns a further lesson in the logic of narrative. On the afternoon of her fateful Saturday—and to visit Loewenthal at his factory on a Saturday evening, as she does, is very obviously extra-curricular: this, in everyday terms, is a

[4] *OC*, p. 564.   [5] *OC*, p. 565.

'free', not a necessary, visit[6]—Emma gives herself to her anonymous sailor and then sets off straight away afterwards for her rendezvous with Loewenthal. Face to face with her predestined victim, she feels the urge not so much to avenge her father as to 'punish the outrage suffered for it', that outrage being her own voluntary deflowering by a Nordic seaman. The lesson Emma learns is that what, in a narrative, immediately precedes also justifies. Her own humiliation has intervened between the death of her father and her meeting with Loewenthal, and it is this new event rather than the old one which becomes her justification for what she has to do.

This is a quite minor improvisation in the plot of 'Emma Zunz' since it affects only the motivation of the conclusive event. Emma has planned her own humiliation and planned to shoot Loewenthal, all she has failed to do is to foresee the final connection between the two events. She has given herself to the sailor, despite her great repugnance, so that Loewenthal can be falsely accused of rape and her murder of him thereby justified as an act of revenge: revenge not for her father's disgrace but her own. And such is the power of narrative over those caught up in it that this is exactly what Emma comes to feel, that it is herself she is avenging. She is in fact framing Loewenthal for a crime he has not committed, just as Loewenthal framed her father for a crime *he* had not committed. The two acts are symmetrical. Emma takes the gun with which she shoots her victim from the *cajón*, or office-till, which is where, presumably, the money her father had been accused of stealing would have come from. (It is also in a different *cajón*, at her home, that she has kept the letter telling her of her father's suicide; on the evening before her big day she takes the letter out and tears it up, just as, on Saturday afternoon, she tears up the money she is given by the sailor.) In the world's eyes Emma takes the place of her victim—as in the case of Zaid and Abenjacán, her *Z*unz replaces his *A*aron—as the true culprit of a crime for which someone else has been punished. She has not been raped at all, because her violation was perfectly voluntary. Nemesis, in this instance, brings with it a fresh crime.

Emma, however, has achieved her deliverance through action. She is out of the labyrinth. The fact that she first entered it of her own accord reveals the true nature of this particular form of incarceration, which is one the maker of a fiction brings on himself. No one compels him to negotiate its repeated bifurcations. The minotaur Asterión, in the very brief story of 'La casa de Asterión', complains against the common assumption that he is a prisoner in his Cretan fastness: 'Shall I repeat that not one door is closed, shall I add that there is not one lock?'[7] But if his reclusion is voluntary, delivery from it is still a vast relief. Asterión looks constantly forward to the coming of his 'redeemer' Theseus, and offers little resistance at the last.

Asterión, were it possible to think of him as a psychological entity, suffers from that common disability, a death-wish. But he is not a psychological entity, he is a creature who dwells in a labyrinth and looks forward to release from it. He is an author weary of invention and longing, after the effort of duplication, for a reunification with reality. In the story of 'El inmortal', Marco Flaminio Rufo, the Roman tribune, describes the fate of many of his fellow legionaries stationed beside the Red Sea: 'fever and magic consumed many men who magnanimously coveted the steel'.[8] As literary men, who have lived out their creative fever and practised their magic, these dead legionaries are perhaps the very authors of the City of the Immortals which Rufo himself will soon discover in the desert sands. They have made their contribution and have done with invention.

And just as they 'covet' the steel, so others of Borges's victims 'long for' (*anhelar*) their appointed ends. Fergus Kilpatrick dies in his box in the theatre, according to plan, when a 'longed-for bullet' enters his breast. Hladík, in his prison-cell, at times 'longed impatiently for the final discharge which would redeem him . . . from his vain task of imagining'.[9] The verb which Borges likes to use on these occasions, *anhelar*, is especially propitious because of its connections with breathing. 'Anhelation', literally, is a shortness of breath, and rather than to death Borges's narratives look forward to a falling silent, to an end of narration. There is a nice ambiguity, too, in the idea of Hladík getting a 'discharge', which will be as much a release from his responsibilities as a volley of bullets.

Hladík is exceptional among Borges's imaginers for actually

dying on the page. More usually they are under the threat of extinction but do not achieve it in public. Their deaths may, on the other hand, be prefigured in the story, by the death of other representatives of their own kind. There are several such representatives in one of Borges's most byzantine constructions, 'El jardín de senderos que se bifurcan'. The protagonist of this story is Doctor Yu Tsun, a Chinaman spying for the Germans in England during the Great War who has been caught and is now under sentence of death; he lets on, in a not unexpected parenthesis, that 'his throat now longs for (*anhela*) the rope', and if it is the cessation of breath he is after, then hanging is a doubly suitable conclusion for him. Yu Tsun's statement, or confession of his espionage, has been 'dictated, reread, and signed' by him in the death-cell.

But Yu Tsun is not the only victim in the story. There is, first of all, his fellow spy for Germany, Viktor Runeberg, 'real' name Hans Rabener, whose death inaugurates Yu Tsun's own narration. Runeberg, whose name, or *nom de guerre*, is also that of Borges's supreme heresiarch in the 'Tres versiones de Judas', has been trapped and killed by Richard Madden, an Irishman in the English service (as Yu Tsun is a Chinaman in the German service), who is now after Yu Tsun. Yu Tsun, expecting to speak on the telephone to Runeberg, has spoken instead, in German, to Madden. This, he concludes, 'meant the end of our anxieties and—but this seemed very secondary, or *ought to have seemed so to me*—also of our lives'.[10] (Borges's italics.) Yu Tsun and his dead colleague, Viktor Runeberg, are secret agents whose function expires with the discovery of their secret. As story-tellers they can last only until their story is told. Madden, the counter-espionage man, is the representative in the story of the reader, forever in pursuit of Yu Tsun as he realizes his plot, but forever a step behind. Yu Tsun feels 'hatred' for Madden because they are duplicate selves. Both are in the service of alien powers and Madden has been accused of 'weakness and even of treason'; his redemption lies in the defeat of Runeberg and Yu Tsun.

The second victim in the story, after Runeberg, is an ancestor of Yu Tsun, his great-grandfather Ts'ui Pên, an exemplary figure whom we have already met, shut away in his Pavilion of Limpid Solitude. Ts'ui Pên was a man with two, apparently separate ambitions: 'who was governor of Yunnan but who renounced

[10] *OC*, p. 472.

temporal power in order to write a novel which should be more populous than the *Hung Lu Meng* and in order to build a labyrinth in which all men might lose themselves'.[11] Novel and labyrinth, needless to say, turn out to be one and the same, a fiction on a heroic scale scrupulously based on the principles of bifurcation laid down by Herbert Quain. Ts'ui Pên's great work is full of careful and deliberate contradictions. Its author, however, has been murdered, and murdered, like Runeberg, by a foreigner.

The third casualty of this particular series is Stephen Albert, a famous English sinologist who has finally penetrated Ts'ui Pên's secret and has identified his novel with his labyrinth. Albert, having shared his secret with Yu Tsun (whom he alone addresses, when they meet, as Hsi P'êng, so turning him more openly into the descendant of Ts'ui Pên), is then murdered by his guest, yet again a foreigner. Thus the imminent death of Yu Tsun himself, at the hands of foreigners, is the fourth in the series. There is a conspicuously high mortality rate among literary men in 'El jardín de senderos que se bifurcan'.

No matter how often paths may fork we should bear in mind that they all lead somewhere. Each successive bifurcation is the starting-point of a fiction: or, more accurately, of two fictions, only one of which will normally be realized. During the dialogue between them Stephen Albert reads Yu Tsun an extract from the giant novel written by his ancestor. He reads in fact two drafts of a single 'epic chapter':

In the first, an army marches to a battle through barren mountains; the horror of the rocks and the shadows brings it to despise life and it achieves the victory with ease; in the second, the same army passes through a palace in which there is a festivity; the resplendent battle seems to them a continuation of the festivity and they achieve the victory.[12]

Here we have, very literally, one end approached along two different routes. These routes are systematically differentiated one from the other: they are opposites, one all austerity and asperity, the other pleasant and convivial. They are opposites partly because they must be shown to be exclusive justifications of the end, partly perhaps to show the full extent of the author's freedom as he plots his course towards that end; within such extremes lie innumerable

[11] *OC*, p. 475.   [12] *OC*, p. 478.

other alternative courses. Like Herbert Quain, and like all plotters, Ts'ui Pên has constructed his labyrinthine fiction backwards, not forwards. He is, after all, a Chinaman, and it was Poe's recommendation that 'romance-writers, in general, might now and then find their account in taking a hint from the Chinese, who, in spite of building their houses downwards, have still sense enough *to begin their books at the end'*.[13] (Poe's italics.)

The victory which the army achieves is, let us say, a historical event and a public one; the convergent paths the army follows, both of which provide a sufficient motive for the victory, are secret events. They are fictions made to fit into the interstices of the public record. And the predestined victory of the army is also the predestined victory of the narrator, who achieves his end simultaneously with the soldiers, having himself followed *both* paths, as it were, and enjoyed both the rigours and the satisfactions of narrative invention. The victory is one in his own civil war.

'El jardín de senderos que se bifurcan' is in every way a war story. The history from which it first departs and then ultimately rejoins is the history of the Great War—the *written* history of the Great War. The particular history which the story gives as its authority is that of Liddell Hart, who writes of a British attack having to be postponed for five days in July 1916 because of 'torrential rain'. I have not checked this quotation because it does not matter in the least whether it is accurate; Borges needs a datum point and he has provided himself with one. The idea of postponement is one we are used to by now. The British attack is the appointed end of the fiction; its postponement opens up the gap in the historical narrative which the fiction can fill. In Liddell Hart, so the story claims, that gap is filled by heavy rain—'nothing significant, certainly'; and an insignificant, climatic reason is just what we would expect history to provide, like the uninteresting hypotheses put forward to explain a rabbi's murder by the policeman Treviranus. Rain, an explanation of the delay by natural means, will not do. Instead of rain we get Yu T*sun*, whose statement, we are straightaway assured, 'throws an unexpected light on the case'. (Yu Tsun, as his name implies, belongs to the Dynasty of Light invoked later on in the story; Richard Madden, who pursues him, at a constant interval of time, is at one moment mistaken by Yu Tsun for the moon.) Yu Tsun's plugging of the gap

[13] Poe, *Essays and Stories*, p. 272.

between the projected British attack and its realization is far more exotic and 'interesting' than Liddell Hart's—and far longer too.

Yu Tsun possesses a military secret: he knows where the new British artillery park is situated, at a town called Albert on the River Ancre in Picardy. His problem is how to transmit this bit of information to his Chief in Berlin. His resources are nil, and he is, inevitably, a coward. He has, however, a revolver with one bullet in it and he believes that the sound of a shot, if not the sound of the human voice, may travel from Staffordshire, where he is, to Germany. The solution to his problem, to cut a wonderfully roundabout story short, is to shoot the famous British sinologist, Stephen Albert. The Chief, a tireless reader of the *periódicos*, will learn of the murder and take the hint: the artillery park at Albert on the Ancre will be bombed. Yu Tsun's fiction has thus been directed to the transmission of a *name*. Albert, which is the name of a real town, means something more at the end of the story from what it meant at the beginning, it has been enhanced; the fiction has done its work. But Albert is also the geographical point at which the story rejoins reality and the fact that the town stands on the River Ancre—*ancre* being the French word for 'anchor'—is no doubt the reason why Borges picked it, since Albert is very much an anchor in the real world for the fiction of 'El jardín de senderos que se bifurcan'.

The fiction ends with the bombing of the artillery park, not, explicitly, with the British attack finally taking place. There is no question but that the attack did take place, all that Yu Tsun's narrative has achieved is to lead us up to the moment for its realization by a different route. Liddell Hart travels, so to speak, by the barren mountain route, Yu Tsun by way of the festive palace (the palace is one of Borges's commoner symbols for a fiction, as a most superior style of construction). Yu Tsun has not altered history but he has gratified himself. He, the self-confessed coward, has proved to his Chief that 'a yellow man could save his armies'. With Borges you can, it seems, tell the colour of a man's skin from the function he is asked to fill in the story.

CHAPTER 2

MAN INTO AUTHOR

To make a fiction is to flout that stern censor of our more wishful thoughts, the reality principle. The gratification of authorship is to appear not as our daily selves but as whatever we wish to appear. The author, inescapably, is a more glorious version of the man; this rule holds good even in those perverse cases where the author seems to be someone running himself down. That author is one who seeks admiration by pretending to be a less admirable person than he really is. Through self-denigration he expects to become a distinctive and respected author. He cannot, however hard he might try, avoid glorifying himself.

This process of glorification is one of the fundamental processes of literature, and one I have already touched on. Borges naturally wishes to dramatize it as an essential element of his plots. Authorship is a transformation; it creates authors, who exist only by virtue of what they have published, out of men, who from a literary viewpoint do not exist at all, since they are incapable of representation in a text without undergoing this very transformation. It is a transformation, too, which creates heroes, since there can be no narrative without a hero, even if that hero departs so egregiously from the norms of literary heroism that he is called an anti-hero.

The trajectory of a fiction, for Borges, has therefore to go upwards. A story may begin in infamy, in the 'plebeian character' of the Babylon lottery, it may be, or the obscene practices of the man met with on top of a tower in 'El acercamiento a Almotásim', who urinates, robs corpses of their gold teeth, and purifies himself with buffalo dung; but it tends to glory, to the point where the lottery company in Babylon has eliminated chance from the affairs of that city altogether, or with the questing pilgrim of 'El acercamiento a Almotásim' being apparently on the verge of coming face-to-face with God. This methodical ascent from the sordid to the magnificent is also represented in Borges's beloved Gnostic doctrine of the two spheres, the earthly and the celestial, the second of which both mirrors and compensates for the first.

This compensation must, of necessity, relate dialectically to whatever humiliations or unhappinesses it is compensating for. In the story of 'Los teólogos' one of the heretical sects of *histriones* teaches that every man is really two men (a doctrine which will, I hope, by this stage of the present study look suspiciously familiar), an earthly half and a heavenly half, and that the heavenly half is the exact contradictory of the earthly one (like the two half-Moons in 'La forma de la espada'). This teaching has some unfortunate results on people's behaviour once they have grasped its implications: 'Four months later, a blacksmith from the Aventine, hallucinated by the deceptions of the *histriones*, loaded a great iron sphere on to the shoulders of his small son, so that his double might fly.'[1] The blacksmith understands very well the relation of fiction to fact, and how the nature of our wishful thoughts depends on the nature of our oppressive circumstances. His overburdened son is being offered opportunities for wish-fulfilment as rich as those of Flaubert's St. Antony, mortifying himself in the desert so as to gratify his fancy with lascivious hallucinations.

The commonest of these hallucinations in Borges's work is the hallucination of heroism. His protagonists tend to be cowards because cowards make exemplary heroes, they display to the full the transformation that a fiction effects. Their cowardice is not determined by any psychological imperative, but by the narrative one. Cowardice is the infamy which is loaded on to their shoulders so that their other self, the heroic self, may fly; and the man who loads it on is the blacksmith, or the author at his forge. The relationship of father and son is that of creator and creature; the creator, in the episode of the Aventine blacksmith, has *two* creatures, because, as an author, he must duplicate himself.

It is a lesson in compensation which the supremely archetypal author, Homer, has once received from his father, in the title-piece of *El Hacedor*:

Another boy had insulted him and he had approached his father and had told him the story. The latter had let him speak as if he were not listening or did not understand but took down from the wall a bronze dagger, beautiful and full of power, which the boy had furtively coveted. Now he held it in his hands and the surprise of possession cancelled out the insult he had suffered, but the voice of his father was saying: *Someone must know you are a man*, and there was an order in the voice. The night had blinded the paths; grasping the dagger, in which

[1] *OC*, p. 555.

he sensed a magic strength, he descended the steep slope which surrounded the house and ran to the sea-shore, dreaming that he was Ajax and Perseus and populating the salt-laden darkness with wounds and battles.[2]

Such is the mature, blind Homer's memory of initiation into the life of imagination. This memory of a courageous sortie into the darkness is his inspiration now that he has lost his sight. It is a memory long lost but which had 'shone like a coin in the rain', and the reason why it shines like a coin is surely that it is a story he can exchange for his present infirmity (similarly, in 'La forma de la espada', the infamous John Vincent Moon is said to have got the land he now owns in exchange for the story of his infamy). Within the story itself, he receives a dagger in exchange for the story of his humiliation, and the dagger, like the pen it so closely resembles, is the instrument of his magical redemption. He need only hold it in his hand to be a hero—to be *two* heroes, indeed, both Ajax and Perseus—just like the duellists in that very different story, 'El encuentro', who are turned into heroes by their possession of two fighting knives.

The young Homer's nocturnal adventure ends in his return home 'with the blood-stained blade', but the blade, or *hoja*, could just as well be a sheet of paper, which is also a *hoja* in Spanish. Borges's Homer is poised, equivocally, between the exercise of Arms and that of Letters, he is yet another point of confluence among many in Borges, of a martial strain with a sedentary. The secular debate between Arms and Letters is one raised, interestingly enough, in *Don Quijote*, and raised again by Pierre Menard in his twentieth-century reproduction of that classic work. Cervantes, the old soldier turned writer, settles the question in favour of Arms, and so, necessarily, does Menard, who is far from being a fighting man himself! This is no doubt one of the many points in Menard's text where he expresses opinions exactly contrary to those he actually holds. He, being a great deal more sophisticated than Cervantes where literature is concerned, will appreciate that to argue, in a work of literature, that military glory is preferable to literary glory, is to prove the reverse, when it is an author who is acquiring glory for so arguing.

From Arms and Letters one can pass easily enough, by synecdoche, to the sword and the pen, as the rival instruments whose

---

[2] *OC*, pp. 781–2.

exercise brings glory. It is surely in deference to literary tradition that Borges cultivates the *cuchillero*, the man who wields his knife as if it were a pen: who creates, that is to say, legends through it. The man who wields the pen recognizes a kinship. The legends, moreover, which the knife-fighter creates are a makeweight, the heroic transformation of their social deprivation. Evaristo Carriego, the poet of the Buenos Aires suburbs, becomes a poet, in Borges's account of him, the moment he finds the right analogy between the countries and dramas he reads about and the environment he lives in:

Life was in France, he thought, in the bright clash of steel, or when the armies of the emperor flooded the land, but to me has fallen the twentieth century, the belated twentieth century, and a mediocre South American suburb . . . Carriego was cavilling thus when something happened. A flourish from a laborious guitar, the ill-assorted row of squat houses seen through the window, Juan Muraña touching his hat to acknowledge a greeting (Juan Muraña who two nights before *marked* Suárez the Chilean) . . .[3]

Carriego suddenly understands that distance has nothing to do with it, that the suburb of Palermo can be as easily glorified as the France of Alexandre Dumas, and its squalid knife-play be elevated to the heroic level of the sword-fights of noble musketeers.

This, Borges would say, is what literature does, and what it cannot help doing: it unrealizes and makes everything it touches more or less momentous. But there are limits. The idea, above all, that he himself might find, in writing fictions, a compensation for his bookishness, is absurd. His own situation is not to be compared with that of some downtrodden *orillero*, romancing so as to put a braver and a better face on things. Borges romances because he is a professional romancer, anxious to show us what romancing is. I cannot believe that Borges's fictions are born of humiliation, or of a genuine nostalgia for the bravery of those of his ancestors who went to war in South America in the epic days of the nineteenth century. Borges knows full well he has acquired a glory more permanent and widespread than theirs, and that they survive only in what he cares to write about them. His deprecation of himself is a literary affectation, a wish to exhibit himself as an exemplary author, driven to aggrandize himself by the knowledge of his intimate inadequacies.

He is well prepared, in this way, to sacrifice the reputation of the

[3] *OC*, p. 157.

man to the requirements of the author. The author, as we have repeatedly seen, alone exists for Borges; the man behind the author is a fiction. This occlusion of the one by the other is a shock to much orthodox literary opinion. Normally, an author is seen as the derivative of the man, and whatever he writes as being in a high degree determined by the sort of man he is. The man takes precedence, and his freedom, as an author, is greatly restricted by his psychological limitations as a man. It is this common, deterministic mode of argument which Borges upends by according the precedence to the author and seeing the man, if at all, as the derivative form. His own supposed inadequacies as a man do not explain his fiction at all, they are explained *by* it: they are the deductions which would be made from its evidence by just the sort of deterministic reader we have invoked.

But Borges's literary system is too intelligent and too comprehensive to permit of these facile transitions from literature to life. His system is one which invalidates, once and for all, the explanation of a literary fact by a biographical one. Literary facts may be *also* biographical facts, but that does not satisfactorily explain what they are doing in a work of literature. They require a literary explanation, because when they pass from life into literature their meaning changes; they have been chosen, they have been set into a structure. And the structure of a literary work is never, not even in the case of a biography, the equivalent of the structure of a life. Literary meanings can only be established by estimating the value of facts within the economy of the work as a whole. The value of the facts contained in a biography does not lie in their veracity, that all these things actually happened, it lies in the logic of their arrangement, or in what one is quite entitled to call the 'plot' which the biographer has contrived from them.

Authors, with Borges, resist conflation with the men whose names they bear. He asks us to disown the trickery whereby we project, from the written evidence, a human 'personality' which we then hypostatize as somehow independent of, and prior to, that written evidence, but linked to it causally. As readers we encounter authors, never men. If, subsequently, we learn something of the life of the man, apart from his authorship, determinism once again takes over and whatever we have learnt of his life is used to justify something in his work. The *locus classicus* of the whole process of course, is Shakespeare, with whom we get the most author for the least man. The remarkably persistent desire to add a life of Shakespeare to the works of Shakespeare hides the fact that, inasmuch as Shakespeare is the author of these works, the works *are* his life. The old joke goes to the heart of the matter: that if Shakespeare's plays are not by Shakespeare, then they are by someone else of the same name.

For Borges an author begins and ends with his published *oeuvre*. He is little more than a hypothesis. We know that literary works cannot, so far at any rate, come into existence on their own, so we infer from the existence of a particular work to the existence of an author for it. Literary works, like all other phenomena, are the visible effects of the invisible operations of a Will, and we can have no experience of that Will except by its effects. Were we, indeed, to be as fanatically idealist as the inhabitants of Tlön, we might disallow the belief that the intermittent effects of the Will— or successive works of literature bearing the same author's name— argued the existence of some subsisting agent; that, in Tlön, would rank as a materialist heresy.

There is no call to go quite so far, however. Just as Hume brought in the faculty of imagination to supply continuity to the phenomenal comings and goings of Berkeley, so we can allow the author as the enduring synthesis of his admittedly sporadic manifestations of himself. But many will still resent what they see as a radical hiatus between the author and the man, because it robs them of their favourite assumptions about literature being the expression of life, as if living were some kind of dress rehearsal for writing. Borges would free authorship from all such psychological constraints and replace them with formal constraints. He sees it as naïve and derogatory to believe that what we write is determined by what we are, but sensible to believe that what we are, as authors, is determined by what we write.

He seems, at moments, to be saying that we could, given time, write *anything*; and certainly that we could all of us together, given time, exhaust our language's possibilities. Against this extreme, and extremely provocative, doctrine, though, one might set what he writes in the 'Nota sobre (hacia) Bernard Shaw' about a combinatorial literature—an essay written some years after the story of 'La biblioteca de Babel' as it happens:

If literature were no more than a verbal algebra, anyone could produce any book, by dint of trying out variations. The lapidary formula, *All is in flux (todo fluye)* abridges the philosophy of Heraclitus into two words; Raymond Lull would tell us that, given the first word, it is enough to try out the intransitive verbs in order to discover the second and to obtain, thanks to a mechanical accident, this philosophy, and very many others. Suffice it to reply that the formula obtained by elimination would lack value and even sense: for it to have some virtue we need to conceive of it in terms of Heraclitus, in terms of an experience had by Heraclitus, although 'Heraclitus' is nothing more than the presumed subject of that experience.[4]

This sober reasoning puts a brake to some extent on the extravagance of 'El biblioteca de Babel', where the fortuitous composition of the books is no deterrent to the librarians. But Borges is not relapsing into any narrow determinism, whereby Heraclitus's aphorism is the only possible outcome of his experience of life. Indeed, he is making no concessions at all: 'Heraclitus' is the hypothesis advanced by the readers of a number of fragments of a notoriously disjointed pre-Socratic philosophy in order to guarantee the coherence of those fragments. As well as ascribing those fragments to 'Heraclitus', we circumscribe them with 'Heraclitus' so to speak, branding them with that convenient name and so creating an early Greek philosopher. 'Heraclitus' is a postulate, and does not have to correspond with the facts. Provided that we believe the philosophy so labelled to be the work of an actual Greek thinker, all is well. A philosophy created by a mechanical, combinatorial method might be taken perfectly seriously were it to be attributed afterwards to a flesh-and-blood philosopher. We do not know what experiences 'Heraclitus' may have had to determine his particular doctrine, or what kind of experiences could be held to determine any philosophical doctrine, but we know he had experiences because we all have them; the phantom philosopher's freedom to have put forward quite different teachings from those he did put forward is not at risk.

Borges has also made things a bit easier for himself by taking the example of a philosopher, rather than a writer of fiction (although philosophies, as we know, *are* a form of fiction for Borges). As readers of philosophy, we expect its doctrines to be empirically founded, and its propositions verified, wherever possible, from the experience of the philosopher himself. With fiction as such, which

[4] *OC*, p. 748.

is not doctrinaire, the gap between experience and expression is necessarily much wider, and we should not be deluded by obvious consistencies in what authors do write into believing that they could not have written different things altogether. An author is a name on a certain collection of published works; like the name of one of his characters, his own name binds together a variety of characteristics and because they are bound together we find them consistent. The authors whom we postulate, after reading one or more of their books, are more protean images than we might care to admit. It is doubtful whether any author could publish a book which destroyed our belief in his consistency altogether. However incongruous the new evidence seems, we will do our utmost to match it to the old.

It is to jolt us out of these thoughtless prejudices about authorship that Borges toys with ideas of literature as an *ars combinatoria*. He asks only that we understand the principles of the Library of Babel, not that we believe in them. Once we do understand them, we shall take a different view of the relationship between texts and their authors. We shall feel a greater respect for such paragons as Pierre Menard, who has regularly, in the course of his literary career, put his name to opinions contrary to those he holds (*precisely* contrary, which perhaps is cheating), and who preaches that 'Every man must be capable of every idea and I intend that in the future he shall be'. This subversive programme has profound effects on what he calls the 'diffident and rudimentary art of reading', and 'peoples the most sedate books with adventure': 'To attribute the *Imitatio Christi* to Louis Ferdinand Céline or James Joyce, is that not a sufficient renovation of those tenuous spiritual counsels?'[5] If we believed that the foul-mouthed Céline or the bawdy Joyce were really the author of the *Imitatio Christi* it would 'renovate' both book and author.[6] It would entail a considerable revision of our conception of both Céline and Joyce, to envisage

[5] *OC*, p. 450.

[6] It would perhaps surprise and please Borges to know that Céline did once have something to say about the author of the *Imitatio*. Writing in *Candide*, in March 1933, after the publication of *Voyage au bout de la nuit*, he is very flattering to him: 'Thomas à Kempis, who was very pure, knew a thing or two about art, and about souls too. Pity he's dead. Here's how he spoke: "Don't try and imitate the warbler or the nightingale, he said, if you can't! But if it's your lot to sing like a toad, then go to it! And as loud as you can! And let them hear you!"' This particular rendering of Thomas à Kempis by Céline certainly counts, by the sound of it, as a 'renovation' of the original.

them as authors of a manual of piety. We could absorb this new evidence only by talking in terms of a 'conversion', the classic instances of which have always involved just such an exchange of one set of values for their opposites. For Borges, dialectician to the last, has actually made things simpler for us by postulating not moderately unlikely authors for the *Imitatio* but systematically unlikely ones, authors whose every published word contradicts the possibility. There is an important restriction here on the freedom of any author to write anything: since he starts out from what has been written already, he will be led to contradict that. The ideas he gets depend absolutely on the ideas which have already been got; his freedom is to say 'no' to them, even though he may agree with them.

To detach the *Imitatio Christi* from Thomas à Kempis (whose name is not in fact mentioned in 'Pierre Menard'), and reattribute it not to one but, this being Borges, two other authors whom we know to have been born too late and whom we trust to have been temperamentally incapable of writing it, is to prepare us for Borges's ideal, which is an anonymous literature, or books without author's names on them. This is not a new ideal: Borges himself names certain predecessors who also held it—Valéry, Emerson, and Shelley—even if the nomination of his predecessors is not the most telling argument in favour of anonymity. On the other hand, it may be said that if others before Borges have believed the same of literature then that belief transcends such individuals as have subscribed to it; it is an idea drawn from stock, not to be patented by any one person.

But if it is not a new idea, neither is it a fashionable one. Because so few people countenance it, those who do so distinguish themselves in the act—they make their name by proposing anonymity. The vested interests which co-operate against anonymity will always prove stronger than the handful of more Classical thinkers who would prefer to see ideas granted a greater autonomy, free from the name-tags we are so quick to pin to them, and the credit for literary invention going more to language and literary tradition than to the demiurges whose names are published on the covers of books. The prospect of a 'history without names' in art, first mooted many years ago by Wölfflin, seems no nearer fulfilment now than it did then, and the motive of many art historians still seems to be the certain attribution of as many paintings as possible.

In literature, similarly, anonymity is still generally thought intolerable. Where the authorship of a work is unknown, the chances are nowadays that its contents will be tabulated and fed to a computer in order to see if its syntactic idiosyncrasies tally with those of some identifiable contemporary author. Borges is up against the *force majeure* of bibliography, the publishing industry, and the vanity of authors. His call for anonymity is, as he well knows, doomed; perhaps we should take it as the call for vengeance of a librarian, forced to pass his time grimly cataloguing trivial, undistinguishable works under their proud author's name.

But if the ideal of anomymity will never be realized, and may not in any case be seriously intended by Borges, that is no reason for discarding the arguments he has made on its behalf. We *should*, in our literary judgements, allow that an author's native language is as much in control of him as he of it, and that so-called expressiveness in words is conventional not natural. Words do not come singly when we write: one word is associated with other words and those associations are as likely to be accidents of the language itself as of our own life-history. We cannot claim all the credit for them. Nor can we claim the credit for all the meanings which the words we use convey, when the meanings we convey may differ widely from the meanings we believe we are conveying. Most of the meanings to which we put our name are not, in any case, peculiar to ourselves; our thoughts are mostly thoughts which have been thought before and which we may well be remembering from our own reading or conversation. Our powers of appropriation of language far exceed our powers of origination in language. Whoever calls something that he reads 'original' really means 'original for me': originality is something we have not experienced before in reading, not something inherent in the text itself. Pierre Menard's two chapters of *Don Quijote* would strike a reader as highly 'original' if he had never come across Cervantes.

In a recent story, 'Utopía de un hombre que está cansado' ('Utopia of a Man who is Tired'), Borges looks forward, not for the first time, to that final state of a literature where everything has already been written. All the new writer needs to do is to consult the old: 'language is a system of quotations'.[7] Originality is out of the question. Traditional conceptions of authorship could hardly

[7] *El libro de arena*, p. 129.

survive under these extreme conditions, and the one Utopian whom the narrator of the story talks with is wholly anonymous— 'they call me anyone', he says. He is an Anyone among Anyones. But he is not a man among men in the real world, he is a dweller in a definitively idealised world from which every last vestige of unprocessed reality has been excluded. In Borges's Utopia, which is the fantastic end of the literary road, there are only representations, and the sum of representations is now complete. This, it seems, is a land where personal identity is no longer needed, or where it can only be constructed, by whatever Anyone chooses to quote. In this Utopia to create is no more than to compile.

Seen as he should be seen, as an author, Borges's Utopian is thus the author of a *cento*, a scrupulously second-hand work assembled from quotations. He is an author, moreover, only when the *cento* is complete: its completion is also the process by which he identifies himself. To write, for Borges, is to realize oneself as an author, not to express oneself as a man. This, I think, is how we ought to interpret his epilogue to *El Hacedor*:

A man proposes to himself the task of delineating the world. As the years pass he peoples a space with the images of provinces, kingdoms, mountains, bays, ships, islands, fish, dwellings, instruments, stars, horses, and persons. Shortly before he dies, he discovers that this patient labyrinth of lines traces the image of his own face.[8]

A naïve reading of this brief parable would have the practice of literature to be a voyage of 'self-discovery', but that is a banal idea and not Borges's idea at all. His idea is not one of self-discovery but of self-creation; his literary voyager has passed from being a man to being an author. The 'face' whose image he leaves behind him is not his man's face which he wanted to 'express', it is his identity as an author, the 'Heraclitus' whom his readers will evoke so as to endow what he has written with its full human value. As readers, the face of the author is the only face we know, the face of the man stays for ever hidden. As readers of autobiography we trust that the face of the author bears a close resemblance to the face of the man (and we have, with autobiography, the extra assurance that whatever an autobiographer writes is autobiographical, that an obvious lack of resemblance between author and man is as revealing as an imputed resemblance). With fiction, the situation changes,

[8] *OC*, p. 854.

and the resemblance between one face and the other becomes decidedly problematical.

The author, then, is the sum of his inventions. He is to be identified not, as so often happens, with a part of his invention, with this character rather than that, but with all of them. Borges's ideal author, very naturally, is Shakespeare, the 'myriad-minded' dramatist, who is ideal because he is so apparently contradictory, the most gifted in the invention of incompatible characters. No psychological phantasm, constructed to 'explain' his plays, even begins to succeed, because the virtualities of the plays are too rich to be fitted inside so crude a model of the human mind. Shakespeare simply had and wrote down too many thoughts; he disproves, as no one else has done, the psychological determinism which imposes such strict limits on what an author is free to express.

In *El Hacedor* Borges imagines Shakespeare as coming face to face with God:

[Shakespeare] said to him: *I, who have been so many men in vain, wish to be one and I.* The voice of God answered him from a whirlwind: *I am not either; I dreamt the world as you dreamt your work, my Shakespeare, and amongst the forms of my dream was you, who like me were many and no one.*[9]

It is the misfortune of this Shakespeare—who, incidentally, is not named in the piece until he is named by God, right at the end—to be confronted with a resolutely Borgesian Creator, an even greater dreamer than himself. The author who seeks at the last to be re-integrated into a man meets only another author. And behind that author . . . Borges leaves us groping with mingled admiration and dismay among the circular ruins, where the dreamer's final realization, after he has succeeded in imposing his dream on reality, is that he himself is being dreamt. There is to be no way out of literature into life, no way of equating the author with the man.

[9] *OC*, p. 804.

CHAPTER 3

THE USES OF USELESSNESS

BORGES'S Shakespeare, in his request to God, would have us believe that his creative endeavours have been 'in vain'. A last but important question which arises with Borges is what does this apparent pessimism mean? Shakespeare is far from being alone amongst his fictive authors in questioning the value of what he has accomplished. 'There is no intellectual exercise which is not, in the end, useless (*inútil*)', affirms the narrator of the story of 'Pierre Menard', and that particular word, *inútil*, is a key one in assessing the view which Borges ultimately takes of the purpose of literature.

At first sight it is a negative view: to regard something as 'useless' seems to be to disregard it altogether. But nothing which is made can be wholly useless, and certainly nothing which is made with the care and patience required of the maker of a fiction. If a fiction is 'useless' then we need to know what it is useless for. One would have to be far gone in utilitarianism not to be able to grasp that the useless may also be valuable, may indeed be particularly valuable. Borges is only pretending to belittle what he has spent part of his life doing; he is really defending and not condemning 'intellectual exercises' when he calls them 'useless'.

For our own taste, there may be something very old-fashioned, and Art-for-Art's-Sake-ish, about a defence of literature which claims that literature is valuable precisely *because* it is useless, because we cannot do anything with it. This is an argument we associate with more philistine ages than our own, and with the age, principally, of industrialization, when the 'use' of any object was liable to be judged instrumentally and literature valued, or not, according to how far it was seen to act instrumentally on human behaviour. But Borges, one should remember, lives in a society far less bookish even than our own, and one with a very much shorter literary history. His defence of 'uselessness' will seem fresher and more challenging, no doubt, to an Argentinian reader than it may do to us.

Whether or not this is the case, Borges is not being pessimistic with all these repeated evocations of the vanity of literature.

Literature, indeed, is almost the only institution about which he seems to feel optimism; even if it has no future it has a splendid past, and there is enough of it to last us all a lifetime even if its practice were to cease tomorrow. Borges is pessimistic where pessimism is more appropriate, about reality, about human societies and about history. His pessimism in that direction is the corollary of his optimism on the intellectual side, since literature for him is clearly a human achievement which deserves a better reality in which to be stored.

'My stories', writes Borges in the prologue to *El informe de Brodie*, 'like those of the Thousand and One Nights, seek to distract or to move (*conmover*), and not to persuade.'[1] Borges is comparing himself, perhaps, less with the anonymous authors of *The Thousand and One Nights* than with Scheherazade, the explicit narratrix of the tales, whose very life depends on her ability to distract the Caliph, that most bloodthirsty of readers. The structure of that remarkable anthology is such as to give distraction its due. Normally, distraction is looked down on as an inferior if not positively reprehensible withdrawal of the mind from what matters to what does not. 'Intellectual exercises' involve us in a more or less prolonged dissociation from extra-mental realities, and to anyone watching us we are not doing anything at all when we are 'lost' in thought. Our reflections do not immediately change anything in the public domain. But 'intellectual exercises', which pragmatists may deprecate as '*purely* intellectual exercises', are actually an unusually methodical and sustained mode of mental activity in general; a prejudice against them is a prejudice against thought itself. A moment's reflection may be too brief to qualify as an 'intellectual exercise', but it fails only on grounds of duration, not because of the kind of activity it is. The benefits of these momentary distractions are generally admitted, as clarifying our future activity in the world and enabling us to act intelligently where otherwise we would have acted blindly.

There is a degree of 'persuasion' in distraction, just as there is a degree of distraction in persuasion. In either case people must listen to us in order to be distracted or persuaded, and in order to listen to us they must remove their attention from whatever else solicits it. Persuasion too is an intellectual exercise. We all know what Borges means when he says that it is not his aim to persuade; he is

[1] *OC*, p. 1021.

distinguishing himself from those writers who, to fall back on a threadbare word, are 'committed', and who would persuade us by their writing to adopt and afterwards support some ideological position. As the representative of such persuasion, Borges chooses not one of its strident and portentous mouthpieces of the past thirty years, but Aesop.

Persuasion, the making of our listeners to be of one mind with ourselves, ranks amongst what the influential linguistic philosopher, J. L. Austin, calls 'perlocutionary' acts, which are the effects we intend or achieve in the world through our speech. Persuasion can be shown to have taken place by the change we observe in the behaviour of those who have been persuaded; they say and do different things as the result of being persuaded. Distraction and commotion (if that be allowed as the mental state produced in his readers by Borges's desire to *conmover*) are not so readily measured. But they *are* effects, and no experience of distraction or commotion leaves us exactly as we were before we had it. Borges has no interest in the cruder uses of literature; to him those are abuses. He does not believe that, by writing, he can make us morally more commendable, socially more desirable, or politically more decisive, or that it is right to try and do so. Such aims would be futile and tasteless. I incline to read the sinister story of 'El evangelio según Marcos' ('The Gospel according to Mark') as, in part, a parable about the effects of 'persuasion': there the passive, golden-tongued Espinosa (the name means 'thorny' and its thirty-three-year-old holder is, quite unobtrusively, a Christ-figure) persuades the degenerate family of *gauchos* with whom he is marooned in a flood so effectively with his readings to them from St. Mark's Gospel that in the end they set to and crucify him.

Borges's own stories have little to offer audiences of degenerate *gauchos*. They contain no calls or excuses for direct action. But as distractions, they justify themselves, as all literature justifies itself, by filling the time we give to them very profitably. They are incomparable stimulants to thought about literature, and to be made to think about the nature of literature is just as valuable as to be made to think more directly about life. No reader who has rethought for himself one-tenth of what Borges has himself thought about fiction is the same reader of fiction as he was before he read Borges. He will be, by any standard, a better reader, with a fuller understanding of the conventions of all literature. Borges offers not just distraction but the chance to improve our minds while they are distracted. He offers us also, it should not be forgotten, pleasure: the pleasure of observing a high and humorous intelligence at work on artefacts which are as memorable as they are intriguing.

But the strongest of all the possible justifications of mental distraction is that it marks a respite from the inflexible chronology of real life. We tend to think of distraction in spatial terms, as procuring our mental removal from one place to another, from a place we do not like to one we do, as an alibi. With Borges we do better to think of it as procuring our removal from time to eternity. 'Intellectual exercises' deliver us from our complete subjugation by the clock. They take place in time, of course, and the ideas which constitute them occur successively, but they set us as free in time as we can ever be by enabling us to rearrange the events of the past in any order we like, and to invent histories of our own. Nothing symbolizes the freedom of the mind more gloriously for Borges than anachronism, the anachronism which allows him, for instance, to point out that Chesterton refuted an argument of Croce's several years before Croce first made it. This is the anachronism of a reader of books. What Borges means is that he read Chesterton before he read Croce, and that there is no earthly reason why, as readers, we should worry about the chronology of books, or the order they were written in. Literature is a republic, a public affair, and also an eternity, where the only time scale is the one we bring to it ourselves.

There is nothing in the least mystical or extravagant about Borges's notion of eternity. He means by it nothing more far-fetched than the ideal world whose temporality is formed, as Berkeley believed the temporality of our real world to be formed, by the succession of ideas in our minds. Any notion of time other than this was, for Berkeley, an illicit abstraction. It is this Berkelyan conception of time which applies, willy-nilly, to fiction. The only real time scale of a fiction is the one formed by the succession of ideas (or words) which constitute the fiction. That succession of ideas may well contain allusions to another time scale, of which the first is a necessary abridgement: 'two years' on the time scale alluded to last, literally, two words on the first time scale. When we are distracted from time into the eternity of a fiction, therefore, we exchange a temporality regulated, not at all for our comfort, from without, to a thoroughly congenial one regulated from within.

Borges never dreams the impossible dream of stopping time dead; he exploits, as all narrative is bound to do, the possibilities of postponing it. The private time scale of a fiction begins with the withdrawal of the author into the unmolested seclusion of his mind. The clock, which records the public passage of time, stops. But the clock will eventually have to be restarted; the author's retirement must be balanced out by his return to the real world and its insistent chronometry. It is that unavoidable moment which the narrative keeps at bay. The ultimate dénouement is, for the narrator, a metaphorical death, since there is nothing left for him to narrate. It is this metaphorical death which threatens the tirelessly inventive Scheherazade and which she finally avoids, against all the rules, by marrying her audience.

Narratives are often divided, especially by the stodgier analysts of fiction, into a beginning, a middle, and an end. That division is misleading, if it convinces us that these three parts of a narrative are somehow equal. It is more profitable to think of a narrative as nearly all middle. The middle is that justification of the end which takes the beginning as its datum, and the middle of a narrative can be as short or as long as its author wishes. There is, in principle, no limit to the number of episodes he may insert between the beginning and the end; there is always room for one more. Borges, in particular, has always enjoyed speculating into these series which are infinitely extensible, into Lewis Carroll's games with syllogisms, for example, which would defer their conclusion for ever.[2] But he never pretends that this kind of deferment of the inevitable is anything more than a game, an 'intellectual exercise'. The mind is never wholly free of time and there is no ultimate salvation in Borges's eternity. Distraction must have a stop. We can postpone our reunion with reality but we cannot avoid it.

The story which would seem to be most methodically founded on the narrative principle of postponement is that early, and favourite one, 'El Sur'. The 'accident' which befalls Juan Dahlmann early on in the story, and which is the contingency that the story will redeem, is described as fate's way of punishing 'tiny distractions'. Dahlmann is hurrying upstairs to enjoy his new-found copy of *The Thousand and One Nights* when it happens. Satisfaction lies at the top of the stairs, and the stairs, as we saw in the case of that other, even earlier, fiction of deferred satisfaction,

---

[2] 'Avatares de la tortuga' ('Avatars of the Tortoise'), *OC*, p. 257.

'El brujo postergado', are themselves a prefiguration of the 'ascent' the narrative makes, of the immediate, magical elevation of the diffident Dahlmann into a fictional hero. Scheherazade, keeping fate at bay in old Baghdad, is Dahlmann's model, as he pursues his own labyrinthine way to his fate in the South. *The Thousand and One Nights*, that exemplary narration, is a source of light for the man who would make a fiction of his own, and it is the *illustrations* of his copy of the work which serve to 'decorate nightmares' as Dahlmann sinks into the creative fever preceding his last, fateful journey.

It is during that journey that *The Thousand and One Nights* reappears in the story. Dahlmann's departure has already been postponed, as we saw in an earlier chapter, by his discovery that he must wait for a train; the interval of time thus made available to him he has spent in the café, with its large, oddly inspiring cat. He returns to the railway station:

Alongside the last platform but one stood the train. Dahlmann examined the coaches and found one which was nearly empty. He settled his case on the luggage-rack (*red*); when the carriages started off, he opened it and took out, after some hesitation, the first volume of the 1001 Nights. To travel with this book, so bound up with the story of his mishap, was an affirmation that that mishap had been annulled and a happy, secret challenge (*desafío*) to the frustrated forces of evil.[3]

The principle of deferment has even determined, apparently, the position of the train in the station: it is not at the end of the station but just before the end, and it is this train which will, a little later in the story, set Dahlmann down not at the usual station but at another, just before it. Once again his satisfaction is delayed. He does not start reading the book right away because of the 'vision' of what he sees through the window of the train, which is that characteristic sight in Borges, the city 'breaking up' into suburbs, as the landscape passes from an urban to a rural one, or from a sordid to a heroic. Dahlmann reads very little; it is 'felicity' (a state of mind one might well associate with his visit to the cat or *felis* before he started out) which now distracts him from 'Scheherazade and her superfluous miracles'. The 'superfluity' is of two kinds: the miracles are superfluous for Dahlmann because he now finds an equally ideal satisfaction in his reality as in fantasies, and super-

[3] *OC*, p. 527.

fluous also in the sense in which all fictions are superfluous, for Borges, that is to say unnecessary in practical, utilitarian terms. The sequence of Dahlmann's distractions is not yet over. As one would anticipate, the mechanical system of his train journey is disrupted. Looking out on the now wholly rural landscape, Dahlmann feels a suspicion that his journey is not only a geographical one, but also temporal, that he is travelling into the past as well as to the South:

From this fantastic conjecture he was distracted by the ticket-inspector who, looking at his ticket, warned him that the train would leave him not at the usual station but at another, a little this side of it, which Dahlmann scarcely knew. (The man added an explanation which Dahlmann did not attempt to understand or even to hear, because the mechanism of events did not matter to him.)[4]

The ticket-inspector takes his place in the series of distractions, as an intrusion on Dahlmann's dream. He represents the reality principle, and his 'mechanical' explanations of events are of no interest.

Dahlmann never reaches the *estancia* which was his planned destination. Having got off the train at the obscure station before the usual one, he fetches up not at his ancestral home but at a comparably ramshackle *almacén*. Its owner promises to provide Dahlmann with a *jardinera* to take him on to his destination. A *jardinera* is a kind of open carriage but its obvious associations with the *jardín* or 'garden' makes it a highly appropriate vehicle for any Borgesian hero to travel in, as he picks his way through his 'garden of forking paths'. Dahlmann, in the end, never needs the *jardinera*; he leaves the *almacén* on foot, knife in hand, thanks to the connivance of the ageless *gaucho*, for what he, and we, foresee as his certain death in a duel.

This duel, or ultimate *desafío*, is brought about, very trivially, by the throwing of two pellets of bread. When the first one hits him Dahlmann feels a slight 'brushing' (*roce*) against his face, just as, originally, as he climbed the stairs to his home with his copy of *The Thousand and One Nights*, something had 'brushed against' (*rozó*) his forehead. His response to this first insult is to decide 'that nothing had happened'. He seeks distraction; he again opens

[4] *OC*, p. 528.

his copy of *The Thousand and One Nights* 'as if to stop up (*tapar*) reality'. But a second pellet strikes him and his fate is sealed.

The newly painted door left open on the stairs, the view from the train window, the ticket-inspector, the pellets of bread, all recall Dahlmann from fantasy to 'fact'. But equally they all contribute to the elaboration of the fantasy in which he is the protagonist, the fantasy which, perhaps, we might see as completing the 'incomplete' copy of *The Thousand and One Nights* which he has bought and which he carries with him to the South. The 'challenges' which fate offers to Dahlmann are challenges to prove himself a literary hero, to pursue his fiction to its conclusion. The book with which he travels is a viaticum. It is the instigator of his original mishap, when it causes him to run distractedly up the stairs instead of taking the lift, but it also, as a work of fiction, shows him how to make use of that mishap, and 'annul' it. Like the sanatorium, the book is ambivalent, a source both of pain and of therapy.

The 'forces of evil' are, however, only 'frustrated' not defeated. *The Thousand and One Nights*, that 'happy (*alegre*), secret challenge' to them, does not save Dahlmann in the saloon, when the peons who inexplicably throw bread at him are described by the owner as 'half-merry' (*medio alegres*). They are necessary to Dahlmann just as, we saw, Judas was necessary to Jesus: his narrative cannot function without them. They are his own other, and worse, half, on whom his final happiness depends. For Dahlmann dies, let us assume, happily. His hour has come but it has not come as it might have come; he will die not as the commonplace victim of an accident, and an absurdly trivial accident at that, but as the hero of a legend. The 'secretary of the municipal library in the Calle Córdoba' has done himself proud, his suburban destiny and drudgery have been crowned in glory. The deferment of his end was well worth while, when one appreciates what a cheerful face the process of fiction can put on the dismal fact of death.

That process, for Borges, is a serial one; in his eternity we can at least pretend, as the Eleatic Zeno pretended in his paradox, that time is really space, and that we can play divisive games with it without growing any older ourselves as we do so. Borges, with his love of symmetrical compositions, of events arranged in series, and of narratives whose end is also in their beginning, exemplifies as few writers do what the Formalist Eichenbaum claims to be 'the general principle of verbal art's being structured step by step, with progress arrested'.[5] He has every right repeatedly to symbolize his own constructions as edifices. We do not think of buildings as being extended in time, although, as we walk around them, they are. In just the same way, a fiction is an architectural structure which we extend in time by reading it.

The most grandiose architect to be found in Borges is the Chinese emperor Shih Huang Ti, celebrated for having inaugurated the Great Wall of China and for having burnt all the books published before his own time. This emperor, according to Borges, prohibited the mention of death and 'shut himself up in a figurative palace' with as many rooms as the year has days. These data, if they really are data, 'suggest that the wall in time and the fire in space were magical barriers intended to detain death'.[6] Shih Huang Ti is a master of artifice, clearly, and a man after Borges's own heart. He may, indeed, have called himself Huang Ti after 'the legendary emperor who invented writing and the compass'. The 'figurative palace', in which the divisions of the solar cycle have become the divisions of a comfortably enclosed space, is the ideal construction of a man adept at deferment. The emperor Huang Ti is dead, but while he lived he taught valuable lessons in the detainment of death.

And one of his ideal constructions, the Great Wall, is still there. For the final paradox of such constructive Idealism is that it adds to the stock of real things. Borges, as a maker of fictions, has made material objects—books—out of his immaterial speculations. The mirror, which represents the objects in the world, is itself an object in the world. Once they have acquired this real, durable form, an author's 'intellectual exercises' become a factor in the intellectual experience of whoever reads them. They are, in a double sense, an imposition: a product of the printing-press and a make-believe. And as real objects they also enter into the unimaginably complex system of causes and effects of which history consists. We cannot know what effects a particular work of literature will cause, but we can be sure that it will not be without effect. It exists, in Borges's own terms, at the point of intersection between a past and a future.

[5] *Readings in Russian Poetics*, p. 16.
[6] *OC*, pp. 633–4.

Behind it there extends the pyramid of causes of which it is itself the effect; ahead of it, as a speculation, the pyramid of effects of which it will be the cause. For better or for worse, the pyramid of effects which stretched ahead of Borges's exemplary fictions when they were first published included the present study.

BIBLIOGRAPHY

BORGES

The bibliography of Borges is complicated by his own suppression of certain earlier writings, by variations in content between successive editions of the same title, and by a suitably Borgesian duplication of particular items, which appear in more than one book. The bibliography given here has been simplified; anyone who wants the full story of Borges's publications, and the publications on him, should consult Horacio Jorge Becco's *Jorge Luis Borges: Bibliografía total, 1923–1973*, Buenos Aires, Casa Pardo, 1973.

Fiction

Historia universal de la infamia, Buenos Aires, Ediciones Tor, 1935. Reprinted by Emecé Editores with minor additions as Volume Three of *Obras completas* in 1954.

El jardín de senderos que se bifurcan, Buenos Aires, Editorial Sur, 1942.

Ficciones (1935–44), Buenos Aires, Editorial Sur, 1944. This contains the eight stories already published as *El jardín de senderos que se bifurcan*, together with six new ones. Reprinted by Emecé with the addition of three more stories in 1956 as Volume Five of the *Obras completas*.

El Aleph, Buenos Aires, Editorial Losada, 1949. Four stories were added to the second edition of 1952. Reprinted by Emecé in 1957 as Volume Seven of the *Obras completas*.

El informe de Brodie, Buenos Aires, Emecé Editores, 1970.

El libro de arena, Buenos Aires, Emecé Editores, 1975.

In English:

Ficciones, trans. Anthony Kerrigan and others, New York, Grove Press, 1962; London, Weidenfeld and Nicolson, 1962 (paperback, London, John Calder, 1965).

The Aleph and other stories, 1933–1969, trans. Norman Thomas di Giovanni, New York, Dutton, 1970; London, Cape, 1971. The contents do not coincide with the Spanish-language editions of *El Aleph*.

A Universal History of Infamy, trans. Norman Thomas di Giovanni, New York, Dutton, 1972; London, Allen Lane, 1973.

Doctor Brodie's Report, trans. Norman Thomas di Giovanni, New York, Dutton, 1972; London, Cape, 1974.

Essays

Inquisiciones, Buenos Aires, Editorial Proa, 1925.

El tamaño de mi esperanza, Buenos Aires, Editorial Proa, 1926.

El idioma de los Argentinos, Buenos Aires, Manuel Gleizer, 1928.

Evaristo Carriego, Buenos Aires, Manuel Gleizer, 1930. Reprinted with additions by Emecé in 1955 as Volume Four of the *Obras completas*.

Discusión, Buenos Aires, Manuel Gleizer, 1932, Reprinted with suppressions and additions by Emecé in 1957 as Volume Six of the *Obras completas*.

Historia de la eternidad, Buenos Aires, Editorial Viau y Zona, 1936. Reprinted with additions by Emecé in 1953 as Volume One of the *Obras completas*.

Otras inquisiciones (1937–1952), Buenos Aires, Editorial Sur, 1952. Reprinted with minor suppressions and additions by Emecé in 1960 as Volume Eight of the *Obras completas* (trans. Ruth L. C. Simms, *Other Inquisitions*, Austin, University of Texas Press, 1964), 1964.

Prólogos, Buenos Aires, Torres Agüero, 1975.

Poetry

Fervor de Buenos Aires, Buenos Aires, Serrantes, 1923.

Luna de enfrente, Buenos Aires, Editorial Proa, 1925.

Cuaderno San Martín, Buenos Aires, Editorial Proa, 1929.

El Hacedor, Buenos Aires, Emecé Editores, 1960. Volume Nine of the *Obras completas* (trans. Mildred Boyer and Harold Morland, *Dreamtigers*, Austin, University of Texas Press, 1964).

Para las seis cuerdas, Buenos Aires, Emecé Editores, 1965.

Elogio de la sombra, Buenos Aires, Emecé Editores, 1969 (trans. Norman Thomas di Giovanni, *In Praise of Darkness*, New York, Dutton, 1974; London, Allen Lane, 1975).

El otro, el mismo, Buenos Aires, Emecé Editores, 1969.

El oro de los tigres, Buenos Aires, Emecé Editores, 1972.

The numerous and varied anthologies of Borges's poetry published by Emecé are not listed. In English there is *Selected Poems, 1923–1967*, ed. Norman Thomas di Giovanni, New York, Delacorte Press, 1972; London, Allen Lane, 1972.

Other anthologies of Borges in English are *Labyrinths*, New York, New Directions, 1961; London, Penguin, 1970, which contains stories, essays, and a few short prose pieces from *El Hacedor*; and *A Personal Anthology*, New York, Grove Press, 1967; London, Cape, 1968, a translation of Borges's own *Antología personal*, Buenos Aires, Editorial Sur, 1961.

Collaborative works

With Adolfo Bioy Casares:

Seis problemas para don Isidro Parodi, Buenos Aires, Editorial Sur, 1942.
Dos fantasías memorables, Buenos Aires, Oportet y Haereses, 1946.
Un modelo para la muerte, Buenos Aires, Oportet y Haereses, 1946.
Los orilleros. El paraíso de los creyentes, Buenos Aires, Editorial Losada, 1955.
Crónicas de Bustos Domecq, Buenos Aires, Editorial Losada, 1967.

With Margarita Guerrero:

Manual de zoología fantástica, Mexico/Buenos Aires, Fondo de Cultura Económica, 1957. Reprinted, with variations, as *El libro de seres imaginarios*, Buenos Aires, Editorial Kier, 1967 (trans. Norman Thomas di Giovanni in collaboration with the author, *The Book of Imaginary Beings*, with additions, New York, Dutton, 1969; London, Cape, 1970).

With Delia Ingenieros:

Antiguas literaturas germánicas, Mexico/Buenos Aires, Fondo de Cultura Económica, 1951.

With María Esther Vásquez:

Literaturas germánicas medievales, Buenos Aires, Falbo Librero, 1966.

Complete Works

The nine volumes of the *Obras completas* published by Emecé were in 1974 consolidated into the one-volume *Obras completas*. The original separate Emecé volumes are also available in the Libro de Bolsillo series published in Madrid by Alianza.

Books on Borges as a writer of fiction

ALAZRAKI, JAIME, *La prosa narrativa de Jorge Luis Borges*, Madrid, Gredos, 1968.
——*Jorge Luis Borges*, New York and London, Columbia Univ. Press, 1971 (Columbia Essays on Modern Writers, No. 57).

BARNATÁN, MARCOS R., *Borges*, Madrid, Epesa, 1972.
BARRENECHEA, ANA MARÍA, *La expresión de la irrealidad en la obra de Jorge Luis Borges,* Mexico, Colegio de México, 1957.
BASTOS, MARÍA LUISA, *Borges ante la crítica argentina, 1923–1960*, Buenos Aires, Editorial Hispanamérica, 1974.

BERVEILLER, MICHEL, *Le Cosmopolitanisme de Jorge Luis Borges*, Paris, Didier, 1973.

BOSCO, MARÍA ANGÉLICA, *Borges y los otros*, Buenos Aires, General Fabril, 1967.

BURGIN, RICHARD, *Conversations with Jorge Luis Borges*, New York, Holt, Rhinehart and Winston, 1969.

CHARBONNIER, GEORGES, *Entretiens avec Jorge Luis Borges*, Paris, Gallimard, 1967.

CHRIST, RONALD J., *The Narrow Act: Borges's Art of Allusion*, New York Univ. Press, 1969.

COHEN, J. M., *Jorge Luis Borges*, Edinburgh, Oliver and Boyd, 1973.

COZARINSKY, EDGARDO, *Borges y el ciné*, Buenos Aires, Editorial Sur, 1974 (contains Borges's own early film criticism).

DUNHAM, LOWELL, and IVASK, IVAR (eds.), *The Cardinal Points of Borges*, Norman, Univ. of Oklohoma Press, 1971.

FERRER, MANUEL, *Borges y la nada*, London, Tamesis Books, 1971.

GUTIÉRREZ GIRARDOT, RAFAEL, *Jorge Luis Borges, ensayo de interpretación*, Madrid, Insula, 1959.

CAHIERS DE L'HERNE, *Jorge Luis Borges*, Paris, 1964.

IBARRA, NÉSTOR, *Borges et Borges*, Paris, L'Herne, 1969.

IRBY, JAMES E., MURAT, NAPOLEÓN, and PERALTA, CARLOS, *Encuentro con Borges*, Buenos Aires, Galerna, 1968.

JURADO, ALICIA, *Genio y figura de Jorge Luis Borges*, Buenos Aires, Universitaria de Buenos Aires, 1964.

MATAMORO, BLAS, *Jorge Luis Borges o el juego trascendente*, Buenos Aires, A. Peña Lillo, 1971.

MILLERET, JEAN DE, *Entretiens avec Jorge Luis Borges*, Paris, Belfond, 1967.

MURILLO, LUIS A., *The Cyclical Night: Irony in James Joyce and Jorge Luis Borges*, Cambridge, Mass., Harvard Univ. Press, 1968.

OCAMPO, VICTORIA, *Diálogo con Borges*, Buenos Aires, Editorial Sur, 1969.

PÉREZ, ALBERTO C., *Realidad y suprarrealidad en los cuentos fantásticos de Jorge Luis Borges*, Miami, Ediciones Universal, 1971.

PRIETO, ADOLFO, *Borges y la nueva generación*, Buenos Aires, Letras Universitarias, 1954.

RODRÍGUEZ MONEGAL, EMIR, *Borges par lui-même*, Paris, Seuil, 1970.

SHAW, D. L., *Borges: Ficciones*, London, Grant and Cutler, 1976.
STABB, MARTIN S., *Jorge Luis Borges*, New York, Twayne, 1970.

TAMAYO, MARCIAL, and RUIZ DÍAZ, ADOLFO, *Borges, enigma y clave*, Buenos Aires, Nuestro Tiempo, 1955.

WHEELOCK, K. CARTER, *The Mythmaker: A Study of Motif and Symbol in the Short Stories of Jorge Luis Borges*, Austin, Univ. of Texas Press, 1969.

NARRATIVE

I give here a short list of books particularly useful in the study of narrative or, more broadly, of the theory of fiction.

BARTHES, ROLAND, *Essais critiques*, Paris, Seuil, 1964 (tr. *Critical Essays*, Northwestern Univ. Press, 1972).
——*S/Z*, Paris, Seuil, 1970 (trans. Richard Howard, *S/Z*, London, Cape, 1975).
BOOTH, WAYNE, *The Rhetoric of Fiction*, Univ. of Chicago Press, 1961.
BREMOND, CLAUDE, *Logique du récit*, Paris, Seuil, 1973.

CULLER, JONATHAN, *Structuralist Poetics*, London, Routledge and Kegan Paul, 1975.

FORSTER, E. M., *Aspects of the Novel*, London, Arnold, 1927.
FRYE, NORTHROP, *Anatomy of Criticism*, Princeton Univ. Press, 1971.

GENETTE, GÉRARD, *Figures I, II, and III*, Paris, Seuil, 1966, 1969, 1972.
GREIMAS, A. J., *Sémantique structurale*, Paris, Larousse, 1966.
——*Du sens*, Paris, Seuil, 1970.

JAKOBSON, ROMAN, *Questions de poétique*, Paris, Seuil, 1973.
JAMES, HENRY, *The Art of the Novel*, New York, Scribner, 1947.

KERMODE, FRANK, *The Sense of an Ending*, New York, Oxford Univ. Press, 1967.
KRISTEVA, JULIA, *Le Texte du roman*, The Hague, Mouton, 1970.

LUBBOCK, PERCY, *The Craft of Fiction*, London, Cape, 1921.
MATEJKA, LADISLAV, and POMORSKA, KRYSTYNA (eds.), *Readings in Russian Poetics*, Cambridge, Mass., MIT Press, 1971.
ORTEGA Y GASSET, *Ideas sobre la novela*, Madrid, 1925 (tr. *Notes on the Novel*, Princeton Univ. Press, 1948).
PRINCE, GERALD, *A Grammar of Stories*, The Hague, Mouton, 1973.
PROPP, VLADIMIR, *Morphology of the Folktale*, Bloomington, Indiana Research Centre in Anthropology, 1958.

RICARDOU, JEAN, *Problèmes du nouveau roman*, Paris, Seuil, 1967.
——*Pour une théorie du nouveau roman*, Paris, Seuil, 1971.
——*Le Nouveau roman*, Paris, Seuil, 1973.
ROUSSEL, RAYMOND, *Comment j'ai écrit certains de mes livres*, Paris, Pauvert, 1963.

TODOROV, TZVETAN, *Littérature et signification*, Paris, Larousse, 1967.
——*Poétique*, Paris, Seuil, 1968.
——*Grammaire du Décaméron*, The Hague, Mouton, 1969.
——*Introduction à la littérature fantastique*, Paris, Seuil, 1970.
——*Poétique de la prose*, Paris, Seuil, 1971.
——(ed.), *Théorie de la littérature*, Paris, Seuil, 1965.

VALÉRY, PAUL, *Cahiers I* and *II*, Paris, Gallimard, 1972 and 1974.

INDEX

INDEX